D1565248

Stepfamilies and the Law

Stepfamilies and the Law

Margaret M. Mahoney

Ann Arbor
THE UNIVERSITY OF MICHIGAN PRESS

Copyright © by the University of Michigan 1994
All rights reserved
Published in the United States of America by
The University of Michigan Press
Manufactured in the United States of America
⊗ Printed on acid-free paper

1997   1996   1995   1994   4 3 2 1

*A CIP catalogue record for this book is available from the British
Library.*

Library of Congress Cataloging-in-Publication Data

Mahoney, Margaret M., 1948–
     Stepfamilies and the law / Margaret M. Mahoney.
        p.   cm.
     Includes bibliographical references and index.
     ISBN 0-472-10519-1 (acid-free paper)
     1. Domestic relations—United States.   2. Stepfamilies—United
States.   I. Title.
KF505.M34   1994
346.7301'5—dc20
[347.30615]   94-21260
                                                                    CIP

For my parents, Clara and James Mahoney

Acknowledgments

I regard this work as a contribution to the important debate that is taking place in the United States about the role of nontraditional families. The voices engaged in the debate are many and varied: scholars in the fields of law and the social sciences, professionals who deal with families, and, of course, family members themselves. I have learned a great deal about the subject of stepfamilies by listening to and engaging in discussion with others. I am very indebted to all of these participants in the debate about the future of the American family.

I would like to share the satisfaction of completing this book with several people. First, the legal research for this project was completed in the University of Pittsburgh's Barco Law Library, where I received assistance from the outstanding library staff, especially Spencer Clough, Marc Silverman, and Nickie Singleton. I am indebted as well to numerous faculty colleagues, at the University of Pittsburgh and elsewhere, whose editorial comments on earlier drafts of the manuscript are reflected in the final text. This group includes Jody Armour, Kevin Deasy, Rhonda Hartman, David Herring, and Mark Nordenberg of the Pitt law faculty, and Sarah Ramsey, Professor of Law at the Syracuse University College of Law. From the very beginning of the project, I received guidance and editorial support from Mary Erwin at the University of Michigan Press. I have been greatly assisted as well by the research support of several University of Pittsburgh law students: Jane Auld (class of 1993), Candace Gottschall (class of 1993), Jeffrey Litts (class of 1992), and Christina Walker (class of 1991). Finally, the task of preparing the manuscript was performed with skill and care by LuAnn Driscoll, Deborah Douglass, and Suzanne Leroy.

Contents

CHAPTER 1   **Introduction**

The subject of nontraditional families promises to be an important social and legal issue on the national agenda during the coming decades. This book describes and analyzes the current state of the law in the United States regarding one type of nontraditional family, the step-family.

What makes a family nontraditional? The label is usually attached to any family group that does not consist of a married couple and their biologic or adopted children, the so-called nuclear family. Traditionally, wife-husband and parent-child relationships have received wide recognition in our society; hence, the term "nontraditional" has been used to describe other types of family units. The stepfamily is nontraditional in this sense because there is no biologic or adoptive connection between the stepparent and stepchild.

The preference for the nuclear family finds expression in the legal system through laws that create distinct protections, entitlements, and re-sponsibilities for spouses, parents, and children. These laws govern the family in areas as diverse as child custody, support, inheritance, taxation, child protective services, social benefit programs, tort law, and criminal law. A major purpose of many family-related doctrines is to safeguard the inter-ests of individual family members, especially children, and also to protect the family unit. The traditional emphasis on the nuclear family has effec-tively prevented many individuals, who live in other family situations, from enjoying the same type of legal recognition and protection.

Many Americans today do not reside in traditional nuclear families. Indeed, the 1990 Census revealed that just twenty-one percent of house-holds consisted of a married couple residing with their own children.[1]

Selected materials from chapter 1 appear in an article by the author entitled *A Legal Definition of the Stepfamily: The Example of Incest Regulation*, which ap-pears in Volume 7 of the BRIGHAM YOUNG UNIVERSITY JOURNAL OF PUBLIC LAW.

1. *See* 1991 STATISTICAL ABSTRACT OF THE UNITED STATES, BUREAU OF THE CENSUS, U.S. DEP'T OF COMMERCE [hereinafter 1991 STATISTICAL ABSTRACT], No. 61, HOUSEHOLDS—STATES: 1980 AND 1990, at 48 (reporting a total of 91,947,000 households in 1990); BUREAU OF THE CENSUS, U.S. DEP'T OF COMMERCE, CURRENT POPULATION REPORTS, SPECIAL STUDIES SERIES P23–180, MARRIAGE, DIVORCE AND

Other common household arrangements included married couples without children (twenty-nine percent),[2] unmarried adult partners who reside together with or without children (three percent),[3] single parent families (eleven percent),[4] stepfamilies (six percent),[5] and individuals living alone (twenty-five percent).[6] These figures represented a significant increase in the number of nontraditional family households; for example, the number of single parent households increased forty-one percent between 1980 and 1990, and the number of stepfamily households increased thirty-six percent during the same decade.[7]

According to the 1990 Census, approximately 5.5 million married-couple households contained at least one stepchild under age eighteen. This number constituted twenty-nine percent of all married-couple households with children. The total number of stepchildren residing in these families was 7,208,000.[8] Indeed, demographers predict that a high proportion of children, perhaps one in three, can be expected to spend some childhood years residing in a stepfamily.[9] In an earlier era, when divorce and the birth of children outside of marriage were less common, most stepfamilies were formed upon the remarriage of a widow or widower, who was the parent of minor children. Today, many stepfamilies are still formed under these circumstances, but most come into being when

---

REMARRIAGE IN THE 1990's (October 1992) [hereinafter CURRENT POPULATION REPORTS], 10 (Table L) (reporting 19,598,000 married couple households with biologic and adopted children in 1990).

2. *See* 1991 STATISTICAL ABSTRACT, *supra* note 1, No. 62, HOUSEHOLDS, 1980 AND 1989, AND PERSONS IN HOUSEHOLDS, 1989, BY TYPE OF HOUSEHOLD AND PRESENCE OF CHILDREN 48 (reporting 27,265,000 married-couple households without children in 1989).

3. *Id.*, No. 53, UNMARRIED COUPLES, BY SELECTED CHARACTERISTICS, 1970 TO 1989, AND BY MARITAL STATUS OF PARTNERS, 1989, at 44 (reporting 2,764,000 unmarried-couple households in 1989).

4. CURRENT POPULATION REPORTS, *supra* note 1, at 10 (Table K) (reporting 9,700,000 single parent families in 1990).

5. *Id.* at 10 (Table L) (reporting 5,578,000 stepfamily households in 1990).

6. 1991 STATISTICAL ABSTRACT, *supra* note 1, No. 62, HOUSEHOLDS, 1980 AND 1989, AND PERSONS IN HOUSEHOLDS, 1989, BY TYPE OF HOUSEHOLD AND PRESENCE OF CHILDREN 48 (reporting 22,708,000 householders living alone in 1989).

7. CURRENT POPULATION REPORTS, *supra* note 1, at 10 (Table K).

8. CURRENT POPULATION REPORTS, *supra* note 1, at 10 (Table L).

9. *See* Paul C. Glick, *Remarried Families, Stepfamilies and Stepchildren: A Brief Demographic Profile*, 38 FAM. REL. 24, 26 (1989) (basing projection about future number of stepchildren on statistics regarding the likelihood of parenthood, divorce, and remarriage among young married persons); *see also* Frank F. Furstenberg, Jr., *The New Extended Family: The Experience of Parents and Children after Remarriage*, *in* REMARRIAGE AND STEPPARENTING 42, 44 (Kay Pasley & Marilyn Ihinger-Tallman eds., 1987) (placing estimate at one in four children).

the custodial parent marries for the first time or remarries following a divorce.[10]

The demographic information provided by the Census Bureau further classifies stepfamilies according to the gender of the stepparent. Not surprisingly, the large majority (ninety-one percent) of stepparents are men; this statistic mirrors the fact that most single custodial parents are women. Still, more than a half million children resided in the home of a father and stepmother in 1990.[11]

In counting the number of stepfamily households in America, the Census Bureau defines a stepfamily as the household unit created when an individual marries and resides with the custodial parent of minor children. Notably, the Census Bureau's definition of stepfamily does not include the situation where an adult marries the *noncustodial* parent of minor children. Furthermore, the person who cohabits with a custodial parent, outside a formal marriage, does not create a stepfamily under this definition. The same definitional limitations have, for the most part, been invoked in discussions about stepfamilies in the legal context.[12]

To date, lawmakers have been slow to recognize many nontraditional family relationships, including the relationships created between residential stepparents and their stepchildren.[13] Most of the important legal

---

10. *See* Marilyn Ihinger-Tallman & Kay Pasley, *Divorce and Remarriage in the American Family: A Historical Review, in* REMARRIAGE AND STEPPARENTING, *supra* note 9, at 3, 4–11 (describing the substantial decrease in the number of stepfamilies formed upon the remarriage of a widowed parent, and the corresponding increase in the number of stepfamilies formed by the marriage of a custodial parent who is divorced or never before married).

11. CURRENT POPULATION REPORTS, *supra* note 1, at 10 (Table L). Throughout this treatise, the terms "stepparent" and "custodial parent" are used in a gender-neutral fashion. The only exception appears in chapter 8, which describes the laws governing name changes for stepchildren, where the assumptions are made that stepchildren bear the surname of their biologic father when the stepfamily is formed, and that the custodial parent is the mother.

12. There are exceptions to the general rule that legal issues involving stepfamilies arise only in situations where the stepparent marries the custodial parent and resides with the children. *See, e.g.*, Rosenberg v. Silver, 762 F.2d 255 (2d Cir. 1985) (recognizing defense of parent-child tort immunity for the husband of an injured child's noncustodial mother, who did not reside with the child). Furthermore, the definitions can become blurred in families where unmarried parents share the joint legal and physical custody of their children. Arguably, upon the marriage of either parent in this situation, the new spouse would be regarded as a stepparent even under the limited definition of that term.

13. *See, e.g.*, Katharine T. Bartlett, *Rethinking Parenthood as an Exclusive Status: The Need For Legal Alternatives When the Premise of the Nuclear Family Has Failed*, 70 VA. L. REV. 879 (1984); Jennifer Jaff, *Wedding Bell Blues: The Position of Unmarried People in American Law*, 30 ARIZ. L. REV. 207 (1988); Nancy D.

issues that affect family members, in the areas of support, custody, inheritance, torts, workers' compensation, and criminal law, are regulated at the state level. Here, the starting premise is that stepparents and their stepchildren are legal strangers to each other. The current "law of stepfamilies" consists of a series of limited exceptions to this principle. Furthermore, with respect to many important issues, there is no uniform treatment of the stepparent-child relationship from one state to another. Thus, a comprehensive definition of the stepfamily in American law has yet to be formulated.[14]

The protection of the law is typically invoked by stepfamily members, who have established relationships of economic and emotional interdependence, at times of crisis or transition within the family. Frequently, the failure to recognize the stepparent-child relationship in these circumstances results in direct hardship for individual family members. For example, the associational interests of a residential stepfather and his preschool-age stepdaughter were placed in jeopardy when their family was disrupted by the custodial mother's sudden death. At that time, the biologic father, who had not contacted nor supported his child during the preceding two-year period, sought and obtained custody. Although the stepfather had served as the child's psychological father during the same period, no legal recognition was extended to the stepfather-child relationship in this situation.[15]

Another stepchild endured economic hardship when his mother's request for child support was denied, even though the boy had become dependent upon his stepfather over an extended period of time. In this case, the stepfather encouraged the mother to terminate the biologic father's relationship with the child, promised to adopt the child, served as the child's father during the parties' seven-year marriage, and continued to serve as the primary custodian for more than a year following their divorce. Still, no future support payments were required when the stepfather subsequently chose to terminate the relationship with his stepson.[16]

Polikoff, *This Child Does Have Two Mothers: Redefining Parenthood to Meet the Needs of Children in Lesbian-Mother and Other Nontraditional Families*, 78 Geo. L.J. 459 (1990); Rebecca L. Melton, Note, *Legal Rights of Unmarried Heterosexual and Homosexual Couples and Evolving Definitions of "Family*,*"* 29 J. Fam. L. 497 (1991).

14. In 1987, the Family Law Section of the American Bar Association began work on the Model Act Establishing Rights and Duties of Stepparents. The Act defines stepparent as "a person who is married to the person who . . . has custody of a minor child." The Act addresses three key issues relating to stepparent rights and duties: the right to discipline, support duties, and custody and visitation rights. *See* Joel D. Tenenbaum, *Legislation for Stepfamilies—The Family Law Section Standing Committee Report*, 25 Fam. L.Q. 137 (1991) (including a tentative draft of the Model Act).

15. *See* Milam v. Milam, 376 So. 2d 1336 (Miss. 1979), *discussed in* chapter 7.

16. *See* Ulrich v. Cornell, 484 N.W.2d 545 (Wis. 1992), *discussed in* chapter 2.

In a final illustration, the exclusion of stepfamilies from the definition of criminal incest left another important interest of stepchildren unprotected. A stepfather, who had engaged in sexual activity with his stepdaughter, was acquitted of this criminal charge because the relevant statutory definition of incest was restricted to biologic families. The Mississippi Supreme Court, which announced this result, also expressed dissatisfaction with the underlying rule of law.

> [W]e regret that a man should go unpunished, if guilty of so gross a violation of moral law, of domestic virtues, of the obligations of a citizen. . . .
> [A]lthough the violator of a most sacred obligation will escape merited justice in this world, through the neglect of the law makers to provide for such a case, he cannot escape the just judgment of that Higher Court, where the sins and the secrets of all will be exposed, and suitably adjudged.[17]

As illustrated by stepfamily cases in the fields of incest, child support, and custody, the exclusive focus of the law on traditional nuclear families leaves other people unprotected in their personal relationships. In recent years, scholars of the family have criticized this gap between current legal norms and the actual family experiences of many individuals in our society.[18] Besides the direct legal burdens imposed on nontraditional families, an additional cost associated with the narrow definition of family is the absence of clear and positive roles for stepfamily members.

Researchers have consistently observed that people entering stepfamilies have no clear expectations about family roles.[19] Furthermore, for whatever reasons, many cultural expectations about the stepfamily, reflected in our language and in the popular culture, are negative.[20] Notably, Cinderella, who was mistreated by her stepmother, is the stereotypical

---

17. Chancellor v. State, 47 Miss. 278, 280–81 (1872). The current Mississippi statutes criminalize sexual relationships between stepparents and their stepchildren. *See* appendix to chapter 11.

18. *See* Marie Witkin Kargman, *Stepchild Support Obligations of Stepparents*, 32 FAM. REL. 231 (1983); Bartlett, *supra* note 13; Mark A. Fine, *A Social Science Perspective on Stepfamily Law: Suggestions for Legal Reform*, 38 FAM. REL. 53 (1989); Margaret M. Mahoney, *Stepfamilies in the Law of Intestate Succession and Wills*, 22 U.C. DAVIS L. REV. 917 (1989); Margaret M. Mahoney, *Support and Custody Aspects of the Stepparent-Child Relationship*, 70 CORNELL L. REV. 38 (1984); Polikoff, *supra* note 13.

19. *See* Fine, *supra* note 18, at 55; David M. Mills, *A Model For Stepfamily Development*, 33 FAM. REL. 365 (1984).

20. *See* BRENDA MADDOX, THE HALF-PARENT: LIVING WITH OTHER PEOPLE'S CHILDREN 32–37 (1975) (discussing the negative connotations of stepfamily terminology).

stepchild of fiction. Indeed, the term "stepchild" is used in many contexts as shorthand for "second class," as illustrated by the following titles of two recent law review articles: *Secondary Trading: Stepchild of the Securities Law,* and *Stepchild of the New Lex Mercatoria: Private International Law from the United States Perspective.* Of course, these negative portrayals do not necessarily depict or influence the reality of modern stepfamilies. Still, scholars of the family have concluded that the absence of clear and positive role models creates adjustment problems over time within many stepfamilies.[21]

It is possible that the current state of the law contributes to the problem of ambiguity about stepfamily roles. Clearly, the legal system has failed to recognize, on any consistent basis, that the relationship between stepparent and child entails enforceable rights and duties. The actual impact of the law upon the feelings and behavior of individuals in stepfamilies is, of course, difficult to measure. Nevertheless, Professor of Psychology Mark A. Fine found it "plausible that the lack of legal precision is one among many factors which perpetuates the uncertain status that stepfamilies have in our culture."[22] Another scholar, Professor Gary B. Melton, whose work in the field of legal psychology has focused on the relationship between law and human behavior, made the following general observation about the impact of formal legal status on nontraditional families.

> The adoption of a broad definition of family often both brings law into harmony with changing social reality and promotes ends consistent with public policy.
> . . . The degree of legal recognition that various relationships attain is likely to affect their stability and individuals' sense of satisfaction with them.[23]

The traditional family law system is concerned with the protection of individuals, especially children, who form economic and emotional interdependencies within the family. Another important goal, highlighted in the observations by Professors Fine and Melton, is the enhancement of certainty and stability in family relationships. These purposes deserve the

---

21. *See* Marilyn Coleman & Lawrence H. Ganong, *The Cultural Stereotyping of Stepfamilies, in* REMARRIAGE AND STEPPARENTING, *supra* note 9, at 19, 19–41 (examining anecdotal and empirical evidence which supports the conclusion that widespread negative stereotyping produces harmful effects in stepfamilies); Judith Grant, *The New Family and the Old Ideology, in* WOMEN AND STEPFAMILIES 214 (Nan Bauer Maglin & Nancy Schniedewind eds., 1989) (criticizing the social and legal "ideology of biologism," which creates internal family problems by failing to validate nontraditional family models).

22. Fine, *supra* note 18, at 55.

23. Gary B. Melton, *The Significance of Law in the Everyday Lives of Children and Families,* 22 GA. L. REV. 851, 854, 856 (1988).

attention of scholars and lawmakers who analyze the legal status of step-families.

Criticism of the status quo is the first and easiest step in evaluating the current laws that regulate stepfamilies. It is more difficult to affirmatively define a legal stepparent-child status, which would recognize and protect stepfamily members while preserving a family law system that is fair, certain, predictable, and not unduly burdensome on those who must enforce the laws. In defining the stepparent-child status, two important questions must be answered. First, what constitutes a legally significant stepparent-child relationship? Second, what rights and responsibilities should be associated with stepfamily membership?

The simplest answer to the first inquiry appears in the Census Bureau's definition of stepfamily: the relationship formed whenever an individual marries the custodial parent of a minor child and thereafter resides with the child. This basic definition is employed in a number of the existing state laws that recognize stepfamilies for specific purposes. For example, the Missouri stepparent support statute provides, in a straightforward manner, that "[a] stepparent shall support his or her stepchild to the same extent that a natural or adoptive parent is required to support his or her child as long as the stepchild is living in the same home as the stepparent."[24]

However, many scholars and lawmakers have concluded that something more than marriage and a shared residence should be required before legal consequences attach; additional criteria generally relate to de facto relationships established over time in the stepfamily. According to this analysis, legal rights and duties should exist only if the residential stepparent assumes an active custodial role, for example, by participating in the child's education, discipline, and moral training, or by making financial contributions to the child's support.

Indeed, judges have developed a legal standard, called the in loco parentis doctrine, which embodies this approach to identifying legally significant relationships outside the biologic or adoptive family. In loco parentis, which in Latin means "in the place of a parent," applies not only to stepfamilies, but to any situation where an adult informally assumes custodial responsibility for a child. The courts have applied the doctrine, however, only in certain fields of law. For example, stepparents who stand in loco parentis to their stepchildren have frequently been accorded the same treatment as biologic parents in the areas of workers' compensation and parent-child tort immunity. Conversely, the courts have rejected the in loco parentis doctrine as a basis for stepfamily claims in many other important fields, including inheritance and wrongful death.

---

24. Mo. Ann. Stat. § 453.400 (Vernon 1986); *see also* N.H. Rev. Stat. Ann. § 546–A:1, –A:2 (1987); Or. Rev. Stat. § 109.053 (1990); S.D. Codified Laws Ann. § 25–7–8 (1992); Utah Code Ann. § 78–45–4.1, –4.2 (1992); Wash. Rev. Code Ann. § 26.16.205 (West Supp. 1993).

Like the common law in loco parentis doctrine, many of the state statutes that recognize stepfamilies for a specific purpose are limited to those situations where the stepparent and child are tied together by more than the stepparent's marriage to the child's parent. For example, the New Jersey inheritance tax statute establishes preferential rates and exemptions for bequests made to "any child to whom the decedent . . . stood in the acknowledged relation of a parent, provided such relationship began at or before the child's fifteenth birthday and was continuous for ten years thereafter."[25] Similarly, the crime of "sexual abuse by a parent, guardian, or custodian" in the West Virginia Code applies to "the spouse" of a parent "where such spouse shares actual physical possession or care and custody of a child."[26] Each of these statutory standards, like the common law in loco parentis standard, requires the assumption of some form of responsibility by the stepparent before legal rights and duties are imposed.

The use of this type of differential standard is supported by the findings of social scientists who have studied families. Researchers have found that the relationships actually established between stepparents and their stepchildren vary widely from one family to the next, for example, in the level of commitment, amount and quality of personal interaction, and the degree of economic and custodial responsibility assumed by the stepparent.[27] Variable factors that appear to influence these matters include the age of the child when the stepfamily is formed, the length of the marriage, the presence of a noncustodial parent, and the presence of stepsiblings in the family.[28] The empirical information about the wide range of stepfamily experiences, coupled with private and societal expectations in this field, support the efforts by lawmakers to develop standards that segregate those stepfamilies where meaningful family ties exist.

The creation of legal standards that are premised on actual relationships in the stepfamily is also consistent with the theories of family scholars who have addressed the question of legal status outside the nuclear family in a more comprehensive fashion. Thus, one widely discussed theory, which was disseminated during the 1970s by the authors of a book entitled *Beyond the Best Interests of the Child*, emphasized the importance of psychological, rather than biologic, parenthood. The psychological parent is defined as "one who, on a continuing, day-to-day basis, through interaction, companionship, interplay, and mutuality, fulfills the child's psychological

---

25. N.J. STAT. ANN. § 54:34–2.1 (West 1986).

26. W. VA. CODE ANN. § 61–8D–1 (4), (5) (1992).

27. *See* Judith Zucker Anderson & Geoffry D. White, *An Empirical Investigation of Interaction and Relationship Patterns in Functional and Dysfunctional Nuclear Families and Stepfamilies*, 25 FAM. PROCESS 407 (1986); Furstenberg, *supra* note 9.

28. *See* Fine, *supra* note 18, at 55–56; Lawrence H. Ganong & Marilyn Coleman, *The Effects of Remarriage on Children: A Review of the Empirical Literature*, 33 FAM. REL. 389, 402–03 (1984).

needs for a parent, as well as the child's physical needs."[29] According to this theory, the laws should protect relationships between children and their psychological parents, because disruption of these bonds would be harmful to the children.

A more recent and more refined proposal appears in Katharine T. Bartlett's article, *Rethinking Parenthood as an Exclusive Status: The Need For More Legal Alternatives When the Premise of the Nuclear Family Has Failed.* Professor Bartlett has proposed that adult-child relationships outside the nuclear family should be recognized whenever the following criteria are met.

> The first criterion is that the adult have had physical custody of the child for at least six months. . . .
>
> "Mutuality" is a second criterion for psychological parenthood. To meet this criterion, the adult must demonstrate that his motive in seeking parental status is his genuine care and concern for the child. . . . Mutuality also denotes that the child perceives the adult's role to be that of parent. . . .
>
> As a final criterion for psychological parenthood, the . . . adult [must] prove that the relationship with the child began with the consent of the child's legal parent or under court order. This requirement is designed to avoid enhancing incentives for child-snatching.[30]

According to Professor Bartlett's own analysis, a stepparent might qualify as a parent figure under this test, at the same time that the stepchild's two biologic parents retain their legal roles.[31]

Once the limitations on legally significant stepparent-child relationships have been established, under the in loco parentis doctrine or some other standard, the remaining questions involve the scope of legal rights and responsibilities within the stepfamily. The logical starting point in this analysis is that stepfamilies could be treated like biologic families; that is, the same legal rights enjoyed by biologic parents and children could be extended to qualifying stepparents and their stepchildren. Indeed, a num-

---

29. JOSEPH GOLDSTEIN, ANNA FREUD, & ALBERT J. SOLNIT, BEYOND THE BEST INTERESTS OF THE CHILD 98 (1973).

30. Bartlett, *supra* note 13, at 946–47. Additional standards for recognizing nontraditional adult-child relationships appear in Polikoff, *supra* note 13 (advocating recognition of functional parent-child relationships that are initially created with the consent of a legally recognized parent); Note, *Looking For a Family Resemblance: The Limits of the Functional Approach to the Legal Definition of Family*, 104 HARV. L. REV. 1640, 1646, 1655 (1991) (describing a functional parent-child relationship that "shares the essential characteristics of a traditional relationship and fulfills the same human needs," including the child's physical, emotional, and financial needs).

31. *See* Bartlett, *supra* note 13, at 951.

ber of the existing laws dealing with stepfamilies for specific purposes treat them on a par with biologic families. For example, under the New Jersey inheritance tax statute quoted previously, both biologic children and qualifying stepchildren, who receive bequests upon the death of a parent or stepparent, enjoy the same preferential tax rates and exemptions.[32] A second illustration of equivalent treatment of parent-child and stepparent-child relationships appears in the laws governing the discipline of children. In most states, stepparents who stand in loco parentis to their stepchildren are entitled to discipline them, and are subject to the same limitations on the use of force as biologic parents.[33]

The biologic family is not, however, the only model for defining legal rights in the stepfamily. For example, state lawmakers have established entirely different child support responsibilities for parents and stepparents. In most jurisdictions today, stepparents have no enforceable obligation whatsoever to support their stepchildren. But even in the eighteen states where lawmakers have imposed a statutory stepchild support duty,[34] it is much less significant than the corollary responsibility of biologic and adoptive parents. Most notably, the obligation of stepparents does not survive the termination of the marriage which created the stepfamily.[35] Of course, this durational limitation stands in stark contrast to the universal rule in the biologic family, where support obligations continue at least until children reach the age of majority. Professor David L. Chambers has pointed out that the current law of support in stepfamilies (no obligation following divorce) and in natural families (full support responsibility during every child's minority) does not exhaust the available options. Thus, for example, lawmakers could establish a postdivorce stepparent obligation that endures for a shorter period of time than the duty of biologic parents.[36]

Indeed, in thinking about a legal definition of the stepfamily status, it is both liberating and overwhelming to consider all of the available options. As to each legal issue, the inquiry must be whether the family-related policies that justify regulation in the biologic family also extend to the stepfamily; and if so, what form of regulation is appropriate in this nontraditional family setting. The task of segregating eligible stepparents and stepchildren, and

---

32. *See* N.J. STAT. ANN. § 54:34–2.1 (West 1986).

33. *See, e.g.,* TEX. PENAL CODE ANN. § 9.61(a)(1) (West 1974) (authorizing reasonable use of force by parents, stepparents, and others standing in loco parentis).

34. The law of stepparent support, including the state statutes, is discussed fully in chapter 2.

35. *See, e.g.,* Deal v. Deal, 545 So. 2d 780 (Ala. Civ. App. 1989). *But see* N.D. CENT. CODE § 14–09–09 (1991) (extending stepparent support duty "during the marriage and so long thereafter as [the stepchildren] remain in [the stepparent's] family").

36. David L. Chambers, *Stepparents, Biologic Parents, and the Law's Perception of "Family" after Divorce, in* DIVORCE REFORM AT THE CROSSROADS 102, 127–29 (Stephen D. Sugarman & Herma Hill Kay eds., 1990).

then identifying appropriate legal rights and responsibilities for them, is a difficult and complex one. The absence of any comprehensive definition of stepfamily rights in the law can be explained in part by the difficulty of the undertaking.

Surely, one attractive feature of the traditional model of the family is its simplicity: two biologic parents and their children, with immutable rights and responsibilities, is an easy model for everyone to work with. Parents, children, employers, teachers, doctors, and other third parties all know that the two parents have an exclusive claim to and responsibility for their children. In reality, the addition of a residential stepparent complicates a child's daily life in many ways. Developments in the law, acknowledging the stepparent's presence, would complicate the legal picture as well, with some resulting uncertainty about the lines of authority and responsibility within the family. This is especially apparent when the biologic parent who is not married to the stepparent plays an active role in the child's life. The challenge for the legal system is to formulate laws that fairly reflect and define the interests of family members without creating undue confusion or uncertainty.[37]

The practical difficulties involved in expanding the legal definition of the family are apparent. But the cumulative decision of lawmakers to keep their distance from the subject of stepfamilies is rooted as well in a philosophical reluctance to move away from the nuclear family as an exclusive legal model. The traditional system of family law is premised on the important assumption that the biologic mother and father have exclusive relationships with their children. Within this framework, the legal recognition of stepparent-child relationships calls into question established social and legal assumptions about the family. Stepfamily members and others seeking a broader legal definition of the family have frequently encountered stiff resistance, because their position is viewed as a threat to traditional values.

The remaining chapters explore in detail the current law of stepfamilies. The various issues affecting stepfamilies are typically raised one-by-one in the state courts and legislatures. Each time the question of legal status for stepparents and stepchildren is raised, the particular lawmakers appear to balance anew all of the competing interests regarding stability and protection for stepfamily members, on the one hand, against the reluctance to complicate the system by moving away from the preference for nuclear families. Different weight has been assigned to these competing values, depending upon the particular legal context and the philosophical

---

37. The tension between the goals of fairness, on the one hand, and certainty and predictability, on the other, permeates the system of family law. *See generally* Mary Ann Glendon, *Fixed Rules and Discretion in Contemporary Family Law and Succession Law*, 60 Tul. L. Rev. 1165 (1986); Carl E. Schneider, *The Tension Between Rules and Discretion in Family Law: A Report and Reflection*, 27 Fam. L.Q. 229 (1993).

disposition of the decision maker. The overall result of this process is an unsettling lack of consistency from issue to issue and from state to state in the legal definition of the stepfamily. Still, it is fair to summarize the current law as denying legal recognition to stepfamilies, subject to a number of specific judicial and legislative exceptions in the laws of each state.

The increasing number of individuals who are living in nontraditional families, especially stepfamilies, is necessarily changing the way in which Americans think about the family. For lawmakers, the task of translating these social realities into a responsive system of family laws in the future is a challenging one. Only when this challenge has been met will the basic goals of the family law system be realized for the families of the twenty-first century.

CHAPTER 2   **Child Support**

I. Introduction

The marriage of a parent who is the custodian of minor children raises questions about financial support for the children in the new stepfamily. Under existing laws, both the mother and father are required to support their minor children, and these duties are undisturbed by one parent's marriage to a new spouse/stepparent. Furthermore, under the legal principles described in this chapter, the new spouse is generally not required to provide for the stepchild's support. The following materials catalog and discuss a number of limited exceptions, which have been fashioned by the courts and legislatures, to these traditional rules regarding support in the stepfamily. A detailed examination reveals that few significant deviations have been made from the premise that enforceable child support obligations are imposed exclusively upon the natural parents.[1]

The actual arrangements made by family members to pay for a stepchild's expenses may or may not coincide with their legal responsibilities. For example, the stepparent may assume a share of the child support burden, even though not legally required to do so. The impact of the underlying support laws upon this type of voluntary family behavior is a matter of speculation. One aspect of the status quo is not speculative, however; when conflicts between family members are resolved in the courtroom, stepparents are rarely required to provide support to their stepchildren. The legal doctrines in this field reaffirm the right of stepparents to make their own decisions about child support.

There are two underlying principles embodied in this legal approach to stepfamily responsibility. The first involves a strong, pro-marriage policy,

---

1. For general discussion of the laws governing stepparent support, see DAVID L. CHAMBERS, *Stepparents, Biologic Parents, and the Law's Perception of "Family" After Divorce, in* DIVORCE REFORM AT THE CROSSROADS 102 (Stephen D. Sugarman & Herma Hill Kay eds., 1990); Robert J. Levy, *Rights and Responsibilities for Extended Family Members?*, 27 FAM. L.Q. 191 (1993); Margaret M. Mahoney, *Support and Custody Aspects of the Stepparent-Child Relationship*, 70 CORNELL L. REV. 38 (1984); Sarah H. Ramsey & Judith M. Masson, *Stepparent Support of Stepchildren: A Comparative Analysis of Policies and Problems in the American and British Experience*, 36 SYRACUSE L. REV. 659 (1985); R. Michael Redman, *The Support of Children in Blended Families*, 25 FAM. L.Q. 83 (1991).

coupled with an assumption that stepparent support duties would discourage marriage and the formation of new stepfamilies. Here, the analysis of stepfamily responsibility enters the realm of speculation. Surely, people marry for a variety of reasons, only some of them financial. And, in terms of financial incentives, additional support responsibility in the stepfamily would likely be an added incentive for custodial parents to marry. Nevertheless, lawmakers have frequently expressed the view that greater financial responsibility in the stepfamily would deter marriage by the parents of minor children.

The second principle reflected in the existing rules places emphasis on the biologic parent-child relationship as the exclusive model of family responsibility. According to this viewpoint, it would simply be unfair to impose economic responsibility upon adults for children whom they did not bring into the world. This limited definition of economic justice has been sorely tested in many stepfamilies, where members form relationships of financial and emotional dependency. A competing definition of economic fairness in this situation would recognize the responsibility of stepparents in order to protect the reasonable expectations of dependent stepchildren. As described in this chapter, several legal and equitable doctrines, which establish stepparent responsibility in limited circumstances, are premised on this alternative view of fairness within the stepfamily. These doctrines constitute minor exceptions to the general principle that stepparents have no financial responsibility for their minor stepchildren.

II. The Support Obligation of Parents

It is a basic legal principle in the United States that all parents have a duty to support their minor children. This responsibility was recognized by society as a moral obligation before it was embodied in law. Thus, William Blackstone described the economic responsibility of parents in his famous eighteenth-century summary of English law in the following manner.

> The duty of parents to provide for the *maintenance* of their children, is a principle of natural law; an obligation . . . laid on them not only by nature herself, but by their own proper act, in bringing them into the world: for they would be in the highest manner injurious to their issue, if they only gave their children life, that they might afterwards see them perish. By begetting them therefore, they have entered into a voluntary obligation, to endeavor, as far as in them lies, that the life which they have bestowed shall be supported and preserved.[2]

The modern support duty, imposed by state law on all parents, is designed to assure the economic welfare of children. The duty extends to both par-

---

2. 1 WILLIAM BLACKSTONE, COMMENTARIES *447.

ents equally, according to their respective financial abilities, whether or not they are married to each other.[3] There are no legal avenues for avoiding this personal obligation; it is discharged only upon the child's death, emancipation, or age of majority, or upon termination of the parent-child relationship by the state.[4]

In spite of this emphasis on parental responsibility, the direct enforcement of child support duties is generally unavailable as long as the child and parent reside together. Of course, most parents in this situation support their children voluntarily, without regard to the existence or enforceability of legal duties. When conflicts arise, however, the common law doctrine of family privacy generally bars any lawsuit for support by one family member against another.[5] The privacy doctrine, which reflects the view that both the family and society are best served by minimal state intervention in the intact family, has been applied by judges to other issues besides child support. In *McGuire v. McGuire,*[6] for example, the Supreme Court of Nebraska held that a wife who resided with her husband was not entitled to sue him for spousal support, although such suits were allowed between separated spouses. The privacy doctrine is not absolute; in cases of economic neglect, for example, the state may intervene to protect needy family members.

Although the family privacy doctrine restricts the direct enforcement of support duties while the child and parent reside together, lawsuits may be initiated during this period by third parties. Thus, welfare authorities and creditors, who provide goods and services for a child's support, may sue the parent for reimbursement, even if the child and parent are members of the same household. In this manner, the indirect enforcement of parental responsibility may occur, even in the intact family.

Not surprisingly, the family privacy doctrine is set aside when family members no longer reside together. Thus, direct orders for child support from the noncustodial parent are common in separation and divorce proceedings. Similarly, support suits initiated by the custodial mother against the noncustodial father, to whom she has never been married, are commonplace. Courts routinely order noncustodial parents to pay support in these situations, in amounts based on the needs of the child and the financial abilities of both parents. Nevertheless, inadequate support from noncus-

---

3. The gender-neutral imposition of support duties in the family is a fairly recent development. William Blackstone explained the earlier view, that fathers were primarily responsible for child support, in the following manner: "[T]he mother finds a thousand obstacles . . . that stifle her inclination to perform this duty: and besides, she generally wants ability." *Id.*

4. For example, a general discharge of the parent's debts in a bankruptcy proceeding does not discharge past and future child support obligations. *See* 11 U.S.C. § 523(a)(5) (1988). Similarly, a promise by one parent to assume the total responsibility for child support does not discharge the other parent's duty to their child.

5. *See generally* HOMER H. CLARK, JR., THE LAW OF DOMESTIC RELATIONS IN THE UNITED STATES 256–57 (2d ed. 1988) (discussing the family privacy doctrine).

6. McGuire v. McGuire, 59 N.W.2d 336 (Neb. 1953).

todial parents has been a contributing factor in the unacceptable and growing rate of poverty among U.S. children. Indeed, the problem of child poverty, which has become the focus of national concern,[7] affects a disproportionate number of children who reside in single parent families.

The Aid to Families with Dependent Children Program[8] is designed to fill the economic gap when parents fail to meet their children's needs. Ironically, as discussed in section X, the income of residential stepparents must be counted in determining stepchild eligibility for assistance, even though stepparents owe no child support obligation under state law. Nationwide, the Aid to Families with Dependent Children Program, along with other public assistance programs, has not succeeded in eliminating the problem of poverty among children, including stepchildren.

This system of parental and public responsibility for children is the necessary backdrop for analyzing the topic of stepparent support. In one sense, stepparent support duties may be regarded as a new financial resource in a system that is currently failing to meet the economic needs of many children. Of course, many additional considerations, explored in the remainder of this chapter, enter into the analysis of this issue. The background information about parental support is instructive in another sense as well. Namely, the creation of a general stepparent support duty would raise many of the same issues that have been addressed by the current laws regulating parental support. For example, any new stepfamily obligation would likely be subject to the same limitations on enforceability under the family privacy doctrine. Finally, stepparent support duties, however they are defined, must be integrated with the well-established rules of parental support described in this section; such an integrated system must clearly define the relative duties of all responsible adults toward the same child.

III. The in Loco Parentis Doctrine

Under common law principles, marriage alone does not obligate the stepparent to support his or her stepchild. However, the courts have developed a doctrine called in loco parentis, whereby the stepparent's behavior in the family may result in a limited support duty. A classic formulation of this common law doctrine appears in the 1914 opinion of the Arizona Supreme Court in the case of *Harris v. Lyon*.

> The universal rule is that a stepfather, as such, is not under obligation to support the [stepchildren], but that, if he takes the children

---

7. The national debate about the child support crisis has produced federal laws in the area, which impose certain requirements on the states regarding the matter of enforcement. *See* Harry D. Krause, *Child Support Reassessed, in* Divorce Reform at the Crossroads, *supra* note 1, at 166, 169–74 (discussing federal law requirements).

8. *See* 42 U.S.C. §§ 601 to 605 (1988 & Supp. 1990).

into his family or under his care in such a way that he places himself in loco parentis, he assumes an obligation to support them, and
acquires a correlative right to their services.[9]

The legal relationship created between stepparent and child under the in
loco parentis doctrine does not encompass all of the economic rights and
duties of the natural parent-child relationship. For example, no inheritance
rights are established between them.[10] As expressed by the court in *Harris*,
the primary economic consequence of the doctrine is the recognition of
mutual obligations regarding support and services between the stepparent
and child.

The creation of an in loco parentis relationship depends in each case
upon the intention of the stepparent to assume this status. In *Harris v.
Lyon*, for example, the stepfather revealed the necessary state of mind by
voluntarily assuming responsibility for his stepdaughter following his wife's
death. The Lyons had been married when Mrs. Lyon's daughter, Emma
Harris, was ten years old. When Mrs. Lyon died one year later, the stepfather established an in loco parentis relationship with Emma Harris, based
on the following behavior.

> The . . . stepfather to Emma, was a party to an arrangement that
> she should live with her grandmother, he to furnish her housing,
> clothing, food, and medical attention and generally to provide for
> them. . . . [T]he grandmother's position was that of housekeeper,
> largely subject to the orders and directions of the [stepfather who]
> . . . exercised the parental rights of controlling and supervising the
> conduct, education, and employment of Emma, and at one time cor-
> poreally chastised her for disobedience. . . . The rights, powers, and
> duties claimed and exercised by him over the child were such as
> only a parent could lawfully claim and exercise.[11]

As a result, the Arizona Supreme Court ruled that Mr. Lyon was not entitled
to reimbursement from Emma Harris's property for the child support expenses that he incurred during the five-year period following her mother's
death.

Harris v. Lyon involved the informal assumption of custodial responsibility for a stepchild who resided in the home of a relative. More often,

---

9. Harris v. Lyon, 140 P. 825, 826 (Ariz. 1914). In her treatise entitled THE
STEPFATHER IN THE FAMILY (1940), Adele Stuart Meriam observed that the in loco
parentis doctrine was first applied by a court in the United States in 1849. *See id*. at
23–26 (citing Williams v. Hutchinson, 5 Barb. 122 (N.Y. App. Div. 1849), *aff'd*, 3 N.Y.
(3 Comstock) 312 (1850); Lantz v. Frey and Wife, 14 Pa. 201 (1850)).

10. *See* chapter 3, which explores the rights of stepparents and stepchildren
under the laws of intestate succession.

11. *Harris*, 140 P. at 826–27.

stepparents establish de facto relationships with their stepchildren during the period of marriage to the child's custodial parent, when the parties reside together in the same household. In this situation, the stepparent who shares custodial responsibility with his or her spouse may, by virtue of this behavior, assume a child support obligation. The Missouri Court of Appeals reached this conclusion in *Schwieter v. Heathman's Estate*, based on the following testimony by the custodial mother.

> She said that [her husband, the stepfather] loved her son as much as if he were his own and that when they were married he took the boy into their home as a member of the family. She said that the treatment accorded [the stepson] was the same as that accorded his half sister, who was born of the [marriage], and that [the stepfather] referred to him as "my boy."[12]

Based on this evidence, the court ruled that the stepfather stood in loco parentis to his stepson and, therefore, could not seek reimbursement for past child support expenses from the estate of the boy's father.

In practice, the presence or absence of the natural parents is not a critical factor in determining whether a stepparent stands in the place of a parent. Thus, in *Schweiter*, the presence of both the custodial mother and the noncustodial father did not prevent the court from concluding that the mother's second husband had assumed an in loco parentis status. The stepson, therefore, was entitled to support from the stepfather as well as both natural parents. Conversely, the absence of both natural parents in *Harris v. Lyon* did not appear to influence the Arizona Supreme Court's analysis of the stepfather-stepdaughter relationship.

The crucial element of intent under the in loco parentis doctrine is always within the stepparent's exclusive control. The courts in *Schweiter* and *Harris* found the necessary intent to assume a parental role, based on each stepfather's conduct in caring for his stepchild. On the other hand, a stepparent can prevent the application of the in loco parentis doctrine, and the corresponding support duty, by clearly expressing a contrary intent through words and actions. For example, the stepparent who maintains a record of support expenses, and consistently expresses the intention to seek reimbursement from the natural parents or from the child's estate, will usually avoid economic responsibility.

The outcome in *Harris v. Lyon* illustrates the extent of the stepparent's control over the in loco parentis status. As discussed earlier, the stepfather there had assumed in loco parentis responsibility for his stepdaughter, Emma Harris, for a period of five years following his wife's death. Thereafter, he changed his behavior and effectively destroyed the in loco parentis status. The litigation in *Harris* arose when Emma Harris became the

---

12. Schwieter v. Heathman's Estate, 264 S.W.2d 932, 933 (Mo. Ct. App. 1954).

owner of valuable property, and her stepfather became the guardian of this estate. In the lawsuit by the stepfather, requesting reimbursement from his stepdaughter's newly acquired property for past and future child support expenses, the Arizona Supreme Court authorized reimbursement only for future expenses. According to the court, the stepfather's recent behavior, in seeking a formal appointment as guardian and requesting reimbursement from his stepdaughter's estate, marked the end of his in loco parentis status.[13]

It becomes more difficult for a stepparent to prove the intention not to stand in loco parentis to a stepchild when they reside in the same household. In these circumstances, the child will likely derive benefit from the stepparent's financial contributions to household expenses, which creates a presumption that the stepparent intends to assume responsibility for the child. The presumption is rebuttable, however, by unequivocal expressions of a contrary intent, such as those of the stepfather in the Minnesota case, *In re Besondy*.[14] There, the stepfather entered into an oral agreement with his wife, at the time of their marriage, that certain government benefits payable to her son, based on his father's military service, would be the primary source of support for the child. The Minnesota Supreme Court ruled that this agreement negated the presumption of the stepfather's in loco parentis status.

> [A] stepfather is, of course, not bound to maintain the children of his wife by a former husband. But if he voluntarily assume [*sic*] the parental relation and receives them into his family under circumstances such as to raise a presumption that he has undertaken to support them gratuitously, he cannot afterwards claim compensation for their support. . . . The arrangement made with the stepfather [regarding the military benefits] . . . is sufficient to rebut the presumption that he took the child into his family to support in loco parentis. . . .[15]

The stepfather accordingly was entitled to reimbursement from the accumulated military benefit funds for the support he had provided to his stepson.

In *Besondy*, as in each case discussed previously, the question of stepparent support under the doctrine of in loco parentis arose when the step-

---

13. Other courts have similarly held that the stepparent who provides support to a stepchild as the guardian of the child's property does not stand in loco parentis to the child. *See, e.g.*, Probate Court of Providence v. Higgins, 191 A. 260 (R.I. 1937). *See generally* MERIAM, *supra* note 9, at 61–68 (discussing cases where stepparents served as the guardian of property).

14. *In re* Besondy, 20 N.W. 366 (Minn. 1884).

15. *Id.* at 367. (Material quoted in the text is out of sequence.)

father sought reimbursement for child support he had already provided. As a general rule, no one is entitled to reimbursement for satisfying his or her own debt, including a child support debt. In contrast, nonobligated parties who provide support, including the stepparent who does not stand in loco parentis, are entitled to reimbursement from either the child or the natural parent. This dichotomy was highlighted in the *Harris v. Lyon* case, where the stepfather was entitled to recover the support he provided to his step-daughter, but only for the period following his appointment as her guardian, which terminated his own support duty. In this manner, the in loco parentis doctrine governs the rights of stepparents to reimbursement for past step-child support.[16]

The creation of the in loco parentis relationship has an additional economic implication for the parties: the stepparent becomes legally entitled to the value of the stepchild's services. In the typical parent-child relationship, parents are entitled by law to the value of their children's services in exchange for supporting them. Hence, children are not entitled to compensation for services rendered to their parents, and wages paid to children by third parties belong to the parents. In the stepfamily, the stepparent who stands in loco parentis to a stepchild has the same rights as a parent with regard to the child's services.

Absent the in loco parentis status, however, the stepparent is treated as a stranger for this purpose, and the child or the child's representative may recover the value of services rendered to the stepparent. The California Court of Appeals applied this principle in *Wardrobe v. Miller*,[17] holding that a father was entitled to recover the value of services provided by his two sons to their stepfather, who failed to prove his in loco parentis status. The father, Mr. Wardrobe, had obtained legal custody of his children following a divorce from their mother. Eleven years later, following a family quarrel, the Wardrobe children moved to the farm of their mother and stepfather, the Millers, for a period of two months. During this time, Mr. Miller provided room and board for the stepchildren and treated them like his own children, while the two boys worked on the Miller farm. Following the children's return to the Wardrobe household, Mr. Wardrobe successfully sued to recover the excess of the value of his sons' labor on the Miller farm over the value of their room

---

16. Stepparents were entitled to reimbursement for support provided to step-children, based on a finding that the stepparent owed no duty to the child, in the following cases: Anonymous Wife v. Anonymous Husband, 739 P.2d 794 (Ariz. 1987) (reimbursement from natural father); Kempson v. Goss, 62 S.W. 582 (Ark. 1901) (reimbursement from property of stepchildren); *In re* Besondy, 20 N.W. 366 (Minn. 1884) (reimbursement from property of stepchild). Conversely, recovery was denied to stepparents, based on a finding that the stepparent had assumed a support obligation, in the following cases: Schwieter v. Heathman's Estate, 264 S.W.2d 932 (Mo. Ct. App. 1954) (no reimbursement from estate of deceased natural father); Norton v. Ailor, 79 Tenn. 563 (1883) (no reimbursement from estate of deceased stepchild).

17. Wardrobe v. Miller, 200 P. 77 (Cal. Dist. Ct. App. 1921).

and board there. The court dismissed the stepfather's argument, that the husband who receives his wife's children by a former marriage into his family and supports them presumably does so as a parent, because the "mere temporary relation" established between the parties failed to trigger this legal presumption. In the absence of any in loco parentis relationship, or corresponding right of the stepfather to the children's services, Mr. Wardrobe was entitled to recover the value of his sons' labor.[18]

Although the in loco parentis doctrine refers to the duties of parents and children regarding child support and services, there is a major distinction between the legal position of parents and the stepparent who stands in loco parentis. The rights and duties of parents, including the support duty, are imposed by law and enforceable in appropriate circumstances. In stark contrast, the rights and duties of the stepparent who stands in loco parentis to his or her stepchild are created by the voluntary assumption of responsibility, which is terminable at will by the stepparent. Thus, the limited legal effect of the in loco parentis doctrine is to place the force of law behind the prior voluntary decisions of stepparents regarding the assumption of parental responsibility.

The enforcement of the obligations that arise under the in loco parentis doctrine is retrospective only, relating to support and services already provided in the stepfamily. Examination of cases such as *Harris* and *Miller* reveals the limited context in which the courts may disagree with stepparents about the existence of their in loco parentis status. Both of these cases involved after-the-fact assessments of stepfamily behavior, when one party sought reimbursement for support or services already provided. In this context, the courts looked to each stepfather's past behavior to determine his actual intention regarding the assumption of parental responsibility. In *Harris*, for example, the stepfather was not allowed to recover for support provided in the past, even though he later denied any intention to assume a support duty, because his earlier conduct proved a contrary intent.

As to questions of current and future child support, the in loco parentis doctrine leaves total discretion in the hands of the stepparent. The supporting stepparent can simply change his or her mind at any time. Thus, unlike the support obligation of natural parents, the in loco parentis doctrine provides no financial security for stepchildren. Most commonly, the stepparent exercises this right to unilaterally terminate child support when marriage to

---

18. *See also* Worcester v. Marchant, 31 Mass. (14 Pick.) 510 (1833). In *Worcester*, the stepfather was denied recovery for his stepson's services from the captain of a whaling ship, on the theory that the stepfather was not obligated to support the boy and was not entitled to the value of his services. The court also denied the claim of the mother against the ship's captain, on the theory that upon marriage she "ceased to have the power of controlling her own actions, and the power of supporting and educating her child." *Id.* at 512. *See generally* MERIAM, *supra* note 9, at 43–47 (summarizing cases in which stepparents asserted their rights to the earnings of their stepchildren).

the child's custodial parent terminates by death or divorce. As described in the next section, the in loco parentis doctrine imposes no continuing support obligation on the unwilling stepparent in this situation.

IV. Postdivorce Responsibility under the in Loco Parentis Doctrine

When the marriage between a stepparent and the stepchild's custodial parent ends in separation or divorce, the stepparent and child may cease to have any contact with each other, based on either the agreement of the parties or the custodial parent's unilateral decision in this matter. On the other hand, the stepparent may continue a relationship with the stepchild, either as the primary caretaker or in some other role. Even if the stepparent-child relationship continues in this fashion, the in loco parentis doctrine imposes no financial responsibility on the stepparent following separation or divorce. [19]

The case of *Jackson v. Jackson*[20] illustrates this limiting feature of the in loco parentis doctrine. In *Jackson*, the Court of Appeals in the District of Columbia held that no child support order could be entered against a stepfather following his marital separation from the mother of his stepdaughter. The Jacksons had married when Mrs. Jackson's daughter from a previous marriage was four years old. During their nine-year marriage, "[t]he husband [had] accepted Vicki as part of the family and treated her as if she were his own daughter,"[21] clearly establishing an in loco parentis relationship. When the spouses separated, Mrs. Jackson found employment in New Jersey and moved there with Vicki and a daughter who had been born during the Jacksons' marriage. The *Jackson* court described the continuing relationship between Mr. Jackson and his stepdaughter during this period as follows.

> [S]ince the separation the husband has continued to pay Vicki's tuition, with supporting expenses; . . . [t]here has been some communication between the stepchild and the husband during this period although he has seen her infrequently, and . . . according to his tes-

---

19. The right of the stepparent to have continuing contact with the child following divorce, contrary to the wishes of the custodial parent, is discussed in chapter 7, which explores the issues of stepparent custody and visitation rights. Although the courts addressing these issues have sometimes invoked the in loco parentis doctrine and have occasionally suggested that a corresponding support duty might be appropriate, no such duty has been clearly established in the cases involving stepparent custody and visitation. *See, e.g.*, Gribble v. Gribble, 583 P.2d 64, 68 (Utah 1978).

20. Jackson v. Jackson, 278 A.2d 114 (D.C. 1971).

21. *Id.* at 114.

timony the husband feels a moral obligation to Vicki and will continue to support her willingly without an order of court.[22]

Mrs. Jackson subsequently filed the lawsuit against her husband, seeking an order of child support for her two children. Although the appellate court in *Jackson* upheld the resulting support order in favor of the Jacksons' daughter, the same court refused to recognize any continuing legal responsibility on the part of Mr. Jackson for his stepdaughter, Vicki.

According to the court, the pivotal factor in the decision not to order child support payments was the stepfather's own view of the matter.

> [A]lthough he feels a moral obligation to contribute in some measure to her support, he vigorously contests the court's authority to enter such an order. At this point it is clearly his intention to no longer continue as one in loco parentis to the stepchild.[23]

This analysis reaffirmed the general rule that the stepparent's intentions govern the question of future support under the in loco parentis doctrine.

The self-imposed moral obligation undertaken by Mr. Jackson, unlike the court-ordered support requested by his wife, could be terminated by him at any time. Another difference between Mr. Jackson's moral duty and a legal support obligation involved the amount of child support. The lower court, believing that a legal duty existed, ordered Mr. Jackson to pay a greater amount of support than he had been voluntarily providing. Thus, absent any legal duty, both the duration and amount of future payments remained solely within the stepfather's discretion.

Notably, the Jacksons were separated but not divorced at the time of the lawsuit, and the stepdaughter had moved with her mother to another state. The same general rule regarding future support for stepchildren has been applied whether the stepfamily unit has been disrupted by separation, divorce, or the death of the custodial parent. Furthermore, even when a stepparent maintains much closer contact with the stepchild following a breakdown of the marriage, the in loco parentis doctrine establishes no continuing support duty.

In *Deal v. Deal*,[24] for example, the mother and stepfather executed an agreement at the time of their divorce whereby the stepfather obtained custody of the couple's two children as well as his wife's two daughters, ages fourteen and seventeen, who had resided in the Deals' home during their marriage. The agreement, which was incorporated into the decree of the Alabama divorce court, provided that Mrs. Deal would pay $500 per month to her former husband as support for her four children. Six months after the

---

22. *Id.* at 115.
23. *Id.*
24. Deal v. Deal, 545 So. 2d 780 (Ala. Civ. App. 1989).

divorce, apparently due to the mother's dissatisfaction with visitation arrangements, she requested the court to award custody of all four children to her, and to order Mr. Deal to pay child support. The Alabama trial court left custody of the two children of the Deals' marriage with their father, but shifted custody of the two stepdaughters to Mrs. Deal and ordered Mr. Deal to make monthly support payments for them.

On appeal, the court reversed the support order for the two stepdaughters with the following explanation.

> It has long been established by Alabama law that a *former* stepfather is under no legal obligation to support his *former* minor stepchildren. . . . Although there is argument made that [Mr. Deal] acted in loco parentis through his intent to care for the unadopted former stepchildren while in his custody, that argument is without merit.[25]

According to this reasoning, the in loco parentis relationship, and the stepparent's responsibility for support, cannot continue after the marriage ends, whatever the evidence of continuing ties between stepparent and stepchild.

In contrast, Pennsylvania law apparently recognizes that the in loco parentis relationship between stepparent and child may continue after the marriage ends. Nevertheless, the same negative result is reached on the issue of postdivorce support, because no financial responsibility whatsoever is associated with the continuing stepparent status. This rule was announced in the case of *Commonwealth ex rel. McNutt v. McNutt*,[26] which involved the request of a custodial mother for an initial order of child support from the stepfather five years after the parties' divorce. The stepdaughter, Melissa, had resided in the family home for the eight years of the McNutts' marriage, from the time she was two months old. Following the divorce, Mr. McNutt established a visiting relationship with Melissa, who continued to call her stepfather "Daddy." Based on this record, the trial court determined that the in loco parentis status had survived the divorce, and ordered Mr. McNutt to make future support payments to his stepdaughter. On appeal, the *McNutt* court affirmed that the stepfather's in loco parentis status had survived the divorce, but reversed the order of stepchild support. According to the court, the trial court's recognition of postdivorce support responsibility "carr[ied] the common law concept of in loco parentis further than we are willing to go."[27]

In addition to the straightforward question of stepchild support rights under the in loco parentis doctrine, which has received a uniformly negative response in the courts, other economic issues involving stepparents

---

25. *Id.* at 781 (emphasis added) (citations omitted).

26. Commonwealth *ex rel.* McNutt v. McNutt, 496 A.2d 816 (Pa. Super. Ct. 1985).

27. *Id.* at 817 (citation omitted).

and stepchildren may arise at the time of divorce. The absence of continuing stepparent support responsibility under the common law in loco parentis doctrine has affected the analysis of these additional issues, which arise from time to time under state alimony and equitable distribution laws.

Under the law of alimony, the financial need of the recipient spouse is a crucial factor in determining the level of payments following divorce.[28] As a practical matter, when a stepparent and custodial parent divorce, the actual level of the custodial parent's future needs will be increased by his or her continuing custody of the stepchild. Stepparents have argued, however, that any reference to the stepchild's future expenses would, in effect, create an unacceptable postdivorce stepparent support duty. Courts that accept this argument have refused to consider child support expenses in setting the amount of alimony owed by the former spouse/stepparent to the custodial parent following divorce.[29]

In addition to child support and spousal support, the divorce courts have jurisdiction over marital property. The laws in most states provide that marital property must be divided in an equitable manner, based on numerous factors relating to the circumstances of the parties and the marriage.[30] A stepparent's in loco parentis status may affect the property rights of the parties under this equitable distribution doctrine.

One factor that influences the distribution of marital property is the contribution of each partner to the acquisition or dissipation of their assets. If a stepparent provided financial support to his or her stepchild during the marriage, this "drain" on the economic resources of the marriage may be viewed as a negative contribution by the other partner, the custodial parent. In *In re Marriage of Peterson*,[31] for example, the stepfather argued that "[n]o authority need be cited to establish that two minor boys will cause wear and tear to the home, in addition to the consumption of marital income."[32] The Montana Supreme Court, however, refused to authorize any increase in Mr. Peterson's share of the assets at divorce, because he had voluntarily assumed in loco parentis responsibility for his stepsons during the marriage.

---

28. For a general discussion of the law of alimony, see CLARK, *supra* note 5, at 619–708.

29. *See* Needel v. Needel, 489 P.2d 729, 732 (Ariz. Ct. App. 1971); Wood v. Wood, 143 S.E. 770 (Ga. 1928); Harrison v. Harrison, 503 So. 2d 116, 119 (La. Ct. App. 1987). *But see* Commonwealth *ex rel.* Bulson v. Bulson, 419 A.2d 1327, 1329 (Pa. Super. Ct. 1980) (suggesting that alimony payments to custodial mother should reflect the needs of her child because former husband/stepfather had assumed a child support duty).

30. For a general discussion of the law regulating the equitable distribution of property at divorce, see CLARK, *supra* note 5, at 589–618.

31. *In re* Marriage of Peterson, 683 P.2d 1304 (Mont. 1984).

32. *Id.* at 1306.

By way of contrast, in *Burgess v. Burgess*,[33] the Alaska Supreme Court permitted the stepfather to receive credit in the property distribution for his stepchild support contributions during the marriage. The crucial distinction between the analysis in the *Peterson* opinion and the *Burgess* decision relates to the existence of a stepparent support obligation during marriage. Unlike the *Peterson* court, which held that the stepfather had established an in loco parentis relationship with his stepsons, the Alaska Supreme Court ruled that the stepfather in *Burgess* had not assumed any responsibility for his wife's children during their marriage. Therefore, his "gratuitous" past contributions to child support enhanced his claim to marital property in the equitable distribution proceeding.

Typically, the family home is one of the most important assets subject to equitable distribution, and state statutes frequently authorize the divorce courts to issue special orders affecting the family home. For example, the Maryland courts may issue two types of orders: one describing the ownership interest of each spouse following divorce, and another permitting exclusive use and occupancy of the home by one spouse for a period up to three years. In *Bledsoe v. Bledsoe*,[34] the state high court ruled that the exclusive use statute, which authorized orders in favor of the "spouse with custody of a minor child who has need to live in that home,"[35] did not apply in the stepfamily setting. In reaching this result, the court relied upon the absence of any stepparent support responsibility following divorce under Maryland law.

> It would be inconsistent to find that a spouse has no legal duty to support stepchildren, that the ordinary acceptation of the word child excludes stepchildren, and then torture the statute to find an intent to expel a spouse from his or her home based on an obligation to protect the children of the other spouse . . . .[36]

This ruling denies stepchildren the benefit of the exclusive use statute, which was intended "to permit the children of the family to continue to live in the environment and community which is familiar to them."[37]

Indeed, as discussed in this section, stepchildren generally are not regarded as the children of the family for economic purposes when the marriage between their custodial parent and stepparent ends in divorce. The in loco parentis doctrine, with its feature of voluntary participation by the stepparent, establishes no continuing economic ties between the par-

---

33. Burgess v. Burgess, 710 P.2d 417 (Alaska 1985).
34. Bledsoe v. Bledsoe, 448 A.2d 353 (Md. 1982).
35. *Id.* at 356.
36. *Id.* at 359.
37. *Id.* at 356.

ties. As discussed in the next two sections, stepchildren have attempted to rely, in the alternative, on the law of contracts or the doctrine of equitable estoppel as a basis for enforcing support responsibility against their stepparents following divorce.

V. The Law of Contracts

The law of contracts enables family members to enter into enforceable agreements that affect their economic rights and responsibilities. Yet there are limits on the ability to modify, by contract, the family support responsibilities imposed by state law. For example, public policy requires that the resources of both parents remain available for child support; this policy disallows any contract that would discharge the future obligation of either parent. No corresponding policy disfavors the creation of *additional* sources of support for children. Thus, a stepparent's promise to provide financial support to stepchildren is enforceable, even though state law imposes no support duty on stepparents. In this manner, the law of private contracts provides an avenue for establishing the economic responsibility of stepparents for their stepchildren.

The most straightforward support contract involves a written agreement, wherein the stepparent agrees to support the stepchild in exchange for other promises made by the custodial parent. Such contracts may be executed during any period prior to the marriage between the parties, during the marriage, or following a breakdown of the marriage. The stepparent may agree to assume responsibility for periods of time both during and after the marriage.

Consider the following agreement executed by Margaret Kelly and William McMahill shortly before their marriage in 1879, containing William's promise to support Margaret's two children.

> [I]n consideration of a marriage about to be entered into by and between the said parties, it is agreed that neither party shall, by reason of said marriage, have any right, title or interest in the property of the other during their joint lives, nor afterwards, except that the said Margaret shall live with the said William with her two children, and be supported by him. William is to instruct said children while they stay with him, as a father, and not charge them anything, nor shall there be any charge for the labor of said children.[38]

Under this antenuptial agreement, William became entitled to the value of his stepchildren's services in exchange for his promise of support. As de-

---

38. McMahill v. Estate of McMahill, 113 Ill. 461, 464 (1885).

scribed in section III, the same exchange of support and services is the essence of the common law in loco parentis relationship. Margaret Kelly and William McMahill, in effect, created that status by their contract.

The responsibility of the stepparent who agrees to support a stepchild is defined by the terms of the contract, not by the law of parental support. This distinction was illustrated in the *McMahill* case. Following William's death, Margaret claimed a family support allowance, available under Illinois law if the decedent was survived by a spouse and minor children to whom he owed support. The court in *McMahill* held that William's promise to support his stepchildren, although enforceable during his lifetime, did not create a child support duty under state law. Therefore, Margaret was not entitled to receive the family support allowance from William's estate.

Consistent with the reasoning employed in *McMahill*, the highest court in Maryland has drawn an important distinction between the enforceable promise to provide child support and a legal child support obligation. The court ruled in *Brown v. Brown*[39] that the remedies available to enforce a stepparent's promise to pay child support were limited to those established by contract law. The stepfather's promise in *Brown* was contained in the following provision of the separation agreement that he and his wife executed in anticipation of their divorce.

> The husband and wife acknowledge that a child, . . . age 6, was born to wife prior to the marriage of the parties. That despite the fact that the husband is not the natural father of [the child], in consideration of his love for the child and other good and valuable consideration, the husband agrees to pay support to the wife for [the child] . . . to continue until the child becomes eighteen years of age, is emancipated or dies, whichever first occurs.[40]

The Maryland divorce decree expressly approved the terms of the Browns' separation agreement and incorporated the stepfather's promise to pay child support. Two years later, the mother sued the stepfather after he fell into arrears in making the promised child support payments.

The *Brown* court determined that the stepfather's promise was enforceable and that the mother was entitled to pursue remedies for breach of contract, such as damages or specific performance. The mother, however, preferred a different theory and a noncontractual remedy; she wanted the court to imprison her former husband for civil contempt, based on his failure to comply with the divorce court's order. The *Brown* court denied this relief. Under state law, the contempt remedy was available only for the breach of judicial orders relating to the satisfaction of family support duties. According to the court, "the obligation of the [stepfather] here to support his

---

39. Brown v. Brown, 412 A.2d 396 (Md. 1980).
40. *Id.* at 397.

stepchild is contractual, and consequently quite different from a father's noncontractual duty to support his natural or adopted child."[41] Therefore, the only remedies available were those established by contract law.

The written contracts in the *McMahill* and *Brown* cases created clear and enforceable stepparent support responsibilities, based solely on principles of contract law. The law of contracts also recognizes many agreements based on verbal understandings between the parties. When stepfamily members fail to reduce their understandings about child support to writing, however, difficult questions frequently arise about the existence of a binding contract, as well as the precise terms of the agreement.

As a threshold matter, the Statute of Frauds doctrine may prevent the creation of enforceable oral contracts regarding stepparent support. The doctrine is designed to prevent fraudulent claims based on alleged oral agreements by requiring written proof of certain categories of contracts.[42] For example, the Oklahoma Supreme Court in *Byers v. Byers*[43] refused to recognize the promise of a husband, made during his wife's pregnancy prior to their marriage, relating to support for her unborn child, on the ground that the alleged contract violated the Statute of Frauds.

> Any contention by [the wife] that . . . by his promise Husband assumed an enforceable duty of support which is in the nature of a contractual obligation, is . . . doomed to failure. The promise, if any was made, is not in writing. Any oral promise made upon consideration of marriage, other than one which falls into the category of mutual promises to marry, is unenforceable.[44]

Even if the Statute of Frauds barrier is overcome,[45] the custodial parent still faces a difficult task in establishing an oral contract regarding post-divorce stepchild support. Proof of a stepparent's statements to the custodial parent, that "I will care for your children as if they were my own," is generally inadequate for this purpose. The problem with this form of proof relates to the limitations of the in loco parentis doctrine, which permits the stepparent to withdraw support at any time. Courts have held that most oral statements about stepfamily status merely indicate the stepparent's intention to create an in loco parentis relationship. Thus, additional evidence is

---

41. *Id.* at 402.

42. For a general discussion of the Statute of Frauds doctrine, see 3 SAMUEL WILLISTON, A TREATISE ON THE LAW OF CONTRACTS §§ 448–86 (3d ed. 1960 & Supp. 1991).

43. Byers v. Byers, 618 P.2d 930 (Okla. 1980).

44. *Id.* at 933.

45. *See, e.g.,* T. v. T., 224 S.E.2d 148, 152 (Va. 1976) (partial performance of oral contract by custodial mother rendered stepfather's support promise enforceable in spite of Statute of Frauds).

required in order to establish a binding commitment to pay future child support.[46]

The same problem arises when the custodial parent attempts to rely upon a pattern of conduct in the stepfamily, with the stepparent assuming an active parental role, to prove the stepparent's intention regarding future support. This type of behavior by the stepparent is also consistent with an in loco parentis status in the stepfamily. Therefore, even though the law of contracts generally recognizes "implied promises" based on a pattern of behavior,[47] additional evidence is required to establish the stepparent's implied promise regarding future child support.[48] Even the combination of oral statements about treating the stepchild as a natural child coupled with a pattern of family behavior may be inadequate to break out of the restrictions imposed by the in loco parentis doctrine.[49]

Custodial parents typically face a difficult task in marshaling the special facts that will convince a receptive court that unwritten understandings within the stepfamily transcend the limitations of the in loco parentis doctrine. In *T. v. T.*,[50] the Virginia Supreme Court ruled that the custodial mother had carried this burden, and ordered the stepfather to assume the responsibility of a biologic parent following divorce. In reaching this unusual result, the court relied upon three factual elements of the case. First, the stepfather did not deny his oral promise to marry the mother and care for her unborn child "as if it were his own."[51] Second, the mother had acted in reliance upon his promise; she abandoned her plans to move to another state, obtain a job there, and surrender her child for adoption at birth. The third factor influencing the decision to impose continuing support responsibility on the stepfather was the conduct of the parties during the marriage, which was consistent with a mutual understanding that the stepfather had assumed the role of a natural father. For example, the stepfather's name appeared on the child's birth certificate, and he held the child out as his own in many public and private settings. On the basis of the stepfather's oral promise, supported by this additional evidence, the court in *T. v. T.*

---

46. *See, e.g.*, Albert v. Albert, 415 So. 2d 818 (Fla. Dist. Ct. App. 1982) (holding that proof of a stepfather's statements, that he would treat his stepchild as his own child, did not change the rights and duties imposed under the in loco parentis doctrine).

47. For a general discussion of the law of implied contracts, see 1 ARTHUR L. CORBIN, CORBIN ON CONTRACTS § 18 (1963 & Supp. 1992).

48. *See, e.g.*, Hippen v. Hippen, 491 So. 2d 1304 (Fla. Dist. Ct. App. 1986) (rejecting implied contract theory). *But see* Lewis v. Lewis, 381 N.Y.S.2d 631 (Sup. Ct. 1976) (recognizing implied contract).

49. *See, e.g.*, Clevenger v. Clevenger, 11 Cal. Rptr. 707 (Dist. Ct. App. 1961).

50. T. v. T., 224 S.E.2d 148 (Va. 1976).

51. *Id.* at 149.

ruled that an enforceable unwritten contract obligated the stepfather to provide future child support.[52]

One of the several factors relied upon by the Virginia Supreme Court in *T. v. T.* was the pattern of conduct, which led to economic dependence within the stepfamily. This same factor plays an important role in assessing stepparent responsibility under an alternative theory, known as the doctrine of equitable estoppel, which is discussed in the next section. Indeed, the proponents of a stepparent support duty have frequently relied upon both contract and estoppel theories to support their claims. Absent an express written contract, however, the likelihood of obtaining child support from an unwilling stepparent under either theory is minimal.

VI. The Doctrine of Equitable Estoppel

The equitable estoppel doctrine is applied by judges in numerous legal contexts to avoid unfair results when one individual has relied, to his or her detriment, upon the words or actions of another. Thus, one noted commentator has explained the general function of this equitable doctrine as follows.

> The word [estoppel] means simply that someone is "stopped" from claiming or saying something; usually he is stopped from saying the true facts or claiming a lawful claim, and usually this is because of some prior inconsistent statement or activity. . . . Equitable estoppel . . . is based on ethical principle . . . .[53]

Within the stepfamily, equitable estoppel may prevent a stepparent from denying the existence of a child support obligation, even in the face of legal rules that fail to recognize stepparent responsibility.

Custodial parents typically invoke the equitable estoppel doctrine in the aftermath of divorce, when the spouse who supported a stepchild during the marriage seeks to terminate this responsibility. Although the stepchild has no legal right to future support in this situation, the stepparent may be estopped from denying future responsibility. However, as discussed in this section, the doctrine has been applied too restrictively to create any

---

52. *See also* L. v. L., 497 S.W.2d 840, 842 (Mo. Ct. App. 1973) (finding enforceable promise where mother "asked for and received an express assurance that the husband would not later reject the child"); *cf.* Spellens v. Spellens, 317 P.2d 613, 620–22 (Cal. 1957) (holding that custodial mother was entitled to a hearing on the issue of an alleged oral contract).

53. Dan B. Dobbs, Handbook on the Law of Remedies 41–42 (1973).

meaningful exception to the traditional rule that stepparents are not required to support their stepchildren.[54]

The estoppel doctrine requires proof of three basic elements: representations by the stepparent regarding the assumption of parental responsibility, reliance of the custodial parent and/or stepchild on these representations, and resulting detriment to the parent or the child. In the typical estoppel case, where an in loco parentis relationship has been established by the stepparent, the custodial parent and stepchild can easily prove the first two elements of representation and reliance.[55] The stumbling block in many cases relates to the third element, the requirement of detriment to the custodial parent and stepchild resulting from the stepparent's conduct. Although residence with the stepparent for a period of years will have inevitably altered many financial and emotional aspects of their lives, the custodial parent and stepchild may be unable to prove that the stepparent's role had a detrimental effect.

In making this analysis, the courts have restricted the meaning of "detriment" under the equitable estoppel doctrine to financial detriment. Thus, all of the nonfinancial aspects of a stepparent's involvement in the stepfamily, such as emotional dependency, are routinely excluded from consideration.[56] Furthermore, financial detriment has been narrowly defined in most support cases to mean lost access to the financial resources of the noncustodial parent resulting from the stepparent's conduct. This narrow definition excludes the consideration of other types of financial reliance, unrelated to the noncustodial parent, that may develop in the stepfamily. For example, the custodial parent may decide to forego career opportunities during the marriage in order to make other contributions to the family. Such a decision, made in reliance upon the stepparent's representations about

---

54. Indeed, some courts have refused to recognize the equitable estoppel theory in the stepparent support context. *See* H.M. v. Delaware *ex rel.* DDS/Foster Care, No. 80A–FE–23 (Del. Super. Ct. Sept. 9, 1981) (LEXIS, States library, Del file); R.D.S. v. S.L.S., 402 N.E.2d 30, 34 (Ind. Ct. App. 1980).

55. The necessary "representation" by the stepparent under the equitable estoppel doctrine usually exists if the stepparent assumed the role of parent and financial provider during the marriage. An additional and limiting aspect of this requirement was established in the California case of Clevenger v. Clevenger, 11 Cal. Rptr. 707 (Dist. Ct. App. 1961), which is frequently cited as the seminal case extending the theory of equitable estoppel to the issue of stepparent support. There, the California court held that the stepfather would be estopped from denying future parental responsibility only if he had represented that he was the child's natural father and the child believed this lie. *See also* Johnson v. Johnson, 152 Cal. Rptr. 121 (Ct. App. 1979). Other jurisdictions have not followed the lead of California as to this particular feature of the representation requirement.

56. *But see* M.H.B. v. H.T.B., 498 A.2d 775, 780 (N.J. 1985) (concurring opinion) (recognizing "personal" as well as financial detriment under doctrine of equitable estoppel).

present and future support, is likely to affect the economic welfare of the stepchild following divorce. Nevertheless, this type of information is generally disregarded under the equitable estoppel doctrine.

Not surprisingly, the narrow definition of financial detriment, requiring proof that the stepparent's conduct destroyed the child's access to the noncustodial parent as a source of support, results in very few successful claims. This conservative approach to the issue of stepchild support under the equitable estoppel doctrine is perfectly consistent with the general principles, discussed in section I, that have long regulated issues of legal responsibility for children within the family. The equitable doctrine has done little to change the traditional assumptions that biologic parents are solely responsible for their children's support, and that the requirement of any contribution from other adults would be inherently unfair. Thus, the Maryland Court of Appeals rejected the equitable estoppel theory as a basis for ordering child support from a stepfather, who had resided with and supported his stepson for sixteen years, with the following explanation.

> In this case, [the husband] knew that [his wife's son] was not his son and, nevertheless, treated him as his son and as a member of [his] family. Such conduct is consistent with this State's public policy of strengthening the family, the basic unit of civilized society. . . . We believe that [the stepfather] should not be penalized for his conduct . . . .[57]

The financial detriment requirement has become the doctrinal key to balancing these traditional concerns against the child's competing interest in future support, under the equitable estoppel doctrine. One clear instance of financial detriment, narrowly defined to require the unavailability of the natural parent due to the conduct of the stepparent, was established in *Johnson v. Johnson.*[58] There, the child's support claim against the biologic father was regulated by an early version of the Michigan paternity statute, which permitted support suits against unmarried fathers only by mothers who had remained unmarried from the date of conception until the date of birth. Because the mother's marriage to the stepfather during her pregnancy automatically terminated the natural father's support duty under this law, the stepfather was required to provide future child support under the equitable estoppel doctrine. Modern statutes no longer impose such limitations on child support actions against unmarried fathers, and a finding of

---

57. Knill v. Knill, 510 A.2d 546 (Md. 1986).

58. Johnson v. Johnson, 286 N.W.2d 886 (Mich. Ct. App. 1979). *But see* Taylor v. Taylor, 279 So. 2d 364 (Fla. Dist. Ct. App. 1973) (refusing to find a stepfather estopped from denying his support obligation even though their marriage during the mother's pregnancy terminated her right to sue the father for support under the Florida support statute).

financial detriment in the stepfamily typically depends upon a more complex analysis of the facts of each case.

The recent decision of the Wisconsin Supreme Court in *Ulrich v. Cornell*[59] illustrates the difficulty faced by the custodial parent who must prove that the stepparent's participation in the stepfamily eliminated the noncustodial parent as a future source of support. Upon her marriage to the stepfather, the custodial mother in *Ulrich* dropped a pending lawsuit for support against the noncustodial father and, instead, initiated a lawsuit that terminated the father's parental rights. At the same time, the stepfather initiated an adoption proceeding that was never finalized due to financial problems.[60] When the marriage ended in divorce seven years later, the parties agreed that the stepfather would retain primary custody of his stepson. Fifteen months later, the court amended this custody arrangement and awarded primary custody to the mother, who simultaneously requested future support from the stepfather under the theory of equitable estoppel. The trial court and intermediate appellate court determined that the stepfather's conduct had resulted in the noncustodial father's unavailability, and held that the stepfather was, therefore, equitably estopped from denying his own responsibility for the stepchild.

The Wisconsin Supreme Court reversed, stating in a conclusory fashion that "[t]he facts simply do not give rise to an unequivocal representation of intent to support the child, reliance on the representation by the natural parent or detriment . . . as a result of reliance."[61] Regarding the stepfather's conduct, the court merely observed that it was "admirable conduct which hopefully is experienced by every stepchild [and] the state has an interest in promoting rather than discouraging such conduct."[62] The opinion failed to

---

59. Ulrich v. Cornell, 484 N.W.2d 545 (Wis. 1992). The facts of the case discussed in the text are taken from both the opinion of the Wisconsin Supreme Court and the opinion of the state Court of Appeals, which appears at 369 N.W.2d 890 (1991).

60. The stepfather's agreement to adopt the stepchild in *Ulrich* suggests an alternative theory for imposing future support liability, the doctrine of equitable adoption. This doctrine first arose in the context of the law of intestate succession, *see* chapter 3, where inheritance rights were established for children who could prove an unperformed promise by the property owner to adopt them. The doctrine was applied by the Nevada Supreme Court in Frye v. Frye, 738 P.2d 505 (Nev. 1987), a case factually similar to *Ulrich*, as the basis for imposing postdivorce support responsibility on a stepfather. Other jurisdictions have refused to extend the equitable adoption doctrine beyond the inheritance context to the issue of child support. *See, e.g.*, Ellison v. Thompson, 242 S.E.2d 95 (Ga. 1978). *See generally* George A. Locke, Annotation, *Modern Status of Law as to Equitable Adoption or Adoption by Estoppel*, 97 A.L.R. 3d 347, § 9 (1980) (collecting cases involving child support claims).

61. *Ulrich*, 484 N.W.2d at 549.

62. *Id.*

explore the issues of reliance and detriment in light of the natural father's legal unavailability following the stepfather's intervention in the child's life.

Even when the noncustodial parent remains legally available for support, the voluntary contributions of a residential stepparent may render the collection of child support from the noncustodial parent unnecessary while the stepfamily is intact. The likelihood of a later successful lawsuit against the noncustodial parent may be diminished by this assumption of total economic responsibility within the stepfamily unit for a period of time. Many judges have taken the view, however, that this situation is not "detrimental" to the child under the estoppel doctrine. As one judge observed, "[the stepparent] should not be penalized for [the custodial parent's] lack of diligence" in collecting support from the other parent.[63]

A recent decision of the Maryland Court of Appeals underscored this observation by denying a stepfather's future responsibility following sixteen years of marriage, because the natural father might still be identified and available for future support. The stepfather in *Knill v. Knill*[64] had lived with and supported his stepson from birth until the time of divorce; indeed, the child believed that the stepfather was his natural father. In the divorce proceeding, the man identified by the mother as the biologic father stated that he had never before been approached about this matter and did not know whether he was, in fact, the child's father. On this record, the *Knill* court refused to hold the stepfather responsible for future support.

> [The stepson] incurred no financial loss as a result of his relationship with [the stepfather]. The evidence fails to support even an inference that [the stepfather's] voluntary support caused [the mother] to forego the possibility of pursuing support from [the] natural father. . . . The availability and accuracy of genetic testing refutes any suggestion that the passage of time has compromised the likelihood of a successful paternity action . . . against [the] natural father.[65]

Consequently, the decision of the divorce court, that the stepfather must continue to provide support under the doctrine of equitable estoppel, was reversed on appeal.

The timing of the child's birth during the marriage, as in the *Knill* case, calls into play a legal presumption that the stepfather/husband is the child's natural father. The presumption, which "place[s] the burden of persuasion on the party arguing for illegitimacy,"[66] is usually rebuttable by proof that

---

63. DeNomme v. DeNomme, 544 A.2d 63, 66 (Pa. Super. Ct. 1988) (quoting the trial court).

64. Knill v. Knill, 510 A.2d 546 (Md. 1986).

65. *Id.* at 551.

66. CLARK, *supra* note 5, at 152.

the husband could not be the father, based on blood tests or other evidence.[67] Of course, the issue of equitable estoppel arises only when the presumption has been overcome and the stepfather's nonpaternity has been established. In *Knill*, for example, the husband's nonpaternity was a stipulated fact.

As a practical matter, the creation of a meaningful relationship between the child and the natural father is highly unlikely in cases such as *Knill*, where the stepson was born during the marriage between his mother and stepfather, and the stepfather assumed an in loco parentis role from the time of his birth. Nevertheless, as the opinion in *Knill* demonstrates, the fact that the stepfather's role actually foreclosed the past participation by the father does not necessarily satisfy the detriment requirement under the equitable estoppel doctrine.

The burden of proving financial detriment may be even greater when the claim for support is made against a stepparent who married the custodial parent of older children, who had an established relationship with their noncustodial parent. In *Miller v. Miller*,[68] for example, the custodial mother married the stepfather, Mr. Miller, when the children of her first marriage were six and nine years old. The former husband had remained involved in his daughters' lives until their mother remarried. Thereafter, the stepfather actively discouraged any continuing relationship between his stepdaughters and their father by prohibiting visitation and destroying the father's support checks. Nevertheless, when the Millers divorced after eight years of

---

67. In order to rebut the presumption of legitimacy of a child born during marriage, the stepfather/husband may be required to raise the issue of his nonpaternity in a timely fashion. *Compare* Fairrow v. Fairrow, 559 N.E.2d 597 (Ind. 1990) (relieving former husband of child support duty after eleven years, upon discovery of his nonpaternity) *with* Hartford v. Hartford, 371 N.E.2d 591 (Ohio Ct. App. 1977) (holding former husband's motion to set aside support order three years after divorce, based on his nonpaternity, was not timely) *and* Banta v. Banta, 782 P.2d 946 (Okla. Ct. App. 1989) (applying two-year statute of limitations to bar determination of nonpaternity).

For many years, the state of Ohio regarded the presumption of paternity as conclusive in the situation where a man married a pregnant woman with knowledge of her condition. This irrebuttable presumption was premised on a belief that, by entering into marriage in these special circumstances, "the husband has voluntarily assumed the burden of supporting the child." *See* Hall v. Rosen, 363 N.E.2d 725, 727 (Ohio 1977) (relying on Miller v. Anderson, 3 N.E. 605 (Ohio 1885)); *see also* Tyler v. Tyler, 671 S.W.2d 492 (Tenn. Ct. App. 1984). The Ohio legislature modified the doctrine in 1982, making the presumption of paternity rebuttable by clear and convincing evidence. *See* Johnson v. Adams, 479 N.E.2d 866 (Ohio 1985) (discussing the 1982 statute).

68. Miller v. Miller, 478 A.2d 351 (N.J. 1984), *discussed in* Karlene K. Knaub, *Equitable Estoppel May Be Applied to Prevent Stepparent From Denying Obligation to Support Stepchildren After Divorcing Natural Parent*—Miller v. Miller, 16 SETON HALL L. REV. 127 (1986).

marriage, the New Jersey Supreme Court held that Mr. Miller would be liable for continuing support only if the natural father was totally unavailable to provide support in the future and his "unavailability [was] due to the actions of the stepparent."[69] The stepchildren in *Miller* faced an especially difficult burden in proving the current unavailability of their noncustodial father, given their prior history with him.

On rare occasion, courts have been willing to impose postdivorce stepparent support duties under the equitable estoppel doctrine. As a doctrinal matter, this result involves a redefinition of the "financial detriment" requirement, recognizing that reasonable expectations about future support may develop in the stepfamily and the failure to fulfill those expectations may place stepchildren in economic jeopardy. For example, in *Nygard v. Nygard,*[70] the Michigan Court of Appeals determined that the stepfather's conduct caused financial detriment to his stepchild because "[the stepfather] should have been cognizant of the fact that he reduced the chances that either the natural father or mother of the child would begin a proceeding whereby the natural father's paternity could be established."[71] Thus, the court's willingness to make an assumption about the impact of the stepfather's presence in the stepfamily on the availability of the natural father resulted in an order of future support for the child under the equitable estoppel doctrine.

The expanded definition of financial detriment in *Nygard* reflected the court's desire to reach a just result. The stepfather had married the child's mother during her pregnancy, stating that he regarded the mother and child as a "package deal," and that he would treat the child as his own.[72] At the time of divorce, two and one-half years later, the court found "it equitable to hold [the stepfather] responsible for child support payments," because this result permitted "injustice . . . to be avoided."[73] Of course, this broad definition of the equitable estoppel doctrine represents the minority view in this country.[74]

In summary, the prevailing definition of the equitable estoppel doctrine, illustrated in cases like *Ulrich, Knill,* and *Miller,* requires proof that the stepparent's conduct permanently eliminated the noncustodial parent as a source of future child support. This rule, which has drastically limited the number of successful support claims, reaffirms the two most compelling

---

69. *Miller,* 478 A.2d at 359.

70. Nygard v. Nygard, 401 N.W.2d 323 (Mich. Ct. App. 1986).

71. *Id.* at 326 n.1.

72. *Id.* at 325.

73. *Id.* at 326–27.

74. *See also* Marshall v. Marshall, 386 So. 2d 11 (Fla. Dist. Ct. App. 1980); Lewis v. Lewis, 381 N.Y.S.2d 631, 633 (Sup. Ct. 1976) (holding stepfather estopped from denying future support responsibility because mother was "justified in relying upon [his] sincerity in being responsible for the child").

features of stepchild support law. First, the duty of the natural parent is immutable; and second, the courts are extremely reluctant to impose financial responsibility upon unwilling stepparents.

VII. Stepchild Support Statutes

Legislatures in more than a dozen states have addressed the topic of stepchild support in statutes that include the residential stepparent as a source of support in certain specified situations.[75] However, all of these statutes place significant limitations on the financial rights of stepchildren. Most notably, the legislation fails to create any enforceable support rights following termination of the marriage that created the stepfamily.

One type of stepchild support statute, illustrated by the following provision of the Montana Code, simply codifies the common law in loco parentis doctrine.

> A married person is not bound to support his spouse's children by a former marriage; but if he receives them into his family and supports them, it is presumed that he does so as a parent and, where such is the case, they are not liable to him for their support nor he to them for their services.[76]

This is the classic formulation of the in loco parentis doctrine as it appears in many judicial opinions. As discussed in sections III and IV, the rights of the parties regarding support and services under the common law doctrine are severely limited. Because the stepparent is permitted to unilaterally terminate the in loco parentis status at any time, it provides no legal basis

---

75. *See* DEL. CODE ANN. tit. 13, § 501(b) (1981); HAW. REV. STAT. § 577–4 (1985); IOWA CODE ANN. § 252A.2(1), .3(1) (West Supp. 1993); KY. REV. STAT. ANN. § 205.310 (Baldwin 1991); MO. ANN. STAT. § 453.400 (Vernon 1986); MONT. CODE ANN. § 40–6–217 (1992); NEB. REV. STAT. § 28–706 (1989) (criminal nonsupport); NEV. REV. STAT. ANN. § 62.044 (Michie 1986); N.H. REV. STAT. ANN. § 546–A:1, –A:2 (1987); N.Y. FAM. CT. ACT § 415 (McKinney 1983); N.Y. SOC. SERV. LAW § 101 (McKinney 1992); N.D. CENT. CODE § 14–09–09 (1991); OKLA. STAT. ANN. tit. 10, § 15 (West 1987); OR. REV. STAT. § 109.053 (1990); S.D. CODIFIED LAWS ANN. § 25–7–8 (1984); UTAH CODE ANN. § 78–45–4.1, –4.2 (1992); VT. STAT. ANN. tit. 15, § 296 (1989); WASH. REV. CODE ANN. § 26.16.205 (West Supp. 1993); WIS. STAT. ANN. § 49.195 (West 1987 & Supp. 1992).

According to a survey of state statutes conducted in 1940, only six states had enacted stepparent support statutes at that time. *See* MERIAM, *supra* note 9, at 69–76 (discussing statutes in California, New Hampshire, New York, North Dakota, Oklahoma, and South Dakota).

76. MONT. CODE ANN. § 40–6–217 (1992); *see also* OKLA. STAT. ANN. tit. 10, § 15 (West 1987) (codifying common law in loco parentis doctrine).

for enforcing current and future support duties. The codification of the in loco parentis doctrine in state legislation has not expanded the support rights of stepchildren as defined under the common law doctrine.

Similarly, the stepchild support statute in Hawaii incorporates the in loco parentis doctrine, connoting voluntary and temporary support at the will of the stepparent. The Hawaii law further restricts the scope of stepparent responsibility by limiting its application to destitute stepchildren as follows.

> A stepparent who acts in loco parentis is bound to provide, maintain, and support the stepparent's stepchild during the residence of the child with the stepparent if the legal parents desert the child or are unable to support the child, thereby reducing the child to destitute and necessitous circumstances.[77]

The limitation of support to stepchildren who are public charges or without proper parental support also appears in the statutes of several other states.[78]

The broadest stepchild support statutes contain neither the in loco parentis limitation nor the needy child restriction. For example, the Missouri law provides that "[a] stepparent shall support his or her stepchild to the same extent that a natural or adoptive parent is required to support his or her child so long as the stepchild is living in the same home as the stepparent."[79] This statutory language would appear to expand the common law rights of stepchildren, by removing the unilateral ability of a stepparent to deny current and future support responsibility as long as the parties reside together.[80]

---

77. HAW. REV. STAT. § 577–4 (1985).

78. *See* DEL. CODE ANN. tit. 13, § 501(b) (1981) (parents unable to provide for child's minimum needs); IOWA CODE ANN. § 252A.2(1) (West Supp. 1993) (public charge); KY. REV. STAT. ANN. § 205.310 (Baldwin 1991) (recipient of public assistance); N.Y. FAM. CT. ACT § 415 (McKinney 1983) (recipient of public assistance); N.Y. SOC. SERV. LAW § 101 (McKinney 1992) (same); VT. STAT. ANN. tit. 15, § 296 (1989) ("financial resources of the natural . . . parents are insufficient to provide the child with a reasonable subsistence consistent with decency and health"); WIS. STAT. ANN. § 49.195 (West 1987 & Supp. 1992) (public assistance payments may be reimbursed from restricted list of stepparent assets).

79. MO. ANN. STAT. § 453.400 (Vernon 1986); *see also* N.H. REV. STAT. ANN. § 546–A:1, –A:2 (1987); OR. REV. STAT. § 109.053 (1990); S.D. CODIFIED LAWS ANN. § 25–7–8 (1992); UTAH CODE ANN. § 78–45–4.1, –4.2 (1992); WASH. REV. CODE ANN. § 26.16.205 (West Supp. 1993).

80. The Missouri statute quoted in the text is expressly limited to stepparents who reside with stepchildren. The Washington Supreme Court read a similar limitation into the stepparent support statute in that state. *See* Van Dyke v. Thompson, 630 P.2d 420 (Wash. 1981) (ruling that spouse of noncustodial parent does not have statutory child support duty).

The financial obligations created under the common law in loco parentis doctrine and the stepparent support statutes share a major limitation. Namely, stepparents do not continue to owe child support when the marriage to the child's parent comes to an end. The durational limitation on stepparent responsibility is clearly expressed in many of the state support laws, including the following Washington statute.

> The expenses of the family and the education of the children, including stepchildren, are chargeable upon the property of both husband and wife. . . . The obligation to support stepchildren *shall cease upon the entry of a decree of dissolution, decree of legal separation, or death.*[81]

Furthermore, the courts in other states have read the same restriction into statutes that are silent on the issue. For example, the Supreme Court of New Hampshire held that "the [statutory stepchild support obligation] is collateral to the existence of a valid marriage and . . . once the marriage is dissolved the stepparent relationship ceases and with it the obligation to support the stepchild."[82]

The sole exception appears in the North Dakota statute, which extends liability "during the marriage and so long thereafter as [the stepchildren] remain in [the stepparent's] family."[83] This extension enhances the support duty created by the common law in loco parentis doctrine, which automatically terminates with the marriage, even when the stepparent continues to serve thereafter as primary custodian of the child. Of course, the North Dakota provision does not contemplate continuing responsibility in the large majority of cases, where the stepparent assumes a different role following termination of the marriage.[84]

The limitation of stepparent responsibility, to the period of marriage to the custodial parent and residence in the same household with the stepchild, has serious implications for the enforcement of stepparent support duties. The family privacy doctrine, which was discussed in the context of parental support duties in section II, also applies to stepfamilies. The doctrine generally prevents the direct lawsuit of one family member against another, in an intact family. Thus, the stepchild would probably be barred

---

81. Wash. Rev. Code Ann. § 26.16.205 (West Supp. 1993) (emphasis added); *see also* Del. Code Ann. tit. 13, § 501 (1981); Utah Code Ann. § 78–45–4.1, –4.2 (1992); Vt. Stat. Ann. tit. 15, § 296 (1989).

82. Ruben v. Ruben, 461 A.2d 733, 735 (N.H. 1983).

83. N.D. Cent. Code § 14–09–09 (Supp. 1989).

84. A proposal to reform the law of stepparent support, to permit the courts to order postdivorce support payments in appropriate cases, appears in Mahoney, *supra* note 1, at 59–60. Other legal scholars who have analyzed the issue have reached the conclusion that such reform is undesirable. *See* Chambers, *supra* note 1, at 127–29; Ramsey & Masson, *supra* note 1, at 702.

from suing the stepparent for support while the parties reside together in the stepfamily. Of course, the support statutes discharge the stepparent from responsibility at other times, after the marriage terminates or the parties cease to reside together. At no time, then, is the stepchild permitted to enforce the statutory support obligation by a direct lawsuit against the stepparent.

Although not directly enforceable by the child, statutory support duties may have real financial implications for stepfamily members beyond any responsibility voluntarily assumed by the stepparent. The enforcement of statutory support duties may occur at the instigation of third parties, including the stepchild's creditors. For example, welfare officials have relied upon obligated stepparents as a source of private support to offset the public responsibility for poor stepchildren.[85]

Another category of third parties who have attempted to derive financial benefit from the existence of stepparent support duties consists of the noncustodial parents of children who reside with their stepparents. In a number of cases, noncustodial parents have attempted to reduce their own child support obligations on the basis of the stepparent's duty to support the same child. Anticipating these claims, several of the statutes creating stepparent duties expressly state that the responsibilities of the natural parents shall not be diminished.[86] The Utah statute goes further, providing that the stepparent may collect reimbursement from the parent for any contributions made to the stepchild's support.[87] In many families, the allocation of financial responsibility becomes even more complicated when the adults owe support to other children besides the stepchild. The balancing of these various support responsibilities in the complex stepfamily is discussed more fully in the next section.

VIII. The Impact of Remarriage on Preexisting Child Support Obligations

When the two parents who owe support to their minor child live apart, their respective contributions to the child's support are a matter of mutual concern. In the event that the custodial parent remarries, the creation of the new stepfamily may trigger a reassessment of child support responsibility. If state law imposes a support duty on the new stepparent, or if the stepparent

---

85. *See, e.g.,* Department of Social Servs. *ex rel.* Daniel P. v. Robert B., 500 N.Y.S.2d 620 (Fam. Ct. 1986); Stahl v. Dep't of Social and Health Servs., 717 P.2d 320 (Wash. Ct. App. 1986).

86. *See* Mo. Ann. Stat. § 453.400 (Vernon 1986); N.D. Cent. Code § 14–09–09 (Supp. 1989); Or. Rev. Stat. § 109.053 (1990); S.D. Codified Laws Ann. § 25–7–8 (1992); Utah Code Ann. §§ 78–45–4.1, –4.2 (1992).

87. *See* Utah Code Ann. §§ 78–45–4.1, –4.2 (1992).

simply begins to pay for some of the child's expenses, the noncustodial parent may attempt to reduce his or her contribution proportionally. The support laws, however, generally do not authorize such reductions; lawmakers have established the principle that the stepparent's presence as a de facto or legal source of support must not diminish the legal responsibility of natural parents.

The Iowa case of *Mears v. Mears*[88] illustrates the complex economic relationships that may develop between the households of the two parents following divorce, when stepfamilies are subsequently created. When Carla and Robert Mears divorced in 1965, the court awarded primary custody of their two boys, ages five and six, to Carla and ordered Robert to pay child support. Three years later, when Robert's income dropped, the support award was reduced by more than one-half. In 1969, Carla remarried, creating a new household with her new husband and her sons. Her husband's substantial income not only enabled Carla to become a full-time homemaker, but also enhanced the overall standard of living in their household. Meanwhile, Robert married a woman with five children from a former marriage, who received support from their noncustodial father. Although Robert's earned income was increasing and his wife worked outside the home, their combined household income did not equal the amount Robert had been earning when he divorced Carla in 1965.

In 1971, Carla sued Robert for an upward adjustment of child support, to an amount greater than the initial 1965 award. She based this request on a number of factors, including her unemployment, Robert's enhanced earning capacity, and their sons' increased needs. Denying her request, the trial court found, inter alia, "that [Carla's] present husband, as the stepfather of the children, stood in loco parentis to them and was obligated to provide for their needs as long as they are in his home should [Robert's] contribution be insufficient."[89] The Iowa Supreme Court reversed, ruling that the trial court had overstated the stepfather's responsibility and its effect on the father's preexisting obligation.

Instead, the *Mears* court limited the stepfather's duty arising under the in loco parentis doctrine as follows.

> Where a stepfather has taken into his home his wife's children by a former marriage which has ended in divorce or dissolution the question of his duty to support his wife's children while in his home should be limited to the extent their being in his home may have increased the cost of their maintenance by reason of a higher living scale than that experienced during the marriage of their father and mother.[90]

---

88. Mears v. Mears, 213 N.W.2d 511 (Iowa 1973).
89. *Id*. at 514.
90. *Id*. at 518.

Under this approach, the natural parents retained total responsibility for child support "[b]ased upon the standard of living experienced by the children before their mother's remarriage."[91] After assessing the children's needs, based on this unenhanced standard of living, and Robert's ability to pay, the court ordered an increase in the amount of support payable by the noncustodial father for his two boys.

The Iowa Supreme Court's decision in *Mears* underscores the general rule that nothing short of a legal termination of the parent-child relationship will interfere with the parent's primary responsibility to support minor children. The presence of a caring and obligated stepparent does not interfere with this principle, whether the stepparent obligation arises under the in loco parentis doctrine, as in *Mears*, or under a state support statute.[92] The Missouri stepparent support statute embodies this same principle in the following proviso: "However, nothing in this [statute] shall be construed as abrogating or in any way diminishing the duty a parent otherwise would have to provide child support."[93]

As a practical matter, the presence of a contributing stepparent may complicate the factual questions about the proper amount of support owed by the noncustodial parent. For example, the distinction drawn in *Mears*, between the children's actual needs in their household versus their hypothetical needs if the stepfather were not present, may be difficult to quantify. Such practical considerations do not, however, interfere with the theoretical premise that the father's obligation was not reduced by virtue of the stepfather's in loco parentis status in the stepfamily.

The facts of the *Mears* case highlight some additional questions about the allocation of support responsibility between parents and stepparents that may arise when both parents have remarried. First, when Carla Mears requested the upward adjustment of her former husband's child support payments, Robert Mears was residing with his second wife and her five children from a former marriage. Conceivably, Robert may have incurred a limited support obligation to these stepchildren under the in loco parentis doctrine, if he had actually assumed a parental role in their lives. In the *Mears* case, Robert apparently did not take the position that his financial contributions to the five stepchildren ought to affect the amount of support owed to his own children.

Elsewhere, noncustodial parents have raised this issue, with modest

---

91. *Id.* at 519.

92. *See* Thompson v. Thompson, 470 P.2d 787 (Kan. 1970); Barker v. High, 334 S.E.2d 479 (N.C. Ct. App. 1985); Dooley v. Dooley, 569 P.2d 627 (Or. Ct. App. 1977); Klein v. Sarubin, 471 A.2d 881, 884 (Pa. Super. Ct. 1984) ("[A]ssuming that [father] had properly attempted to demonstrate [stepfather's] in loco parentis status, we . . . can conceive of no policy reason for permitting a natural parent to employ such a tactic in order to relieve himself of his support obligation, and impose it on a stepparent . . . .").

93. Mo. ANN. STAT. § 453.400(1) (Vernon 1986).

success, especially in states where statutes expressly create stepparent
duties. For example, the Utah Supreme Court relied upon the state statute
when it ruled that a person's obligation as a stepparent might diminish his
or her obligation as a parent.

> It is . . . proper to consider obligations incurred since the divorce to
> support a "new family," including a step-child. . . . Although the obli-
> gation to support a second family does not replace the obligation to
> support one's natural children, it is certainly a factor to be consid-
> ered in making a modification of a [child support order].[94]

This ruling did not establish any absolute priority between the responsible
adult's child support obligations to both children and stepchildren. Nevertheless, the Utah Supreme Court acknowledged that the residential stepparent's contributions in the stepfamily may directly affect the preexisting
obligation to children residing in another household.

One final question about the effects of remarriage on preexisting child
support obligations involves the noncustodial parent's remarriage to a partner with significant earnings and assets. The issue that arises in this situation is whether the new spouse's resources are relevant in determining the
noncustodial parent's ability to pay child support. For example, in the *Mears*
case, if Robert had married a wealthy woman who provided the financial
support for their household, this circumstance arguably would have enhanced his ability to support his two sons, who resided with their mother.
As a general rule, courts have been willing to consider the new spouse's
actual contributions in this situation, in assessing the noncustodial parent's
ability to pay child support.[95] Of course, Robert's wealthy wife in the hypothetical case would not owe a direct support duty to her husband's children,
because the in loco parentis doctrine and the stepparent support statutes
generally do not extend to nonresidential stepparents.

Thus, the child support obligations of natural parents may be affected
in several different ways by remarriage and the creation of stepfamilies.

---

94. Openshaw v. Openshaw, 639 P.2d 177, 179 (Utah 1981); *see also* Mack v.
Mack, 749 P.2d 478, 483 (Haw. Ct. App. 1988) ("[I]f Father is legally obligated to
support Stepson, then Stepson's presence decreases Father's income available for . . .
child support."); Logan v. Logan, 424 A.2d 403, 405 (N.H. 1980) ("[I]n a modification hearing the trial court should admit and consider evidence of stepparent obligations in determining the ability to support natural children.").

95. *See* State *ex rel.* Mohr v. Mohr, 377 N.W.2d 247, 248–49 (Iowa Ct. App.
1985) ("[Father] has remarried and, although his present wife's income cannot be
used to support a child from a previous marriage, her salary can be considered.");
Commonwealth *ex rel.* Travitzky v. Travitzky, 326 A.2d 883, 885 (Pa. Super. Ct. 1974)
("Certainly, if the second wife was gainfully employed and if her earnings or a portion
thereof was contributed to the family budget, such facts would be relevant in determining the father's ability to pay for his minor children.").

Where the residential stepparent owes a support duty to the stepchildren under state law, as in *Mears*, an allocation of responsibility must be made among the several adults who are legally required to support the same child. Furthermore, a stepparent's support obligation to stepchildren may reduce his or her obligation to the children of a prior marriage. Finally, the resources of one spouse may have an impact on the outstanding support obligations of his or her partner to children who reside in another household. As discussed in the following section, the analysis of this final issue is complicated in the nine states where community property laws define the financial relationship of marriage partners.

IX. The Impact of Remarriage in Community Property States

Analyzing the impact of a parent's remarriage on outstanding child support obligations becomes even more complicated in the nine states—Arizona, California, Idaho, Louisiana, Nevada, New Mexico, Texas, Washington, and Wisconsin—that define the property rights of marriage partners under the law of community property. The essence of the community property system is the shared ownership of certain assets, income, and earnings acquired by the parties during marriage, with each spouse acquiring a one-half interest in the community assets. Application of this principle of economic sharing in marriage to the issue of preexisting child support debts raises the question of the child's access to the obligated parent's one-half interest in a new spouse's earnings and resources. In responding to this question, state lawmakers have been required to balance two competing goals: the protection of marital interests and the enforcement of child support obligations.

To date, the various community property states have taken no uniform approach to determining the impact of remarriage on the resources available for child support.[96] In Louisiana, for example, preexisting child support obligations, which are regarded as debts of the second marriage, are dischargeable from all of the community funds.[97] In contrast, the Arizona legislature has essentially neutralized the impact of community property principles in this context; a state statute provides that "[t]he community property is liable for the premarital separate debts or other liabilities of a spouse, . . . but only to the extent of the value of that spouse's contribution to the community property which would have been such spouse's separate property if single."[98] In Arizona, as in the states that do not establish com-

---

96. *See* W.S. McClanahan, Community Property in the United States §§ 10:1 to 10:13 (1982 & Supp. 1990).

97. *See* La. Civ. Code Ann. arts. 2345, 2362 (West 1985); Connell v. Connell, 331 So. 2d 4, 5–6 (La. 1976).

98. Ariz. Rev. Stat. Ann. § 25–215(B) (1991).

munity property rights during marriage, only the earnings and resources acquired by the obligated spouse are liable for his or her child support debts.

In *Van Dyke v. Thompson*,[99] the Supreme Court of Washington assessed the availability of a nonobligated spouse's wages to satisfy her partner's child support duty, in the absence of a governing statute. The court resolved the issue by analyzing the important state policies involved in this context. At the time of the lawsuit, Sydney Van Dyke was unemployed and owed child support to his nonresident child from a prior marriage. The State of Washington, which had been providing public assistance for the child, attempted to satisfy Sydney's debt by attaching one-half of the wages of his second wife, Sallie Van Dyke. While acknowledging the special "need to support children of a prior marriage," the court held that Sydney's one-half interest in his wife's earnings was not subject to this claim. The court emphasized policies of the state relating to protection of the new marital community: "[T]he rule urged by [the State] would . . . discourage marriage; . . . [and] it would place unwarranted stress upon a second marriage."[100]

The dissenting opinion characterized these considerations as "bugaboos," and chastised the court for failing to vindicate the interest of the state in enforcing child support obligations. The dissenting justice underscored a concern raised by the facts of the *Van Dyke* case, that "[a] new community should not be able to avoid a prior support obligation by deciding that only the nonobligated spouse shall work."[101] According to this alternative assessment of the competing policies, Sydney Van Dyke's one-half interest in his wife's earnings should have been liable for his child support debts.[102]

The issue addressed in *Van Dyke*, regarding a child's access to the noncustodial parent's community property interest in the earnings of the other spouse, is distinct from the question considered in the previous section, as to whether those same resources should be considered in computing the obligated parent's ability to pay child support out of his or her own

---

99. Van Dyke v. Thompson, 630 P.2d 420 (Wash. 1981).

100. *Id.* at 423.

101. *Id.* at 424 (dissenting opinion).

102. Subsequent to the state supreme court's decision in *Van Dyke*, the Washington legislature enacted the following statute, which addresses the issue of the liability of community assets for child support debts.

The obligation of a parent . . . to support a child may be collected out of the parent's . . . separate property, the parent's . . . earnings and accumulations, and the parent's . . . share of community personal and real property. Funds in a community bank account which can be identified as the earnings of the nonobligated spouse are exempt from satisfaction of the child support obligation of the debtor spouse. WASH. REV. CODE ANN. § 26.16.200 (West 1986).

resources.[103] Of course, the *Van Dyke* issue can only arise in a community property state, while the latter issue is not so restricted. The distinction between the two is emphasized in the California Code, which first provides that the earnings of one spouse are not liable for debts incurred by his or her partner prior to marriage, including child support debts;[104] the same statute adds that "[n]othing in this section limits the matters a court may take into consideration in determining or modifying the amount of a support order, including, but not limited to, the earnings of the spouses of the parties."[105] The latter provision is consistent with the general rule nationwide, which was discussed in the previous section.[106]

In summary, parties with children from prior unions, who marry in one of the community property states, may find that their preexisting child support obligations are affected by the marital property laws. The important issue that arises exclusively in these states relates to children's access to the wages and other property acquired by the spouse of their noncustodial parent. The principle of community property provides a theoretical basis for such child support claims, although state lawmakers have reached inconsistent results in assessing them. Thus, the law of marital property adds a level of complication to the analysis of child support responsibility following remarriage in the nine community property states.

X. Stepparent Responsibility under the AFDC Program

The Aid to Families with Dependent Children (AFDC) Program, established by Congress under the Social Security Act of 1935, assists poor families by supplementing the private income and resources available for child support.[107] The involvement of both the state and federal govern-

---

103. *See supra* text accompanying note 95.

104. *See* Cal. Civ. Code §§ 5120.110(b), 5120.150(a) (West Supp. 1992).

105. *Id.* § 5120.150(c).

106. *But see In re* Montell, 775 P.2d 976 (Wash. Ct. App. 1989) (refusing to consider resources of nonobligated spouse in assessing child support obligation of noncustodial parent).

107. *See* 42 U.S.C. §§ 601 to 615 (1988 & Supp. 1990). For a general discussion of the AFDC Program, see Harry D. Krause, Child Support in America: The Legal Perspective 281–479 (1981). Children receive billions of dollars as the beneficiaries of other government programs that assist poor families, including the Medicaid Program, *see* 42 U.S.C. § 1396a (1988 & Supp. 1991) (children eligible for AFDC are eligible for Medicaid), and the Food Stamp Program, *see* 7 U.S.C. §§ 2011–2015 (1988); 7 C.F.R. § 273.1 (1993) (eligibility based on circumstances of household, defined to include "[p]arent(s) living with their natural, adopted or stepchild(ren)"). Furthermore, children may receive benefits under the Social Security

ments in the design and implementation of the multibillion-dollar AFDC Program has led to its designation by the United States Supreme Court as a "scheme of cooperative federalism."[108] One important aspect of this federal-state relationship is the distribution of funds by the federal government to each state, on the condition that the state administer the AFDC Program in conformity with both the Social Security Act and the relevant Health and Human Services Department (HHS) regulations.

Within this federal scheme, two important rules directly affect the eligibility and assistance levels for millions of poor stepchildren. The first excludes stepchildren from eligibility for assistance in those states that have created a statutory stepparent support obligation "of general applicability." The second federal guideline requires welfare officials in the other states to "deem" certain portions of a residential stepparent's income to be available for stepchild support in computing the child's level of need for assistance.

The presence of a stepparent in the family has the most dramatic impact in the first category of states, where stepparent support laws of general applicability have been enacted. The AFDC Program contains a general preference for single-parent families and limits eligibility to "dependent children" who have been "deprived of parental support or care by reason of the death, continued absence from the home . . . , or physical or mental incapacity of a parent."[109] The HHS regulations define "parent" in this context to mean the child's natural or adoptive parent, or a "stepparent who . . . is legally obligated to support the child *under State law of general applicability* which requires stepparents to support stepchildren to the same extent that natural or adoptive parents are required to support their children."[110] Therefore, the stepchild who resides in a household with both a stepparent and custodial parent will fail to satisfy the AFDC test for "dependency" in those states that have enacted stepparent support laws of general applicability.[111]

According to a Health and Human Services Department survey con-

---

Act, without regard to the level of family income, as the surviving beneficiaries of a deceased worker. *See* 42 U.S.C. §§ 402(d), 416(e)(2) (1988 & Supp. 1991); Margaret M. Mahoney, *Stepfamilies in the Federal Law*, 48 U. Pitt. L. Rev. 491, 496–514 (1987) (discussing the eligibility of stepchildren as survivors of covered workers under the Social Security Act).

108. *See* King v. Smith, 392 U.S. 309, 316 (1968).

109. 42 U.S.C. § 606(a) (1988 & Supp. 1991).

110. 45 C.F.R. § 233.90(a)(1) (1992) (emphasis added).

111. Relief is provided for a limited number of poor, two-parent families under the AFDC-U Program, which expands the definition of "dependent child" to include one who has been deprived of parental support by reason of the unemployment of the principal breadwinner in the family. *See* 42 U.S.C. § 607 (1988 & Supp. 1991), *discussed in* Timothy J. Casey, *The Family Support Act of 1988: Molehill or Mountain, Retreat or Reform*, 23 Clearinghouse Rev. 930, 932–33 (1989).

ducted in 1981, six states had stepparent support statutes regarded by HHS as "state laws of general applicability": Nebraska, New Hampshire, South Dakota, Utah, Vermont, and Washington.[112] Two additional current state statutes, in Oregon and Missouri, appear to satisfy the federal standard.[113] In these jurisdictions, the presence of the obligated stepparent in the home renders the child ineligible for benefits, just as the presence of the second parent would prevent eligibility. This result follows, even though the stepparent's obligation is less substantial under state law than the parental support duty.[114]

The remaining states have no stepparent support laws of general applicability. As described elsewhere in this chapter, the majority of states impose no personal responsibility beyond that voluntarily assumed by the stepparent, and others have created limited statutory support duties that apply only to the stepparents of destitute children. Welfare authorities in several states have attempted to rely upon these narrow rules as the basis for automatically excluding stepchildren from AFDC eligibility, but their efforts have been uniformly unsuccessful in the absence of a stepparent support law of general applicability.[115] Thus, the federal guidelines have directly limited the discretion of the states on this important issue.

In the states that do not have stepparent support laws of general applicability, the presence of the stepparent in the home may nevertheless have a negative impact on the family's claim for public assistance, pursuant to a 1981 amendment to the Social Security Act entitled the Omnibus Budget Reduction Act (OBRA).[116] This federal law requires the states to "deem" portions of a residential stepparent's income to be available for stepchild support, in determining the child's level of need for assistance. AFDC benefits are generally available only to the extent that the family's private resources fall below a minimum level, or need standard, established by state law. Prior to 1981 the states were permitted, under federal law, to factor

---

112. *See* 46 Fed. Reg. 46,750, 46,754 (1981).

113. *See* Mo. Ann. Stat. § 453.400(1), (7), (8) (Vernon 1986); Or. Rev. Stat. §§ 109.010, .015, .053 (1990).

114. *See* Bishop v. Missouri Div. of Family Servs., 592 S.W.2d 734 (Mo. 1980) (characterizing the Missouri stepparent support statute as one of "general applicability" under the federal regulation in spite of the limited duration of stepparent responsibility); Concerned Parents of Stepchildren v. Mitchell, 645 P.2d 629 (Utah 1982) (finding that the Utah stepparent support statute qualified under the federal regulation in spite of a provision allowing reimbursement to stepparents from natural parents).

115. *See, e.g.,* Grubb v. Sterrett, 315 F. Supp. 990 (N.D. Ind. 1970); Meagher v. Hennepin County Welfare Bd., 221 N.W.2d 140 (Minn. 1974); *In re* Fowler, 288 A.2d 463 (Vt. 1972).

116. The key provision of OBRA is currently codified in 42 U.S.C. § 602(a)(31) (1988 & Supp. 1991).

stepparent income into this equation, but only to the extent of actual contributions made by the stepparent to the child's support.[117] OBRA reversed this rule and, for the first time, required the states to automatically include a stepparent's resources in the calculation of family income available for child support.[118]

Under OBRA, the stepchild's level of need, and the resulting level of public assistance benefits, is reduced or eliminated by virtue of the stepparent's resources. This reduction occurs whether or not the stepparent actually contributes to the child's support and whether or not state law requires any contribution. For example, in a case arising in Pennsylvania, a custodial mother's remarriage resulted in the complete termination of her daughter's AFDC grant. The mother challenged this action, alleging that her new husband refused to contribute to her child's support; Pennsylvania law left this matter to his sole discretion. The state court upheld the termination of assistance for the stepchild, stating simply that the agency policy of counting the stepfather's income in such cases "complies with federal law in order to avoid curtailment of federal funds to the Commonwealth's AFDC program."[119]

The recognition of a financial role for stepparents in the AFDC Program is inconsistent with the economic treatment of stepfamilies in many other areas of the law. The rationale for creating an exception in the context of public assistance programs is obvious; the Omnibus Budget Reduction Act was enacted to reduce the cost of public assistance programs. A related goal was the allocation of limited public resources to truly needy children. Congress believed that the stepparent deeming provision promoted these goals, apparently based on the assumption that all residential stepparents actually contribute to the support of their needy stepchildren. This assumption is reflected in a Senate Report stating that OBRA was enacted "[to] prevent situations in which children receive AFDC even while they are an integral part of a family which may have substantial income."[120]

---

117. *See, e.g.,* Lewis v. Martin, 397 U.S. 552 (1970) (invalidating a California law that conclusively presumed the income of stepparents to be available for stepchild support); Harper v. New Mexico Dep't of Human Servs., 623 P.2d 985 (N.M. 1980) (invalidating a New Mexico regulation that conclusively presumed that one-half of a stepparent's income, representing the community property interest of the parent spouse, was available for stepchild support).

118. The following amounts of stepparent income are exempt from the AFDC calculation: the first $75 of monthly earned income, the amounts paid by the stepparent for alimony and child support to family members in another household, and a limited amount for the stepparent's own support and the support of other stepfamily household members. *See* 45 C.F.R. § 233.20(a)(3)(XIV) (1992).

119. Shaffer v. Department of Welfare, 485 A.2d 896, 897 (Pa. Commw. Ct. 1985).

120. S. REP. No. 139, 97th Cong., 1st Sess. 1, 506 (1978), *reprinted in* 1981 U.S.C.C.A.N. 396, 773.

The calculation of AFDC grants based on stepparent income, in the absence of any corresponding legal requirement of stepparent contribution to the child's support, jeopardizes the economic well-being of stepchildren. In many stepfamilies, the children actually benefit from voluntary contributions to their support by the stepparent. In other stepfamilies, the reduction in benefits under the stepparent deeming provision may apply financial pressure on the stepparent to support a needy child. As a legal and practical matter, however, stepparents need not fill this financial gap for their stepchildren. To the extent that Congress was wrong in assuming that all residential stepparents with financial means would actually contribute to the support of their needy stepchildren, the law permits children to live in poverty.[121] The absence of stepparent support laws at the state level, combined with the assumption about stepparent responsibility under OBRA, creates this gap in the financial safety net for stepchildren.

---

121. In Brown v. Heckler, 589 F. Supp. 985 (E.D. Pa. 1984), the court upheld the constitutionality of the stepparent deeming provision, on the ground that Congress could reasonably assume that stepparents contribute to the support of their stepchildren. *See also* Kratzer v. Pennsylvania Dep't of Pub. Welfare, 481 A.2d 1380 (Pa. Commw. Ct. 1984).

CHAPTER 3

Property Rights at Death

I. Introduction

The legal system carefully regulates the passage of property at the time of the owner's death. The law of wills enables the owner to designate beneficiaries; the law of inheritance designates the new owners in the absence of a will; and the tax laws allow the state to share in the wealth as it changes hands. The recognition of family relationships in this context is an important aspect of the economic protection that the legal system extends to families. As explored in this chapter, stepfamily members are not treated as family members with any consistency in the laws that regulate the transfer of property at death.

First, the state inheritance statutes, which govern the succession of property when the owner dies without a will, do not include steprelatives as heirs. This refusal to recognize stepfamily relationships is based, in part, on the historical notion that heirship was defined exclusively by blood relationship. In the framework of modern inheritance law, state lawmakers have attempted to name as heirs those categories of close relatives who are most likely to be the objects of bounty within the family. The continuing exclusion of stepparents and stepchildren reflects the view that stepfamily relationships are not likely to involve this type of donative intent.

While the law of inheritance establishes a single set of rules for all property owners who die intestate, the distribution of property under the law of wills is a highly individualized process. Here, the goal is to identify and carry out the individual wishes of the property owner, as expressed in his or her will. Of course, testamentary gifts can be made to stepfamily members or to any other beneficiary. However, in situations where there is ambiguity about the testator's intent to benefit steprelatives, the courts frequently resort to the traditional notion that family wealth is intended to pass through blood lines. For example, a class gift to the testator's children presumably excludes stepchildren. In this situation, the burden generally falls on the surviving stepfamily members to prove that a different disposition was intended by the deceased property owner. Clearly, a carefully drafted will, which avoids this type of ambiguity, is the essential tool for accomplishing testamentary goals within the stepfamily.

The final area in which family relationships play a role in the transfer of property at death is under the state inheritance tax laws. Legislatures in many states have designated certain family members who receive preferential tax treatment, and steprelatives are frequently included in the inheritance tax statutes for this purpose. Perhaps lawmakers have been willing to recognize stepparents, stepchildren, and other steprelatives in this context because their status as beneficiaries in the testator's will is strong evidence of meaningful ties in the stepfamily. In any event, the law of inheritance taxation is one of the few legislative contexts where stepfamily relationships routinely receive this type of recognition.

II. Inheritance Statutes

The law of intestate succession provides for the disposition of property when the owner dies without a will. Historically, these laws established inheritance rights exclusively for blood relatives. Indeed, modern provisions for the owner's surviving spouse and adopted children are the only significant exceptions to the requirement of kinship.[1] Steprelatives, who are related by affinity rather than by blood, have not fared well in this system.

The intestacy statutes enacted in each state attempt to identify the categories of surviving family members who would be the natural objects of bounty of most property owners.[2] Not surprisingly, surviving spouses and children are designated as the primary heirs in this system; only in their absence does the estate pass to other categories of relatives, including parents, siblings, and more distant relatives. With very few exceptions, stepparents, stepchildren, and more distant steprelatives are not regarded as heirs entitled to inherit property under the intestate succession statutes.[3]

When a property owner dies without a will, his or her surviving children inherit at least part of the estate. The meaning of "children" has never been expanded in this context to include stepchildren. Nor have stepparents been included in the category of "parents," who usually inherit if no

---

1. *See* 5 George W. Thompson, Commentaries on the Modern Law of Real Property § 2412, at 254 (repl. ed. 1979).

2. According to the introductory comment to the Uniform Probate Code provisions governing intestate succession, "[t]he Code attempts to reflect the normal desire of the owner of wealth as to disposition of his property at death . . . ." 8 U.L.A. 56 (1983). *See also* Mary L. Fellows et al., *Public Attitudes About Property Distribution at Death and Intestate Succession Laws in the United States*, 1978 Am. B. Found. Res. J. 319, 323–34.

3. *See* Sol Lovas, *When Is a Family Not a Family? Inheritance And the Taxation of Inheritance Within the Nontraditional Family*, 24 Idaho L. Rev. 353, 368–69 (1988) (summarizing the limited inheritance rights of stepchildren); L.S. Tellier, Annotation, *Descent and Distribution from Stepparents to Stepchildren or Vice Versa*, 63 A.L.R.2d 303 (1959 & Supp. 1984) (collecting cases).

spouse or children survive the property owner. Indeed, a number of state inheritance statutes expressly exclude steprelatives from the definition of "child" and "parent."[4] In other jurisdictions, the courts have imposed the same limitation.[5]

For example, in *In re Smith's Estate*,[6] the Supreme Court of Washington held that stepchildren were not the "children" of their deceased stepfather under the heirship provisions of Washington law. The stepfather had executed a will containing two clauses. The first conveyed the sum of one dollar "unto each of my children," and named as "children" the testator's natural son and the four daughters of his wife. The second clause of the will bequeathed the residue of Mr. Smith's estate to his wife. Because Mr. Smith's wife and son died first, his testamentary plan was derailed, and the bulk of his estate lapsed into intestacy. The Washington Supreme Court ruled that Mr. Smith's stepdaughters were not entitled to share as "children" in the intestate distribution of his property, even though he had regarded them as his children during life and designated them as such in his will. As a result, the entire residuary estate passed to Mr. Smith's grandchild as his sole surviving heir.

A unique exception to the general rule applied in *Smith* appears in a 1985 amendment to the California intestacy statute, where stepchildren are

---

4. The Uniform Probate Code defines "parent" and "child" to exclude stepparents and stepchildren. *See* Unif. Probate Code § 1–201(3), (28), 8 U.L.A. 30, 32 (1983). The states that have adopted the Code, along with several other states, incorporate this exclusion into their intestate succession statutes. *See* Ala. Code § 43–8–1(2), (22) (1991); Alaska Stat. § 13.06.050(3), (28) (Supp. 1992); Ariz. Rev. Stat. Ann. § 14–1201(3), (30) (Supp. 1992); Colo. Rev. Stat. § 15–10–201(5), (31) (1987); Del. Code Ann. tit. 12, § 101(1), (3) (1987); Fla. Stat. Ann. § 731.201(3), (24) (West 1976 & Supp. 1993); Haw. Rev. Stat. § 560:1–201(3), (32) (1985); Idaho Code § 15–1–201(4), (32) (Supp. 1993); Me. Rev. Stat. Ann. tit. 18–A, § 1–201(3), (28) (West 1981); Md. Code Ann., Est. & Trusts § 1–205 (1991); Mich. Comp. Laws Ann. §§ 700.3(3), 700.9(1) (West 1980 and Supp. 1992); Minn. Stat. Ann. § 524.1–201(3) (West Supp. 1993); Neb. Rev. Stat. § 30–2209(3), (31) (Supp. 1992); N.J. Stat. Ann. §§ 3B:1–1, 3B:1–2 (West 1983); N.M. Stat. Ann. § 45–1–201(3), (27) (Michie 1989); N.D. Cent. Code § 30.1–01–06(4), (31) (Supp. 1991); S.C. Code Ann. § 62–1–201(3), (28) (Law. Co-op. 1987); Tenn. Code Ann. § 31–1–101 (1), (7) (1984); Utah Code Ann. § 75–1–201 (3), (28) (1993); Wyo. Stat. § 2–4–104 (1980).

5. *See* Houston v. McKinney, 45 So. 480 (Fla. 1907) (stepdaughter did not inherit from stepfather); *In re* Field, 169 N.Y.S. 677 (App. Div. 1918) (stepchildren did not inherit from stepmother); *In re* Marquet's Will, 178 N.Y.S.2d 783 (Sur. Ct. 1958) (stepdaughter did not inherit from stepfather); *In re* Wall's Will, 5 S.E.2d 837 (N.C. 1939) (stepchildren did not inherit from stepmother); *In re* Smith's Estate, 299 P.2d 550 (Wash. 1956) (stepchildren did not inherit from stepfather); *cf. In re* Paus' Estate, 57 N.E.2d 212 (Ill. App. Ct. 1944) (stepfather's niece and nephews did not inherit from his stepdaughter).

6. *In re* Smith's Estate, 299 P.2d 550 (Wash. 1956).

included in the definition of "children" in the following limited circumstances.

> For the purpose of determining intestate succession by a person or his or her descendants from or through a foster parent or stepparent, the relationship of parent and child exists between that person and his or her foster parent or stepparent if (1) the relationship began during the person's minority and continued throughout the parties' joint lifetimes and (2) it is established by clear and convincing evidence that the foster parent or stepparent would have adopted the person but for a legal barrier.[7]

A recent appellate decision in California affirmed the legislative intent to limit the benefit of this provision to stepfamilies in which true family ties have been established between stepparents and children. The court in *In re Estate of Claffey*[8] denied a claim by the children of a noncustodial father to inherit property from his wife. In refusing to recognize the claimants as "children" of their father's wife, the court observed that no "parent/child-like family relationship" had ever been established between them.

The California legislation continues to exclude many stepchildren from inheritance, even in stepfamilies where real family ties have been established. First, stepchildren cannot inherit if they reached the age of majority prior to their parent's marriage to the property owner. Evidently, this limitation is premised on an assumption that the stepparent will have less opportunity in these circumstances to develop affection and donative intent toward the adult children of his or her spouse.

The second statutory limitation, requiring proof that a legal barrier prevented an adoption of the stepchild during the stepparent's lifetime, is more complex. According to the legislative commentary, this "legal barrier to adoption" requirement would be satisfied, "for example, where a . . . stepchild is not adopted because a parent of the child refuses to consent to adoption."[9] Of course, the stepparent's expressed desire to adopt the stepchild in this situation would clearly establish the intention to create a parent-child relationship, which normally entails inheritance rights between the parties. Yet real family ties and donative intentions may exist in many other stepfamilies, where no attempt to adopt has occurred. The "legal barrier to adoption" requirement would prevent inheritance by the stepchildren in these families. Even with these substantial restrictions,

---

7. Cal. Prob. Code § 6408(e) (West 1991). This legislation modified the rule of law that had been established by the courts in California, that stepchildren were not the heirs of their intestate stepparents. *See* Estate of Stewart, 176 Cal. Rptr. 142 (Ct. App. 1981).

8. *In re* Estate of Claffey, 257 Cal. Rptr. 197, 199 (Ct. App. 1989).

9. Cal. Prob. Code § 6408, Law Rev. Comm'n comment at 513 (West 1991).

the California legislation remains the only statutory authority that entitles stepchildren to inherit as the "children" of a deceased stepparent.

Steprelatives have found their way into the statutory intestacy schemes of a few other states, but only as takers by default. Connecticut, Maryland, Ohio, and South Carolina permit stepchildren and their issue to inherit in cases where the property owner is survived by no other heirs.[10] For example, the Ohio statute distributes property, "[i]f there are no next of kin, to stepchildren or their lineal descendants."[11] Few stepfamily members will benefit under this type of law, whose primary purpose is to prevent the escheat of property to the state when the owner dies without any close relatives.

Another type of default provision also includes stepchildren, although in a less direct manner. Statutes in several states distribute property, when the intestate owner has no surviving relatives, to the relatives or heirs of the owner's deceased spouse.[12] Under the Kentucky intestacy law, for example, "[i]f there is no kindred . . . the whole [estate] shall go to the kindred of the husband or wife, as if he or she had survived the intestate and died entitled to the estate."[13] The kindred of the deceased spouse under this provision may include the stepchildren of the intestate property owner. The potential benefit to stepchildren under such a default provision is highlighted by the result in *In re Peer's Estate*.[14] There, the entire estate of a widow, who left no surviving next of kin, passed to the children of her deceased husband under the New York intestacy statute.

A more restricted version of this type of default provision appears in the Washington Code. There, only the estate assets that were earlier received

10. *See* CONN. GEN. STAT. ANN. § 45a–439(a)(4) (West Supp. 1993); MD. CODE ANN., EST. & TRUSTS § 3–104(e) (1991); OHIO REV. CODE ANN. § 2105.06(I) (Baldwin 1987); S.C. CODE ANN. § 62–2–103(6) (Law. Co-op. 1987 & Supp. 1992).

11. OHIO REV. CODE ANN. § 2105.06(I) (Baldwin 1987). Two distinct efforts to narrow the scope of this default provision in the intestacy statute have been rejected by the courts in Ohio. First, the Supreme Court of Ohio, in Kest v. Lewis, 159 N.E.2d 449 (Ohio 1959), rejected a narrow definition of "stepchild" that would have excluded the child born to an unmarried mother prior to her marriage to the intestate property owner. Second, stepchildren have been included as heirs under the default provision even if their parent's marriage to the intestate property owner ended by divorce. *See In re* McGraff's Estate, 83 N.E.2d 427 (Ohio C.P. 1948) (involving status of stepchildren as "heirs" entitled to notice of probate of stepparent's will).

12. *See* ARK. CODE ANN. § 28–9–215(2) (Michie 1987); CAL. PROB. CODE § 6402(e), (g) (West 1991); FLA. STAT. ANN. § 732.103(5) (West Supp. 1993); IOWA CODE ANN. § 633.219(4) (West 1992); KY. REV. STAT. ANN. § 391.010(6) (Baldwin 1988); MO. ANN. STAT. § 474.010(3) (Vernon 1992); NEV. REV. STAT. ANN. §§ 134.200, 134.210 (Michie 1993); R.I. GEN. LAWS § 33–1–3 (1984); VA. CODE ANN. § 64.1–1 (Michie 1991); W. VA. CODE § 42–1–3a–(d) (Supp. 1993).

13. KY. REV. STAT. ANN. § 391.010(6) (Baldwin 1988).

14. *In re* Peer's Estate, 245 N.Y.S. 298 (Sur. Ct. 1930), *aff'd*, 249 N.Y.S. 900 (App. Div. 1930). The New York statute applied in this case has since been repealed.

by the intestate owner from his or her predeceased spouse may later pass by intestacy to the owner's stepchildren.[15] Of course, in the absence of such a statutory provision, the children of a first marriage lose all inheritance rights in their parent's property, if it passes at the parent's death to the spouse of a second marriage.[16] The special default statutes may save such property for the children of a first marriage, but only if the second spouse subsequently dies intestate and with no next of kin, as in *Peer*.

Another type of default provision distributes intestate property to the surviving relatives of the deceased parent of the intestate property owner. This category of beneficiaries may include the property owner's stepparent. In Iowa, for example, a portion of the estate passes to the "heirs" of the intestate owner's deceased parent, but only if the intestate owner left no surviving issue or parent.[17] In *In re Parker's Estate*,[18] the intestate owner's stepmother inherited property under this provision, based on her status as the surviving spouse of her husband, the intestate's deceased father.

In contrast, the corresponding statute in Kansas expressly excludes the intestate owner's stepparent from the category of the parent's surviving relatives who may inherit property. The Kansas statute provides that, "[if] the decedent leaves no surviving spouse, child, issue or parents, the respective shares of his or her property which would have passed to the parents, had both of them been living, shall pass to the heirs of such parents respec-

---

15. *See* WASH. REV. CODE ANN. § 11.04.095 (West 1987); *see also* CAL. PROB. CODE § 6402.5(a)(1), (b)(1) (West 1991) (distributing "portion of the decedent's estate attributable to the decedent's predeceased spouse" to surviving issue of the latter when no spouse or issue of the decedent survive).

16. *See, e.g., In re* Field, 169 N.Y.S. 677 (App. Div. 1918) (denying claim by stepchildren to a share of the assets that their intestate stepmother had earlier acquired through their father's will). The second spouse can surrender testamentary control over property by making a contract to benefit the children of a deceased spouse. Spouses entering into second marriages sometimes execute "mutual wills," wherein they promise to leave all property to the survivor of them in exchange for the survivor's promise to benefit both children and stepchildren. Such contracts are generally enforceable. *See, e.g.*, Shaka v. Shaka, 424 A.2d 802 (N.H. 1980) (enforcing stepmother's oral promise to bequeath property in equal shares to her child and stepchildren); *In re* Young's Estate, 244 P.2d 1165 (Wash. 1952) (enforcing stepmother's written promise, contained in the joint will that she executed with her husband, to benefit his son); *cf.* Oursler v. Armstrong, 179 N.E.2d 489 (N.Y. 1961) (finding evidence insufficient to establish enforceable promise by surviving stepmother to benefit stepchildren). *See generally* Annotation, *Establishment and Effect, After Death of One of the Makers of Joint, Mutual or Reciprocal Will, of Agreement Not to Revoke Will*, 17 A.L.R. 4th 167 (1982 & Supp. 1992).

17. *See* IOWA CODE ANN. § 633.219(2), (3) (West 1992). This provision governs the distribution of the portion of the estate that does not pass to the decedent's surviving spouse.

18. *In re* Parker's Estate, 66 N.W. 908 (Iowa 1896).

tively *(excluding their respective spouses)*."[19] Clearly, the state statutes benefiting relatives of the intestate property owner's deceased parents are designed primarily to prevent the escheat of property, rather than to recognize stepfamily relationships in the law of inheritance.

Intestacy laws do recognize the existence of reconstituted families in another limited fashion, by permitting inheritance by collateral relatives of the half blood. Contrary to the strict common law rule, which disfavored relatives of the half blood, modern intestacy laws typically provide for equal rights of inheritance by relatives of the whole blood and relatives of the half blood.[20] The half-blood doctrine, however, continues to emphasize the importance of blood relationships in the law of inheritance and provides no relief for stepparents or stepchildren.

The doctrine would apply, for example, in the following situation: Wife W marries Husband H and they have two children, C–1 and C–2. Following H's death, W marries H–2 and has a third child, C–3. For a time, the three children reside together in the household of W and H–2; H–2 is the stepfather of C–1 and C–2. Then W and H–2 die. Upon C–1's subsequent death without a will, the only surviving relatives are C–2 and C–3. C–1 and C–2 are siblings of the whole blood, because they had the same parents; C–1 and C–3 are siblings of the half blood, because they had different fathers. Under many state intestacy statutes, C–2 and C–3 would inherit equal shares of C–1's estate.

The half-blood doctrine is limited to collateral relatives, like siblings C–1 and C–3 in the hypothetical, who are related by blood. Thus, if H–2 had died intestate, his stepchildren C–1 and C–2 would have no claim as heirs to his estate under the half-blood doctrine. In *In re Smith's Estate*,[21] the Washington Supreme Court described this limitation on the scope of the state half-blood statute as follows.

> The "kindred" mentioned in [the intestate succession statute], whether of the half blood or of the whole blood, are kindred of the intestate. The meaning of the word "kin" is a blood relation. As between a stepchild and a stepparent there is no blood relationship, but

---

19. Kan. Stat. Ann. § 59–508 (1983) (emphasis added). In Sarver v. Beal, 13 P. 743 (Kan. 1887), a stepfather inherited property, as the surviving spouse of his intestate stepchild's deceased mother, under an earlier version of the Kansas statute which did not contain the exclusionary language.

20. *See* 5 Thompson, *supra* note 1, § 2417, at 266. In some jurisdictions, relatives of the half blood continue to receive less favorable treatment than relatives of the whole blood. *See* Miss. Code Ann. § 91–1–5 (1973) (excluding half-blood relatives if whole-blood relatives of the same degree survive); Va. Code Ann. § 64.1–2 (Michie 1991) (providing that half-blood relatives receive half share); 7 Richard R. Powell, Powell on Real Property 997 (Patrick J. Rohan ed., rev. ed. 1992).

21. *In re* Smith's Estate, 299 P.2d 550 (Wash. 1956).

only that designated as affinity, the relationship which one spouse, because of marriage, has to blood relatives of the other.[22]

In this manner, the *Smith* court construed the provision for inheritance by relatives of the half blood to exclude stepparents and stepchildren.

In summary, the law of intestate succession, which regulates the distribution of property to surviving family members when the owner dies without a will, does not recognize family relationships based on affinity rather than blood. The strength of relationships formed in the stepfamily and the intestate property owner's actual desire to benefit steprelatives are irrelevant in this context. Narrow legislative exceptions permit inheritance only when no "real" heirs survive the property owner, in order to prevent the property from passing by default to the state. Thus, stepparents and stepchildren are rarely entitled to inherit property from each other under the statutory law of intestate succession.[23]

The courts have created an exception to the rigid definition of family relationships in the intestacy statutes through the doctrine of equitable adoption. The doctrine recognizes children as heirs, based on equitable considerations rather than their legal relationship to the property owner. The next section discusses the limited impact of the equitable adoption doctrine on inheritance rights in the stepfamily.

III. The Doctrine of Equitable Adoption

As described in the previous section, inheritance statutes restrict the definition of "children," who are entitled to inherit from an intestate property owner, to biologic and formally adopted children. The judicial doctrine of equitable adoption establishes inheritance rights for other children by treating them as adopted children of the property owner, even though no formal adoption occurred.[24] This equitable doctrine acknowledges that individuals

---

22. *Id.* at 553; *see also* Humphrey v. Tolson, 384 F.2d 987 (D.C. Cir. 1966) (holding that stepchildren could not inherit as half-blood relatives of deceased stepparent); *In re* Paus' Estate, 57 N.E.2d 212, 213 (Ill. App. Ct. 1944) (holding that intestate stepdaughter's estate did not pass under half-blood statute to nieces of her stepfather).

23. A proposal to reform state intestacy statutes to permit inheritance between stepparents and stepchildren and their issue, in cases where de facto family ties existed between the decedent and other stepfamily members, appears in Margaret M. Mahoney, *Stepfamilies in the Law of Intestate Succession and Wills*, 22 U.C. DAVIS L. REV. 917, 928–40 (1989).

24. The formal adoption of children establishes complete inheritance rights between adoptive parents and children. *See* 5 THOMPSON, *supra* note 1, § 2412, at 254. The impact of a stepparent adoption on inheritance rights between the child and his or her biologic relatives is discussed in chapter 9.

sometimes establish de facto parent-child relationships, not recognized by the intestacy statutes, that involve the need and desire of the parties to share economic benefits. However, this equitable expansion of the statutory definition of heirship is severely limited in scope, extending inheritance rights to very few stepfamily members.[25]

The doctrine of equitable adoption creates inheritance rights when "a contract or agreement to adopt a child, clear and complete in its terms, and entered into by persons capable of contracting, . . . has been fully and faithfully performed on the part of the child."[26] Once these elements have been established, the courts generally rely upon contract theory as the basis for allowing inheritance by the equitably adopted child.[27] The doctrine has been formulated by reference to the law of contracts for two reasons. First, the requirement of a promise by the property owner to adopt a nonrelative is strong evidence of the intention to create a relationship involving inheritance rights. And second, by treating the matter as the enforcement of a contract to adopt, the courts have been able to classify the successful claimant as an adopted child under the intestacy statute, thus avoiding the necessity of creating a new category of heirs.

This conservative formulation of the equitable adoption doctrine has prevented the courts from extending relief to many nontraditional families, including stepfamilies, where claims are based upon family ties and donative intent. The typical behavior within most stepfamilies simply does not satisfy the restrictive test for heirship, involving proof of a formal contract to adopt children or incomplete adoption proceedings. Indeed, stepchildren frequently face greater difficulty than other claimants under the equitable adoption doctrine. Thus, "when the alleged adopter is the child's stepparent the courts almost invariably find the proof insufficient on the grounds that the conduct of the parties was as consistent with a normal stepparent-stepchild relationship as it was with a contract to adopt."[28] As a result, stepchildren rarely qualify as equitably adopted children.[29]

---

25. *See generally* Jan E. Rein, *Relatives by Blood, Adoption, and Association: Who Should Get What and Why (The Impact of Adoptions, Adult Adoptions, and Equitable Adoptions on Intestate Succession and Class Gifts)*, 37 Vand. L. Rev. 711, 787–806 (1984) (describing judicial applications of the equitable adoption doctrine); George A. Locke, Annotation, *Modern Status of Law as to Equitable Adoption or Adoption by Estoppel*, 97 A.L.R.3d 347 (1980 & Supp. 1992).

26. Ballentine's Law Dictionary 409 (3d ed. 1969).

27. *See* Rein, *supra* note 25, at 770–87.

28. *Id.* at 781–82; *see, e.g.*, Taylor v. Boles, 13 S.E.2d 352 (Ga. 1941); Capps v. Adamson, 242 S.W.2d 556 (Mo. 1951).

29. *See* C St. Foodland v. Estate of Renner, 596 P.2d 1170 (Alaska 1979); Estate of Stewart, 176 Cal. Rptr. 142 (Ct. App. 1981); Estate of Davis, 165 Cal. Rptr. 543 (Ct. App. 1980); Alexandrou v. Alexander, 112 Cal. Rptr. 307 (Ct. App. 1974); *In re* McCardle's Estate, 35 P.2d 850 (Colo. 1934); Lee v. Green, 126 S.E.2d 417 (Ga. 1962); *In re* Estate of Crossman, 377 N.W.2d 850 (Mich. Ct. App. 1985); *In re*

The denial of inheritance rights to the stepdaughters in *In re Berge's Estate*[30] illustrates the difficulty of proving an equitable adoption in the stepfamily setting. There, the two stepdaughters moved into Mr. Berge's home, at the time of his marriage to their mother, when they were seven and eight years old. During the rest of their childhood, the stepfather educated and supported the two girls, while they worked on his farm. Mr. Berge called them "his girls," and they were generally known by his surname. Following their mother's death, the daughters remained in the stepfather's home until each one married. After his wife died, Mr. Berge stated his intention to leave all of his property to the stepdaughters and to disinherit his heirs, who were relatives living in foreign countries.

Upon the stepfather's death without a will, the Minnesota Supreme Court held that this record failed to establish the elements of an equitable adoption. According to the court, "[t]here [was] no claim or proof of any specific oral or written contract to adopt [the stepdaughters] or to make them decedent's heirs."[31] Having failed to establish a specific contract to adopt, the stepdaughters sought to rely upon the general equitable principle, that "equity regards as done that which ought to be done." The court, however, narrowed the application of this principle to the search for a contract to adopt: "[T]he maxim referred to cannot operate to make a contract for a deceased person where there is no rule of law or equity to support the contention that he ought to have made the contract in his lifetime."[32] Thus, even though the evidence in *Berge* established a close family relationship and the decedent's intention to benefit his stepdaughters, they were entitled to no share of their stepfather's property under the doctrine of equitable adoption.

The outcome in *Berge* highlights the limitations of the equitable adoption doctrine as a remedy for stepchildren who have been excluded from inheritance under the intestacy statutes.[33] No additional theories have been established in the courts to provide relief from the statutory definition of

---

Berge's Estate, 47 N.W.2d 428 (Minn. 1951); Hogane v. Ottersbach, 269 S.W.2d 9 (Mo. 1954); Defoeldvar v. Defoeldvar, 666 S.W.2d 668 (Tex. Ct. App. 1984). *But see* Foster v. Cheek, 96 S.E.2d 545 (Ga. 1957) (recognizing a stepchild's claim, based on stepfather's promise to adopt made to the child's custodial grandparents); Roberts v. Sutton, 27 N.W.2d 54 (Mich. 1947) (finding a contract to adopt based on the stepparent's unsuccessful attempt to formally adopt the stepchild plus years of family devotion).

30. *In re* Berge's Estate, 47 N.W.2d 428 (Minn. 1951).

31. *Id.* at 429.

32. *Id.* at 431.

33. Thus, Professor Homer Clark has proposed recasting the equitable adoption doctrine as "de facto adoption," available in cases where real family relationships exist and the policies of the adoption laws would be promoted by including children in the distribution of family property. *See* HOMER H. CLARK, JR., THE LAW OF DOMESTIC RELATIONS IN THE UNITED STATES 925–27 (2d ed. 1988).

heirship, which excludes stepfamily members.[34] Clearly, the property owner who wishes to benefit stepfamily members at the time of death must execute a will that names them as beneficiaries.

IV. The Law of Wills

Under the law of wills, the intention of the individual testator controls the distribution of property at death. Every property owner is free to make specific testamentary gifts to designated beneficiaries, including stepfamily members. Problems about stepfamily relationships tend to arise, however, in cases where the language in a will is ambiguous and requires judicial construction. The existence of family relationships has been a relevant factor in the process of will interpretation in the three distinct situations described in this section: class gifts to relatives, lapsed gifts to stepfamily members, and bequests to the children of a divorced spouse. In these situations, stepchildren and other stepfamily members have not been consistently regarded as surviving relatives of the testator.

When testamentary gifts are made to a class of beneficiaries, the identity of the individual class members is generally not disclosed in the will. In the stepfamily setting, when property is bequeathed to the children of a named person, a determination must be made whether the class includes stepchildren. Addressing this issue, the following provision of the *Restatement of Property* establishes a rebuttable presumption that stepchildren and other relatives by marriage are excluded from class gifts.

> When the donor of property describes the beneficiaries thereof as "children" of a designated person, the primary meaning of such class gift term excludes stepchildren, sons-in-law, and daughters-in-law of such person, and excludes other persons related to such person only by affinity. It is assumed, in the absence of language or cir-

---

34. *See, e.g.*, Thurn v. McAra, 130 N.W.2d 887 (Mich. 1964) (rejecting stepdaughter's theory that a constructive trust should be imposed on her behalf on property in the hands of her intestate stepfather's five children). In a few cases, stepchildren have been allowed to establish inheritance claims as "legitimated" children under state statutes designed to elevate the status of the "illegitimate" child whose natural parents marry after the child's birth. As a general rule, the biological parenthood of both spouses is required before their marriage will operate to "legitimate" children under these statutes. Thus, their application to stepchildren probably exceeded the scope of the legislation. *See* Thomaston v. Thomaston, 468 So. 2d 116 (Ala. 1985); Binns v. Dazey, 44 N.E. 644 (Ind. 1896); Selby v. Brenton, 130 N.E. 448 (Ind. Ct. App. 1921); C.S. Patrinelis, Annotation, *What Amounts to Recognition Within Statutes Affecting the Status or Rights of Illegitimates*, 33 A.L.R.2d 705 (1954 & Later Case Serv. 1989).

cumstances indicating a contrary intent, that the donor adopts such primary meaning.[35]

Most courts have employed a similar rule of construction, imposing the burden on the steprelative claimant to establish more inclusive boundaries for the class. Absent special evidence revealing the testator's intent to include them, stepfamily members have not been permitted to share in class gifts.[36]

According to the *Restatement*, the requisite evidence of the testator's intent to include steprelatives in a class gift may appear in the language of the will itself. For example, the New Jersey court in *Von Fell v. Spirling*[37] determined in this manner that a residuary bequest "to my children and grandchildren mentioned above" included the testator's stepdaughter and her children. An earlier clause of the will conveyed individual gifts to the testator's natural children and grandchildren, as well as his stepdaughter and four stepgrandchildren, referring to each beneficiary individually as a "child," "grandson," or "granddaughter." The court in *Von Fell* ruled that this earlier language established the testator's clear intent to include the stepdaughter and her children in the bequest of the residuary estate to his children and grandchildren.

Not all courts have been receptive to this type of proof regarding the testator's intent to include steprelatives in a class gift. For example, in *In re Kurtz's Estate*,[38] the Pennsylvania Supreme Court construed a residuary bequest to the testator's "wife and children" to exclude his stepchildren, in spite of an earlier reference in the will to the stepchildren as his children "which came to me by my marriage with my wife." The court's justification for excluding the stepchildren from the residuary gift to "children" was perfunctory: "[The testator] left children of his own which answer this description."[39]

---

35. RESTATEMENT (SECOND) OF PROPERTY § 25.6 (1988). This rule of construction also affects the eligibility of steprelatives as objects of a special power of appointment. *See* RESTATEMENT (SECOND) OF PROPERTY § 20.1 comment (1986).

36. Steprelatives succeeded in establishing the testator's intent to include them in class gifts in the following cases: Coon v. McNelly, 98 N.E. 218 (Ill. 1912); Von Fell v. Spirling, 124 A. 518 (N.J. Ch. 1924), *modified on other grounds*, 128 A. 611 (N.J. Ct. Err. & App. 1925); *In re* Sulzbacher's Estate, 6 N.Y.S.2d 683 (Sur. Ct. 1938); Herrick v. Snyder, 59 N.Y.S. 229 (Sup. Ct. 1899); *In re* Estate of Gehl, 159 N.W.2d 72 (Wis. 1968). In contrast, steprelatives failed in their claims as class members in the following cases: Davis v. Mercantile Trust Co., 111 A.2d 602 (Md. 1955); *In re* Kurtz's Estate, 23 A. 322 (Pa. 1892) (per curiam). *See generally* B.D.R. O'Byrne & J. Kraut, Annotation, *Testamentary Gift to Children as Including Stepchild*, 28 A.L.R.3d 1307 (1969) (collecting cases).

37. Von Fell v. Spirling, 124 A. 518, 519 (N.J. Ch. 1924), *modified on other grounds*, 128 A. 611 (N.J. Ct. Err. & App. 1925).

38. *In re* Kurtz's Estate, 23 A. 322 (Pa. 1892) (per curiam).

39. *Id.* at 322.

In most cases, unlike *Von Fell* and *Kurtz*, no evidence exists within the four corners of the will regarding the testator's intent to benefit step-children. In this situation, courts commonly refer to the testator's circum-stances at the time of the will's execution to help interpret class gifts.[40] For example, reference to the testator's family tree may reveal that the language of a class gift makes no sense, unless steprelatives are treated as family members. Thus, a bequest "to my grandchildren," by a man who never had any natural or adopted children or grandchildren, was construed to mean the grandchildren of his wife, his stepgrandchildren.[41] In a similar vein, class designations typically employ plural nouns, such as "children" or "nieces and nephews," and the fact that the testator had just one natural family member in the named class has been accepted as evidence of the intention to also benefit steprelatives.[42] In this category of cases, evidence about the testator's family tree, coupled with the testamentary language, has supported the claims of steprelatives as class gift beneficiaries.

Other types of evidence, which establish the testamentary intent to include steprelatives in class gifts, relate more directly to the nature of the relationships established in the testator's stepfamily.[43] For example, in *In re Estate of Gehl*,[44] the Wisconsin Supreme Court relied upon strong proof of de facto parent-child relationships between the testator and her six step-children. According to the court, "[t]he entire record is indicative of a family situation, of a mutual exchange of parent-child love, with [testator] exercis-ing all the disciplinary prerogatives of a parent."[45] In the court's assess-ment, this family status continued after the stepchildren had reached adult-hood, as evidenced by lengthy visits between the parties and other types of loving interaction. Based on this record, the court concluded that the testa-

---

40. As a general rule, this type of evidence regarding the testator's circum-stances at the time the will was executed is admissible in a probate proceeding. *See* Thomas E. Atkinson, Handbook of the Law of Wills § 146, at 810 (2d ed. 1953). The types of evidence introduced in stepfamily cases, regarding the testator's family tree and the quality of relationships in the stepfamily, have generally created no problems regarding admissibility.

41. *See* Coon v. McNelly, 98 N.E. 218 (Ill. 1912); *see also* Herrick v. Snyder, 59 N.Y.S. 229 (Sup. Ct. 1899) (holding that bequest "unto the children of my first and second marriage," by a woman who had stepchildren but no natural or adopted children in her second marriage, included the stepchildren).

42. *See In re* Sulzbacher's Estate, 6 N.Y.S.2d 683 (Sur. Ct. 1938) (holding that steprelatives were included in the bequest to nephews and nieces by a testator who had only one natural nephew and one natural niece); *In re* Estate of Gehl, 159 N.W.2d 72 (Wis. 1968) (including stepchildren in the residuary bequest to children by a testator who had only one child).

43. *See, e.g.,* Coon v. McNelly, 98 N.E. 218 (Ill. 1912); *In re* Sulzbacher's Estate, 6 N.Y.S.2d 683, 685–86 (Sur. Ct. 1938); *In re* Estate of Gehl, 159 N.W.2d 72 (Wis. 1968).

44. *In re* Estate of Gehl, 159 N.W.2d 72 (Wis. 1968).

45. *Id.* at 75.

tor intended to include the six stepchildren, along with her son, in the bequest to her "children."

In contrast, the Maryland court in *Davis v. Mercantile Trust Co.*[46] did not find the evidence of close stepfamily relationships to be persuasive. The will in *Davis* included a gift to the seven children of the testator's nieces and nephews. One of the testator's nephews had a stepson, whom the testator mistakenly believed to be the nephew's biologic child. In deciding whether the nephew's stepson should be included in the bequest, the *Davis* court observed that "it [was] clear that the testator had [him] in mind as one of the seven children who would take, although deceived as to his true status . . . [but the] crucial question is whether this designation can prevail over the description as 'child' of a nephew or niece."[47] The court resolved this question by reference to its own narrow view of the meaning of family relationships, which did not include stepfamily relationships.

> [W]e cannot find, under the circumstances, that the testator was indifferent to ties of blood, or had any desire to provide for a putative stepchild whom his nephew was under no legal or moral obligation to support. We think the description in this case is a stronger indication of intent than the numerical designation.[48]

Thus, the rules governing the interpretation of wills place the burden on stepfamily members to establish their right to participate in class gifts. Furthermore, the courts construing words such as "children" and "nephews and nieces" have not been consistently receptive to evidence that the testator intended to include steprelatives. Clearly, the property owner who wishes to benefit stepfamily members should not rely upon class gift designations, but should name them as specific beneficiaries in the will.

Even carefully drafted bequests to individual beneficiaries may be frustrated, however, by various changes in the parties' circumstances between the time a will is executed and the testator's death. Most notably, the doctrine of lapse provides that any bequest intended for a beneficiary who predeceases the testator is ineffective.[49] Lapsed gifts, which by definition cannot pass to the intended person, are generally distributed as intestate property to the testator's heirs. However, many states have enacted antilapse statutes, which pass lapsed bequests instead to the issue of the predeceased beneficiary.[50] Antilapse provisions apply only to those relatives of the

---

46. Davis v. Mercantile Trust Co., 111 A.2d 602 (Md. 1955).

47. *Id.* at 604. Technically speaking, the designation of a fixed number of beneficiaries prevented the bequest in *Davis* from being a true class gift.

48. *Id.* at 605.

49. *See* ATKINSON, *supra* note 40, at 777 (discussing the law of lapsed gifts).

50. *See id.*

testator designated in the statute, and stepfamily members have not always been included as relatives for this important purpose.[51]

In *Sands v. Ross*,[52] for example, the Ohio Probate Court refused to invoke the state antilapse statute in order to save the bequest in a step-father's will intended for the stepdaughter who predeceased him. The Ohio antilapse statute was limited to the "children or other relatives" of the testator. In *Sands*, the testator named his two stepdaughters and a niece as the residuary legatees in his will. When one stepdaughter predeceased the testator, the court refused to pass her one-third share to her surviving children, stating that "stepdaughters are not considered children" under the antilapse statute. As a result, the stepdaughter's bequest lapsed and passed to the testator's (unnamed) heirs under the state intestacy law.

The analysis of this issue yields another lesson for the drafter of wills. When gifts are made to steprelatives, a substitute gift should also be drafted to provide for the contingency of the steprelative's death prior to that of the testator. As illustrated by the outcome in *Sands*, antilapse laws cannot be relied upon to provide substitute beneficiaries in this situation.

Another change in family circumstances that may affect bequests intended for steprelatives is the testator's divorce following the execution of his or her will. In many states, a divorce automatically revokes all bequests in favor of the testator's spouse under any will executed prior to their divorce.[53] This type of change in the will may have an indirect impact on other beneficiaries as well, including stepchildren.

For example, a common testamentary plan designates the spouse as primary beneficiary and names a substitute beneficiary in the event that the spouse dies before the testator. In this situation, failure of the primary gift to the spouse due to divorce raises questions about the validity of the substitute gift as well.[54] For example, the will in *Porter v. Porter*[55] left all of the testator's property to his wife, Sena Porter, but if she failed to survive him, then to her son, the testator's stepson. Another provision stated that Mr. Porter's three children from a prior marriage would receive nothing. Six months prior to the testator's death, his marriage to Sena ended in divorce.

---

51. *Compare* Application of McGuinness, 59 N.Y.S.2d 424 (Sur. Ct. 1945) (permitting bequest to lapse) *and* Sands v. Ross, 89 N.E.2d 99 (Ohio P. Ct. 1949) *with In re* Estate of Cook, 206 A.2d 865 (N.J. 1965) (saving bequest for heirs of deceased stepson). *See generally* C.C. Marvel, Annotation, *Who Are Within Terms "Relation," "Descendant," "Child," "Brother," "Sister," etc. Describing the Legatee or Devisee, in Statute Providing Against Lapse Upon Death of Legatee or Devisee Before Testator,* 63 A.L.R. 2d 1195, §§ 2(b), 3, 4 (1959 & Later Case Serv. 1984) (collecting cases).

52. Sands v. Ross, 89 N.E.2d 99 (Ohio P. Ct. 1949).

53. *See* 5B Thompson, *supra* note 1, § 2629, at 120–21.

54. *See generally* J.R. Kemper, Annotation, *Devolution of Gift Over upon Spouse Predeceasing Testator Where Gift to Spouse Fails Because of Divorce,* 74 A.L.R.3d 1108 (1976 & Supp. 1992) (collecting cases).

55. Porter v. Porter, 286 N.W.2d 649 (Iowa 1979).

The primary gift in the will to Sena was clearly revoked by this event. Mr. Porter was survived by his three children, his former wife Sena, and her son.

The contest in *Porter* arose between the stepson, who was the substitute beneficiary under the will, and the testator's three children, who were his heirs under the law of intestate succession. The children argued that the gift to the stepson, which was conditioned upon Sena's death prior to the testator, failed because this condition had not been met. The Iowa Supreme Court rejected this construction, ruling that the will embodied a clear preference for the stepson over the testator's own children. According to the court, "[t]here is no reason to assume that in all or even most cases a testator estranged from his spouse will also be estranged from alternative beneficiaries under the will, even if they are relatives of that spouse."[56] The court ruled that the entire estate should be distributed to the testator's stepson.

Other courts confronted with the same issue have refused to preserve gifts over to stepchildren. For example, in *In re McLaughlin*,[57] an appellate court in Washington construed literally a condition that the testator's stepchild was entitled to the entire estate if the testator's wife predeceased him. Since the wife's bequest had been revoked by the parties' divorce, rather than her death, her son also lost his claim to the property.

A comparison of the results in *Porter* and *McLaughlin* illustrates the uncertain status of testamentary gifts over to stepchildren when divorce occurs in the stepfamily.[58] Clearly, any person who divorces should execute a new will; in this process, a stepparent can clarify his or her current donative intent regarding children of the former spouse.

In summary, property owners have the power to clarify their own intentions about the disposition of property at death. The designation of stepfamily beneficiaries raises a number of special issues that require careful drafting of the will. With careful drafting, property owners can accomplish their desires to leave property at death to surviving stepfamily members.

---

56. *Id.* at 655.

57. *In re* Estate of McLaughlin, 523 P.2d 437 (Wash. Ct. App. 1974).

58. A number of state legislatures have resolved the ambiguity about bequests to alternative beneficiaries in cases where the primary gift to a spouse is revoked by divorce. For example, the Uniform Probate Code provides that property designated in the will for a former spouse must be distributed as if the spouse had predeceased the testator. UNIF. PROBATE CODE § 2–508, 8 U.L.A. 122 (1983 & Supp. 1992). In the *Porter* situation, the alternative gift to stepchildren, conditioned upon the death of the testator's spouse, would become clearly enforceable under this provision. *See, e.g.*, *In re* Estate of Zimmerman, 328 N.E.2d 199 (Ill. App. Ct. 1975); *In re* Estate of Shelton, 311 N.E.2d 780 (Ill. App. Ct. 1974); Steele v. Chase, 281 N.E.2d 137 (Ind. Ct. App. 1972); *In re* Finlay Estate, 397 N.W.2d 307 (Mich. Ct. App. 1986), *aff'd*, 424 N.W.2d 272 (Mich. 1988); *cf.* Lamontagne v. Hunter, 341 So. 2d 1074 (Fla. Dist. Ct. App. 1977) (applying a similar judicial rule of construction, which requires the estate to be distributed as if the divorced spouse had predeceased the testator).

V. Inheritance Tax Statutes

The transfer of property upon the death of the owner is subject to taxation by both the federal and state governments. Congress and most states have established systems of estate taxation that levy taxes on the total estate value in the hands of the estate administrator. Thus, the identity of the individual beneficiaries is generally not relevant in computing this type of estate tax.[59]

In contrast, a second type of state succession tax, adopted in approximately twenty states,[60] is levied on the receipt of property by individual beneficiaries. Under these inheritance tax laws, the relationship between the decedent and the beneficiary is a relevant factor in determining the amount of the inheritance tax on each bequest. Close relatives of the decedent may pay less tax than other beneficiaries, because they are entitled to larger exemptions and subject to lower tax rates.[61] For example, in Delaware, the highest tax rate paid by a "Class A" beneficiary is 4 percent, while the highest rate paid by the less-favored "Class D" beneficiary is 16 percent; the exemption for a "Class A" beneficiary is $70,000, compared to a smaller, $1,000 exemption for the "Class D" beneficiary.[62]

Stepfamily members have been recognized as preferred beneficiaries in most of the state inheritance tax laws. Most often, recognition is limited to the stepchildren of the decedent. Other categories of steprelatives appearing less frequently in state tax legislation are the decedent's stepparent, the child or other descendant of decedent's stepchild, and the spouse of dece-

---

59. The following states have enacted estate tax laws: Alabama, Arizona, Arkansas, California, Colorado, District of Columbia, Florida, Georgia, Hawaii, Idaho, Illinois, Massachusetts, Minnesota, Mississippi, Missouri, Nevada, New Mexico, New York, North Dakota, Ohio, Oregon, Rhode Island, South Carolina, Texas, Utah, Vermont, Virginia, Washington, West Virginia, Wisconsin, and Wyoming. *See* Inher. Est. & Gift Tax Rep. (CCH) All-States Compendium.

60. *See* Conn. Gen. Stat. Ann. § 12–344 (West Supp. 1993); Del. Code Ann. tit. 30, § 1322 (1985 & Supp. 1992); Ind. Code Ann. § 6–4.1–1–3 (Burns 1991); Iowa Code Ann. § 450.10 (West 1990 & Supp. 1993); Kan. Stat. Ann. § 79–1537 (1989); Ky. Rev. Stat. Ann. § 140.070 (Baldwin 1990); La. Rev. Stat. Ann. §§ 47:2402, 2403 (West 1990 & Supp. 1993); Me. Rev. Stat. Ann. tit. 36, § 3462 (West 1990); Md. Code Ann., Tax-Gen. § 7–204 (1988); Mich. Comp. Laws Ann. § 205.202 (West 1986 & Supp. 1993); Mont. Code Ann. §§ 72–16–301, –313 (1991); Neb. Rev. Stat. §§ 77–2004, –2005.01 (1990); N.H. Rev. Stat. Ann. § 86:6 (1991 & Supp. 1992); N.J. Stat. Ann. § 54:34–2 (West 1986); N.C. Gen. Stat. § 105–4 (1992); Okla. Stat. Ann. tit. 68, § 803 (West 1992); 72 Pa. Cons. Stat. Ann. § 9116 (Supp. 1993); S.D. Codified Laws Ann. § 10–40–21 (Supp. 1993); Tenn. Code Ann. § 67–8–302 (1989). These states have also enacted supplementary estate tax statutes to ensure that the full amount of the federal estate tax credit for state taxes paid is recovered by the state.

61. *See generally* Inher. Est. & Gift Tax Rep. (CCH) 1000–1100 (comparing the operation of estate tax laws and inheritance tax laws).

62. *See* Del. Code Ann. tit. 30, § 1322 (1985 & Supp. 1990).

dent's stepchild.[63] Notably, the Nebraska law includes many steprelatives, as well as relatives-in-law, in a provision referring generally to the "relatives of [decedent's] spouse."[64]

Preferred status under the tax statutes has generally been confined to the precise categories of relationship described by the state legislature. First, the courts have refused to construe statutory language relating to "children" and "lineal descendants" to include stepfamily members.[65] Furthermore, legislative enactments that benefit "stepchildren" have not been extended by the courts to other stepfamily members.[66] Both of these limitations are aptly illustrated by a decision of the Colorado appellate court in a case involving the bequest of decedent's residuary estate to the daughter of her deceased stepdaughter.[67] The Colorado tax statute applicable to this gift listed both "lineal descendants" and "stepchildren" as preferred beneficiaries. Even though the will explicitly referred to the residuary beneficiary as the testator's "granddaughter," the Colorado court decided that she did not qualify as a "lineal descendant" nor as a "stepchild" of the decedent. She was, therefore, not entitled to preferential tax treatment.

An additional constructional issue arises when bequests are made to a stepchild whose parent is no longer married to the testator at the time of the testator's death. In this situation, state tax authorities have taken the posi-

---

63. Steprelatives receive preferential treatment in the inheritance tax laws in Connecticut (stepchild); Delaware (stepchild, lineal descendant of stepchild); Iowa (stepchild); Kansas (stepchild, spouse of stepchild, descendant of stepchild); Kentucky (stepchild, child of stepchild); Louisiana (lineal descendants by blood or affinity); Maine (stepchild, spouse of stepchild, child of stepchild); Maryland (stepchild and stepparent); Michigan (stepchild); Montana (stepchild); Nebraska (relatives of spouse); New Hampshire (stepchild, descendant of stepchild, stepchild of stepchild, and spouses of all these individuals); New Jersey (stepchild); North Carolina (stepchild); Oklahoma (stepchild); Pennsylvania (stepchild, descendant of stepchild); and Tennessee (stepchild).

64. NEB. REV. STAT. § 77–2005.01 (1990).

65. *See, e.g.,* First Nat'l Bank v. People, 516 P.2d 639 (Colo. 1973) ("grandchildren" did not include stepgrandchildren); *In re* Estate of Van Cleave, 610 S.W.2d 620 (Mo. 1981) (en banc) (stepchildren were not equitably adopted "children" of their deceased stepmother); *In re* Plaisted Estate, 253 A.2d 48 (N.H. 1969) ("lineal descendants" did not include stepchildren); *In re* Hopkins' Estate, 125 A.2d 153 (N.J. Super. Ct. App. Div. 1956) ("grandchildren" did not include stepgrandchildren).

66. *See, e.g.,* Estate of Kunkel v. United States, 689 F.2d 408 (3d Cir. 1982) (rejecting a challenge under the Equal Protection Clause to the Pennsylvania statute (since repealed) that applied a reduced inheritance tax rate to stepchildren but not to stepgrandchildren). *But see* Ingram v. Johnson, 133 S.E.2d 662 (N.C. 1963) (construing an inheritance tax statute, which created benefits for children and stepchildren and the "grandchildren" who stand in their place, to include stepgrandchildren).

67. *See* Denver United States Bank v. People, 480 P.2d 849 (Colo. Ct. App. 1970).

tion that the beneficiary's status as a stepchild was derived from the marriage between the stepparent and the child's parent, and that the end of the marriage automatically terminated the stepchild status. The Supreme Court of Colorado rejected this narrow definition of stepparent-child relationships in a case involving a divorced stepmother, with the following explanation.

> [T]he legislature wished to tax those persons who may be loosely classified as "family relations" at a lower rate than persons not related to the decedent. In terms of family relations, it is not at all apparent that the ties that often bind a stepparent to his stepchild will automatically terminate upon a divorce from the child's natural parent. The very fact that the testatrix in this case chose to make the bequest indicates that the relationship engendered by the marriage continued between the testatrix and these children.[68]

Other courts have similarly concluded that the status of stepchildren as preferred beneficiaries under inheritance tax laws does not automatically terminate when the marriage that created the stepfamily relationship comes to an end.[69]

In addition to the provisions expressly referring to stepparents and/or stepchildren, a number of state inheritance tax statutes establish preferred categories for de facto parent-child relationships that are broad enough to include many stepfamily relationships.[70] The following New Jersey statute illustrates this approach to preferential tax treatment.

> The transfer of property passing to any child to whom the decedent for not less than ten years prior to such transfer stood in the mutually acknowledged relation of a parent, provided such relationship began at or before the child's fifteenth birthday and was continuous for

---

68. *In re* Estate of Iacino, 542 P.2d 840, 841 (Colo. 1975).

69. *See* Lavieri v. Commissioner of Revenue Servs., 439 A.2d 1012 (Conn. 1981); Succession of Zaring, 527 So. 2d 417 (La. Ct. App. 1988); Depositors Trust Co. v. Johnson, 222 A.2d 49 (Me. 1966); *In re* Estate of Ehler, 335 P.2d 823 (Wash. 1959); *see also* KAN. STAT. ANN. § 79–1537 (1989) (expressly including the child of a former spouse); Op. Att'y Gen. No. 0–91–005 (N.H. 1991), *digested in* 17 Fam. L. Rep. (BNA) 1471–72 (1991). *But see* Hamilton v. Calvert, 235 S.W.2d 453 (Tex. Civ. App. 1950) (ruling that the statutory tax exemption for stepchildren did not apply when the decedent stepparent was divorced from the stepchildren's natural parent); 84–97 Op. Att'y Gen. 169 (Okla. 1984) (same).

70. In Michigan, Nebraska, New Hampshire, and New Jersey, the tax preferences for individuals involved in de facto family relationships complement other provisions in the inheritance tax laws referring expressly to steprelatives. In contrast, the Indiana and South Dakota statutes recognize in loco parentis relationships and do not expressly refer to any steprelatives.

ten years thereafter, shall be taxed at the same rates and with the same exemptions as the transfer of property passing to a child of said decedent born in lawful wedlock.[71]

The New Jersey statutory requirements, regarding the duration of the relationship (minimum ten years) and the age of the child at its inception (under fifteen years), are more rigid than the standard definition of the common law in loco parentis relationship.

The strict requirements of this type of de facto parent provision have sometimes been eased by liberal judicial construction, to the benefit of stepfamily members. For example, in *In re Estate of Anderson*,[72] the Nebraska Supreme Court broadly construed a statutory provision favoring any beneficiary to whom the decedent stood in the "acknowledged relation of parent" for a period of ten years and who "had his permanent home in the home of the deceased for at least five continuous years during his minority." Margaret Anderson, who claimed the benefit of this provision, first resided with her father and stepmother for a period of two years, from the time of their marriage when she was eight years old. Thereafter, she lived with them during the summer months only, until she married at age twenty-one. The court in *Anderson* concluded that the Nebraska home of Margaret's father and stepmother had served as her "permanent home" during this entire period, thereby satisfying the five-year residence requirement. Therefore, Margaret Anderson was entitled to preferential tax status when she was later named as the primary beneficiary in her stepmother's will.

Of course, the recognition of stepparent-child relationships, along with natural parent-child relationships, creates the possibility of one child having legally recognized relationships with more than two parent figures. In the area of inheritance taxation, state authorities have sometimes attempted to limit the benefit of stepchild preferences, on the basis that each beneficiary should be entitled to a tax preference as to just one "mother" and just one "father." Thus, the Indiana Court of Appeals was required to consider whether a stepdaughter was estopped from claiming preferential status as to her stepmother's estate because she had previously enjoyed the same type of preference at the time of her mother's death.[73] Rejecting the theory that an individual can have only one "mother" for this purpose, the court observed that "[the stepdaughter] had the good fortune to establish familial ties with her stepmother in addition to maintaining a relationship with her natural mother."[74] She was, therefore, entitled to preferential tax status as to the estates of both of the women who bequeathed property to her.

---

71. N.J. STAT. ANN. § 54:34–2.1 (West 1986).

72. *In re* Estate of Anderson, 230 N.W.2d 182, 185 (Neb. 1975).

73. *See* Department of State Revenue v. National Bank, 402 N.E.2d 1008 (Ind. Ct. App. 1980).

74. *Id.* at 1009. *But see* Hart v. Neeld, 122 A.2d 611 (N.J. 1956) (denying preferential tax treatment to a niece/beneficiary based on the existence of an in loco

In summary, state legislatures and courts have been more cognizant of stepfamilies in the area of state inheritance taxation than in the areas of inheritance and the law of wills. Lawmakers may be more willing to recognize stepfamilies in this limited context because the status of the steprelative as a will beneficiary is strong evidence of family ties, and because preferential tax treatment for steprelatives does not interfere with the rights of any other beneficiary or heir. As a result of the broad definition given to family relationships by most state inheritance tax laws, many stepchildren and other stepfamily members are entitled to the favorable exemptions and tax rates reserved for preferred beneficiaries.

---

parentis relationship between the niece and her deceased aunt, because she had earlier qualified as a preferred "child" during the distribution of her mother's estate).

CHAPTER 4 **The Law of Torts**

I. Introduction

The law of torts is "a body of law which is directed toward the compensation of individuals . . . for losses which they have suffered within the scope of their legally recognized interests, . . . as a result of the conduct of another."[1] Family relationships play a significant role in several of the common law and statutory doctrines that define individual rights and duties in this important area of the law. Three of these family-related doctrines are the subject of this chapter: restrictions on the ability of family members to sue each other (immunity), the recognition of protectible interests in family relationships (consortium), and the imposition of responsibility upon parents for the misconduct of their children. In addition, chapter 5 examines state wrongful death statutes, which govern the recovery of damages by surviving family members when a tort victim dies.

As in other fields of law, the stepparent-child relationship is not recognized on a consistent basis in the tort law doctrines that involve family relationships. On the one hand, the doctrines that establish immunity from lawsuits within the family have frequently been extended to stepfamilies. On the other hand, stepfamilies are not included in the laws regulating wrongful death recovery, vicarious family liability, and compensation for injuries to family relationships. As described in this chapter, the legislative and judicial judgments made about stepfamilies in the field of tort law have tended to focus on the public policies underlying each specific legal doctrine, rather than the nature of stepfamilies or the interests of stepfamily members. The result of this process has been the selective recognition of stepfamilies in the law of torts.

II. Immunity

When the tort law principles governing compensation for personal injuries first evolved, judges established general immunity for spouses, parents, and children from liability for all injuries that occurred within the family. In

---

1. W. Page Keeton et al., Prosser and Keeton on the Law of Torts 5–6 (5th ed. 1984) [hereinafter Prosser and Keeton].

recent decades, these doctrines, which bar lawsuits between family members, have been reevaluated; in many states, they have been partially or totally abolished. Thus, a survey of state laws completed in 1991 reached the following conclusion regarding modern family immunity doctrines: "What was once a nearly unanimous position in the states . . . has given way to a patchwork of full, partial or no abrogation of . . . immunity."[2]

The rights of stepfamily members have been defined in this legal con text primarily by the doctrine of in loco parentis. To the extent that immunity survives in a particular jurisdiction for biologic family members, it has generally been extended as well to de facto parent-child relationships under the in loco parentis doctrine. As described in this section, stepfamily members have frequently experienced the benefits and burdens of family tort immunity doctrines when an in loco parentis relationship has been established between stepparent and child.

The concept of family immunity originated in the early common law view of the married woman as having no legal identity distinct from her husband. The resulting legal disabilities of the married woman included the incapacity to sue or be sued without joinder of her husband in the lawsuit. Within this framework, a suit between spouses was theoretically impossible, because the husband would, in effect, be placed in the position of suing himself. Thus, the notion of family tort immunity can be traced back to the view of marriage that existed in another era.[3]

The enactment of the Married Women's Acts by state legislatures in the nineteenth century, which established the separate legal identity of married women, eliminated the theoretical necessity for the tort immunity doctrine. Indeed, at this juncture, lawsuits were permitted between spouses as to contract and property claims. Nevertheless, common law judges refused to abandon the tort immunity doctrine, fearful that personal injury lawsuits between spouses would threaten family harmony and privacy and unduly burden the courts. In recent decades, many state courts and legislatures have reassessed the strength of these same policies in the context of the modern family. The result has been a trend toward finally abolishing tort immunity between husbands and wives.[4]

---

2. Martin J. Rooney & Colleen M. Rooney, *Parental Tort Immunity: Spare the Liability, Spoil the Parent*, 25 NEW ENG. L. REV. 1161, 1161 (1991) (citations omitted).

3. *See* RESTATEMENT (SECOND) OF TORTS § 895F comments b, c (1979) [hereinafter RESTATEMENT] (discussing historical development of immunity doctrine); HOMER H. CLARK, JR., THE LAW OF DOMESTIC RELATIONS IN THE UNITED STATES 370–71 (2d ed. 1988); PROSSER AND KEETON, *supra* note 1, at 901–02.

4. *See* PROSSER AND KEETON, *supra* note 1, at 902–04 (summarizing the trend toward abrogation of spousal tort immunity, and observing that "it may be expected that the trend towards spousal liability for torts will continue"); Wayne F. Foster, Annotation, *Modern Status of Interspousal Tort Immunity in Personal Injury and Wrongful Death Actions*, 92 A.L.R.3d 901 (1979 & Supp. 1992) (summarizing state law of tort immunity between spouses).

Historically, no strict legal disability, corresponding to the disability of married women, prevented lawsuits between minor children and their parents. Still, for many years, the well-documented "history of almost unbridled authority"[5] of parents over their children effectively barred intrafamily lawsuits. Indeed, the first reported U.S. case involving a child's claim for personal injury damages against a parent was *Hewellette v. George*,[6] decided by the Mississippi Supreme Court in 1891.

In *Hewellette*, which is regarded as the seminal case in the area of parent-child tort immunity, the Mississippi Supreme Court extended the theory of family immunity to the relationship between unemancipated children and their parents. As a result, the plaintiff daughter was not permitted to sue her mother for wrongfully placing her in an asylum. In announcing the parent-child immunity doctrine, the Mississippi Supreme Court invoked the same justifications that already supported the well-established rule of spousal immunity, especially the themes of harmony and privacy within the family. Moreover, the outcome in *Hewellette* reinforced the traditional view that the proper status of children in the family and in society subjected them to the "almost unbridled authority" of their parents.[7]

Courts in other jurisdictions quickly adopted the doctrine of *Hewellette*, and carefully refined their reasons for denying compensation to family members for their injuries. First, the principles of family privacy and parental autonomy guaranteed freedom for parents from interference in raising their children. The related goal of family harmony was promoted by avoiding the negative and disruptive aspects of litigation between family members. Finally, judges expressed the view that intrafamily lawsuits would have undesirable economic consequences, including the depletion or reallocation of family resources and an increase in collusive lawsuits against insurance companies.

The dual policies relating to privacy and harmony within the family have emerged from this list as compelling considerations in the present-day

---

5. Gail D. Hollister, *Parent-Child Immunity: A Doctrine in Search of Justification*, 50 FORDHAM L. REV. 489, 493 (1982). *See generally* Barbara Bennett Woodhouse, *"Who Owns the Child?": Meyer and Pierce and the Child As Property*, 33 WM. & MARY L. REV. 995, 1036–59 (1992) (discussing historical development of laws regulating relationships between parents and children).

6. Hewellette v. George, 9 So. 885 (Miss. 1891), *overruled in part by* Glaskox v. Glaskox, 614 So. 2d 906 (Miss. 1992) (creating cause of action between parent and child for negligent operation of automobile).

7. The broad immunity doctrine announced in *Hewellette v. George* extended to both parents and children; neither could be sued for tortious injury to the other. Several aspects of the immunity doctrine, such as the principle of parental autonomy, have no application to lawsuits by parents against their children. Thus, one modern proposal for limiting the immunity doctrine would eliminate protection for children against lawsuits by their parents. *See* CLARK, *supra* note 3, at 380 (collecting recent cases that have imposed this limitation).

analysis of immunity issues.[8] The strength of these family-related policies is reflected in judicial decisions that extend parental immunity to stepfamilies where in loco parentis ties have been established. For example, the opinion of the Connecticut Superior Court in *Bricault v. Deveau* emphasized the importance of family privacy and harmony in this context.

> The reason for the [immunity] rule is that to permit such suits would tend to undermine family unity, bring discord into the family, weaken its government and disturb its peace.
>
> These reasons are as applicable to a stepfather who stands in loco parentis to a stepson as they are to the father-son relationship.[9]

With few exceptions, both the rule and reasoning of the *Bricault* case have been adopted by other courts that have considered the issue of tort immunity in the stepfamily and in other de facto families bound together by in loco parentis relationships.[10] Thus, judicial concern for family harmony and privacy has prevented lawsuits between family members, in both biologic families and stepfamilies.

Despite the importance of the underlying family-related policies, the

---

8. *See* Hollister, *supra* note 5, at 493–508; Rooney & Rooney, *supra* note 2, at 1164–66 (discussing modern justifications for the parent-child immunity doctrine).

9. Bricault v. Deveau, 157 A.2d 604, 605 (Conn. Super. Ct. 1960).

10. *See* Trudell v. Leatherby, 300 P. 7, 9 (Cal. 1931) ("The same vexatious conditions created in the family circle by litigation between parent and child would result from like litigation instituted by a minor against the stepfather or stepmother when the minor has been taken into, and is a member of, the household of the latter."); London Guarantee & Accident Co. v. Smith, 64 N.W.2d 781, 784 (Minn. 1954); Rutkowski v. Wasko, 143 N.Y.S.2d 1, 3–4 (App. Div. 1955); Wooden v. Hale, 426 P.2d 679, 681 (Okla. 1967); Gunn v. Rollings, 157 S.E.2d 590, 591–92 (S.C. 1967); Lyles v. Jackson, 223 S.E.2d 873, 874 (Va. 1976) ("The basis for the [immunity] rule was that litigation by a child against his parent would tend to disturb the peace and tranquility of the home or disrupt the family finances. . . . This same reasoning applies to one standing in loco parentis."). The underlying rules establishing immunity between natural parents and their children, applied to steprelatives in *Trudell, Wooden, Gunn,* and *Lyles,* have been abrogated since the decisions in those cases. *See* Gibson v. Gibson, 479 P.2d 648 (Cal. 1971) (abrogating immunity doctrine); Unah v. Martin, 676 P.2d 1366 (Okla. 1984) (abolishing immunity in auto cases); Elam v. Elam, 268 S.E.2d 109 (S.C. 1980) (abrogating immunity doctrine); Smith v. Kauffman, 183 S.E.2d 190 (Va. 1971) (abolishing immunity in auto cases).

There are a few exceptions to the general rule that courts have extended parental immunity doctrines to in loco parentis relationships. *See* Burdick v. Nawrocki, 154 A.2d 242 (Conn. Super. Ct. 1959) (refusing to extend immunity to stepfather for negligent operation of motor vehicle); Rayburn v. Moore, 241 So. 2d 675 (Miss. 1970) (refusing to extend immunity to stepfather in wrongful death action by stepdaughter); Wilkins v. Kane, 181 A.2d 417 (N.J. Super. Ct. 1962) (refusing to extend immunity for negligence to grandmother who stood in loco parentis to injured child).

blanket rule of parent-child immunity, first announced in *Hewellette v. George*, has not withstood the test of time. In numerous situations, the absolute bar against recovery for personal injuries within the family proved to be inconsistent with the basic goals of the tort law system, relating to fairness and the compensation of victims. Furthermore, in the decades following the decision in *Hewellette*, the failure to compensate injured children came into direct conflict with the emerging social and legal view of children. A scholar who wrote about the immunity doctrine in 1982 summarized this important transition.

> In the ninety years since the initial adoption of the immunity, society's view of the child, and the parent-child relationship, has changed radically. Children are now viewed as individuals with rights of their own, and the parent-child relationship has become more egalitarian.[11]

When lawmakers began to factor the interests of uncompensated children and other injured family members into the analysis, the rule of unqualified immunity was modified in both the biologic family and the stepfamily.[12]

Historically, the first encroachments on the *Hewellette* rule of blanket family immunity took the form of limited exceptions for certain types of tortious behavior. The most compelling exception to parent-child immunity recognizes the right of abused children to sue their parents for damages. Here, the goals of preserving family harmony and parental autonomy have lost their relevance, and conversely, the competing goals of assisting and compensating victims are most compelling.[13] The Alabama Supreme Court balanced the competing interests in precisely this manner, when it announced the following rule of parental tort liability for the sexual abuse of children.

---

11. Hollister, *supra* note 5, at 508.

12. Although the issue of parent-child tort immunity remains primarily a common law subject with little legislative involvement, a handful of state legislatures have become involved in defining the rights of parents and children to sue each other, usually by placing restrictions on existing immunity doctrines. *See, e.g.*, CONN. GEN. STAT. ANN. § 52–572C (West 1991) (creating exception to immunity for negligent operation of aircraft, motor vehicle, or vessel); N.C. GEN. STAT. § 1–539.21 (Supp. 1992) (establishing motor vehicle exception to parental immunity); N.D. CENT. CODE § 9–10–06 (1987) (establishing general rule of liability for all persons for their negligent actions), *applied in* Nuelle v. Wells, 154 N.W.2d 364 (N.D. 1967) (holding parent liable to child). *But see* LA. REV. STAT. ANN. § 9:571 (West 1991) (establishing immunity for parents against tort claims by their children).

13. Other laws that protect abused children include civil dependency and neglect laws, which enable the state to remove children from an abusive home, and criminal abuse statutes. Like the exception to parental tort immunity discussed in the text, these laws assign priority to the goal of protecting children over the interests involved in family privacy and autonomy. *See* chapter 10.

To leave children who are victims of such wrongful, intentional, heinous acts without a right to redress those wrongs in a civil action is unconscionable, especially where the harm to the family fabric has already occurred through that abuse. Because we see no reason to adhere to the doctrine of parental immunity when the purpose for that immunity is no longer served, . . . we are . . . creating an exception to the doctrine, limited to sexual abuse cases only.[14]

The minor plaintiff in *Hurst v. Capitell* sued her stepfather for damages relating to his abusive behavior; she also sued her mother for aiding and abetting in this activity. The trial court had denied both claims under Alabama's general immunity doctrine. On appeal, the Alabama Supreme Court created the limitation on parental immunity for acts of sexual abuse in the family and applied this rule evenhandedly to both the mother and stepfather.

> In creating this exception to the parental immunity doctrine, we make no distinction between natural or adoptive parents or stepparents; the plethora of such cases as [the plaintiff stepdaughter's case] indicates that sexual abuse is not a respecter of parental status.[15]

Accordingly, the *Hurst* case was remanded for trial of the stepdaughter's claims against both her mother and stepfather.

Other jurisdictions have defined an exception from immunity more broadly, to include any injurious activity by a parent that is intentional, willful, or malicious.[16] Thus, the California court in *Gillett v. Gillett*[17] permitted an eight-year-old girl to sue her stepmother, whose beating of the

---

14. Hurst v. Capitell, 539 So. 2d 264, 266 (Ala. 1989).

15. *Id.*; *see also* Wilson v. Wilson, 742 F.2d 1004 (6th Cir. 1984) (holding that Tennessee law permits a stepchild's lawsuit against the stepparent for sexual assault).

16. *See, e.g.*, Gillett v. Gillett, 335 P.2d 736 (Cal. Dist. Ct. App. 1959); Perkins v. Robertson, 295 P.2d 972 (Cal. Dist. Ct. App. 1956) (denying immunity to stepfather for willful or malicious torts). *But see* McKelvey v. McKelvey, 77 S.W. 664 (Tenn. 1903) (denying any "civil remedy . . . for personal injuries inflicted" by stepmother's alleged "cruel and inhuman treatment"); Barranco v. Jackson, 690 S.W.2d 221 (Tenn. 1985) (reaffirming the rule established in *McKelvey*).
Parents and stepparents, who must pay damages in child abuse cases, may be denied reimbursement under their personal liability insurance policies, which typically exclude coverage for liability resulting from the intentional behavior of the insured. *See, e.g.*, CNA Ins. Co. v. McGinnis, 666 S.W.2d 689, 691 (Ark. 1984) ("[F]or a stepfather in such a situation to claim that he did not expect or intend to cause injury, flies in the face of all reason, common sense and experience."); Rodriguez v. Williams, 729 P.2d 627 (Wash. 1986).

17. Gillett v. Gillett, 335 P.2d 736 (Cal. Dist. Ct. App. 1959).

child resulted in injuries that required the surgical removal of her spleen and kidney. Once again, the interest in compensating the victim was strong, while the purposes of the immunity doctrine seemed irrelevant under the circumstances.

> The rationale of the cases refusing to extend immunity to the parent for wilful or malicious torts against his minor children is that the lack of such immunity does not conflict with or inhibit reasonable parental discipline. . . . Since the law imposes on the parent a duty to rear and discipline his child . . . , the parent has a wide discretion in the performance of his parental functions, but that discretion does not include the right wilfully to inflict personal injuries beyond the limits of reasonable parental discipline. . . . A child, like every other individual, has a right to freedom from such injury.[18]

The *Gillett* court easily concluded that the stepmother had violated this standard of behavior, observing "[t]hat the limit of reasonable punishment was passed in this instance and that defendant's violence was willful admits of little debate."[19]

The exceptions for willful or intentional torts, established by the decisions in *Hurst* and *Gillett*, leaves the immunity doctrine undisturbed when personal injuries result from *negligent* behavior within the family. Here, in the absence of any willfully destructive act by the parent, it is more difficult to dismiss the policy concerns relating to family privacy and parental autonomy. Nevertheless, additional exceptions to the general rule of immunity have been recognized in many states for certain types of negligent torts.[20] The most important exception involves automobile accidents.

The Virginia Supreme Court established the rule of family liability for automobile accidents in *Smith v. Kauffman*,[21] a case involving the claim of

---

18. *Id.* at 737.

19. *Id.* at 738–39. The opinion in the *Gillett* case emphasized that the stepmother's behavior exceeded "the limit of reasonable punishment." The parental right to discipline children, which is generally extended to residential stepparents, forecloses any lawsuit by children as to the use of reasonable force by their parents for a disciplinary purpose. *See* RESTATEMENT, *supra* note 3, §§ 147–51 (describing "the privilege which is given in aid of the control, education and training of children, to persons against whom a child may maintain a civil action under the principles of tort law if the privilege is abused"). The application of this doctrine in the stepfamily is discussed in chapter 10.

20. *See* Hollister, *supra* note 5, at 508–11 (discussing the various exceptions to the parent-child immunity rule for negligent torts).

21. Smith v. Kauffman, 183 S.E.2d 190 (Va. 1971); *cf.* Lyles v. Jackson, 223 S.E.2d 873 (Va. 1976) (dismissing lawsuit by stepchildren injured in automobile accident caused by stepfather's alleged negligence, because accident occurred prior to decision of the Virginia Supreme Court in *Smith v. Kauffman*).

a seven-year-old girl against her stepfather's estate. In the opinion of the court, "[t]he very high incidence of liability insurance covering Virginia-based motor vehicles, together with the mandatory uninsured motorist [laws],"[22] affected the traditional doctrine of family immunity in two important ways. First, the financial interests of all family members, including the negligent defendant, would be enhanced if damages were recoverable from the defendant's insurer.[23] Furthermore, family harmony was not jeopardized by this type of litigation, because the family members were not likely to regard each other as true adversaries. The Virginia Supreme Court summarized its views about the immunity rule in auto cases as follows.

> In such litigation, the [immunity] rule can be no longer supported as generally calculated to promote the peace and tranquility of the home and the advantageous disposal of the parents' exchequer. A rule adopted for the common good now prejudices the great majority.[24]

As illustrated by *Smith v. Kauffman*, the pattern of including stepfamilies in the laws governing immunity has been continued in the special rules creating intrafamily liability in limited situations.[25]

The trend in recent decades has moved beyond the recognition of limited exceptions to family immunity, toward a more general abrogation of the doctrine.[26] The *Restatement of Torts* has embraced this approach, providing simply that "[a] parent or child is not immune from tort liability to the other solely by reason of that relationship."[27] The *Restatement* provision

---

22. *Smith*, 183 S.E.2d at 194.

23. The common financial interests of family members in litigation involving potential recovery from an insurance company, as in *Smith v. Kauffman* and *Lyles v. Jackson*, raises the specter of unlawful collusion between the parties. For the most part, in creating exceptions to the immunity rule, the judicial system has trusted its own capacity to identify fraudulent claims by one family member against another, insured family member.

24. *Smith*, 183 S.E.2d at 194.

25. An additional exception to the general doctrine of stepfamily immunity has been recognized in some states if the tort victim dies and a claim is made against the negligent stepfamily member under the wrongful death act. *See* Shiver v. Sessions, 80 So. 2d 905 (Fla. 1955); Deposit Guar. Bank & Trust Co. v. Nelson, 54 So. 2d 476 (Miss. 1951). In contrast, other states have extended the same immunity that applies in the intact stepfamily to the wrongful death context. *See* Lawber v. Doil, 547 N.E.2d 752 (Ill. App. Ct. 1989) (parental immunity); Jones v. Swett, 261 S.E.2d 610 (Ga. 1979) (spousal immunity).

26. *See* Carolyn Andrews, Comment, *Parent-Child Torts in Texas and the Reasonable Prudent Person Standard*, 40 BAYLOR L. REV. 113, 117 n.25 (1988) (summarizing the laws regulating parent-child tort immunity in fifty states and the District of Columbia).

27. RESTATEMENT, *supra* note 3, § 895G(1).

reflects the view that the limited exceptions to immunity under prior law, for automobile accidents and for intentional conduct, did not adequately protect the rights of injured family members.

Even when state courts and legislatures set out to abrogate parent-child immunity in this fashion, however, the underlying family-related policies continue to impose limits on the recovery of personal injury damages. According to a leading treatise, "it is clear that the parent-child relationship remains a special one and that not every act or omission by a parent will be regarded as actionable negligence, even if, as to some other persons, negligence might be found to exist."[28] The *Restatement* continues to acknowledge this special aspect of the parent-child relationship by providing that "[r]epudiation of general tort immunity does not establish liability for an act or omission that, because of the parent-child relationship, is otherwise privileged or is not tortious."[29]

The task of defining a standard of recovery that protects special family interests while compensating injuries in appropriate cases has proved to be a difficult challenge. The *Restatement* attempts to accomplish these dual goals by maintaining immunity for certain categories of family activity; hence, no recovery is permitted when injury results from reasonable "parental discipline," intentional physical contacts that are part of "the intimacies of family life," or thoughtless behaviors that may be regarded as "commonplace incidents in family life."[30] Outside these special categories of family activity, the *Restatement* recognizes liability for injurious behavior within the family.

In 1963, Wisconsin became the first state to adopt this approach, in the case of *Goller v. White*.[31] There, the state high court announced the general abrogation of parent-child tort immunity, except for the following types of negligent conduct.

> (1) [W]here the alleged negligent act involves an exercise of parental authority over the child; and (2) where the alleged negligent act involves an exercise of ordinary parental discretion with respect to the provision of food, clothing, housing, medical and dental services, and other care.[32]

This list of family activities, which remain exempt from liability, is somewhat more specific than the *Restatement*'s exemptions for "discipline" and the "commonplace incidents of family life."

The rule of *Goller v. White* has been implemented in a number of

28. PROSSER AND KEETON, *supra* note 1, at 908.
29. RESTATEMENT, *supra* note 3, § 895G(2).
30. *Id.* § 895G comment K.
31. Goller v. White, 122 N.W.2d 193 (Wis. 1963).
32. *Id.* at 198.

states, including Michigan, where it has been construed broadly to protect parents from lawsuits by their children based on "negligent parental supervision." In *Hush v. Devilbiss Co.*, the Michigan Court of Appeals provided the following explanation for its decision to retain limited parental immunity under this parental supervision doctrine.

> Each parent has unique and inimitable methods and attitudes on how children should be supervised. . . . Allowing a cause of action for negligent supervision would enable others, ignorant of a case's peculiar familial distinctions and bereft of any standards, to second-guess a parent's management of family affairs . . . .[33]

This analysis reflects the court's continuing deference to the traditional notion of family privacy.

In *Hush*, the Michigan Court of Appeals applied the parental supervision doctrine to a grandmother, thereby continuing the traditional, even-handed treatment of biologic parents and de facto parents under the law of tort immunity. In *Hush*, the court ruled that the grandmother, who stood in loco parentis to her fourteen-month-old grandson, was not responsible for the injuries suffered by the child when he was accidentally burned by hot water from a vaporizer. According to the court, her conduct fell within the scope of day-to-day custodial responsibility that is protected under the parental supervision doctrine. Furthermore, the grandmother was entitled to invoke the doctrine as a defense to charges that she acted negligently, because "[s]omeone who voluntarily assumes parental responsibility and attempts to create a home-like environment for a child should be granted immunity from judicial interference to the same extent as a natural parent."[34]

The continuing importance of the in loco parentis doctrine in defining the scope of modern immunity standards is also illustrated by the case of *Rosenberg v. Silver*.[35] The plaintiff in *Rosenberg* sued her noncustodial mother and stepfather for damages, based on their negligence, after she fell down the stairs in their home. The New York law, applied by the federal court in *Rosenberg*, recognized parental immunity for acts involving the negligent supervision of children, even though the doctrine of parent-child immunity had been otherwise abrogated in the state.[36] The federal district court dismissed the case on the ground that the defendants were immune from liability under state law.

---

33. Hush v. Devilbiss Co., 259 N.W.2d 170, 172 (Mich. Ct. App. 1977).
34. *Id.* at 173.
35. Rosenberg v. Silver, 762 F.2d 255 (2d Cir. 1985).
36. The doctrine applied in *Rosenberg*, which granted immunity to parents for their negligent supervision of children, had been earlier established by the New York Court of Appeals in Holodook v. Spencer, 324 N.E.2d 338 (N.Y. 1974).

The appellate court in *Rosenberg* reversed, ruling that the defendants' claim of parental immunity was dependent upon the resolution of two issues at trial. The first issue was whether the dangerous conditions in the defendants' home fell within the scope of the "negligent parental supervision" doctrine. As to this issue, the court stated its own negative view, that "[w]e have difficulty in relating the rule and reasoning of [the negligent supervision doctrine] to the existence of [the] allegedly defective light fixture and railing, dangerous conditions that do not appear to have resulted from the exercise of parental judgment."[37]

The second issue, which was crucial in resolving the stepfather's claim of parental immunity, involved his in loco parentis relationship with the victim. According to the court, "[b]efore a stepfather will be treated as a parent, there must be a factual showing that he intended to assume the duties of a natural father in supporting, educating, and instructing the child and caring for the child's general welfare."[38] In other words, the stepfather would be entitled to immunity only if he stood in loco parentis to the plaintiff and his conduct in maintaining the premises fell within the scope of parental supervision. The *Rosenberg* court remanded the case to the trial court for the resolution of these two issues.

The judicial decisions in *Goller v. White*, *Hush v. Devilbiss*, and *Rosenberg v. Silver* preserved immunity for parents and stepparents as to certain types of injurious behavior that fell within the scope of parental supervision. In contrast, the California Supreme Court has "reject[ed] the implication of *Goller* that within certain aspects of the parent-child relationship, the parent has carte blanche to act negligently toward his child."[39] Instead, the court has adopted a "reasonably prudent parent" standard that applies to every type of activity within the family and permits recovery for any injuries resulting from unreasonable conduct.[40] The California rule has been interpreted by some scholars as the total abolition of any special immunity for

---

37. *Rosenberg*, 762 F.2d at 257.

38. *Id.* at 256. The fact that the defendant mother was not the primary custodian of the injured child did not appear to affect the court's analysis of the parental immunity doctrine in *Rosenberg v. Silver*. Thus, the doctrine was applied to the mother and her husband in the same manner that it would be applied to married parents or to the custodial parent and stepparent. *See also* Thelen v. Thelen, 435 N.W.2d 495 (Mich. Ct. App. 1989). Other jurisdictions have denied immunity to the noncustodial parent and his or her spouse. *See, e.g.*, LA. REV. STAT. ANN. § 9:571 (West 1991) ("The child who is not emancipated cannot sue . . . [t]he parent who is entitled to his custody and control, when the marriage of the parents is dissolved . . . ."), *applied in* Bondurant v. Bondurant, 386 So. 2d 705 (La. Ct. App. 1980) (permitting child's lawsuit against noncustodial father).

39. Gibson v. Gibson, 479 P.2d 648, 652–53 (Cal. 1971).

40. *Id.* at 653. The "reasonably prudent parent" standard established in *Gibson* has been adopted in other states as well. *See* Rooney & Rooney, *supra* note 2, at 1170–71.

parents and children, leaving the protection of special family interests to the application of general tort law standards of negligence.[41] In other words, certain conduct between family members may be regarded as reasonable and nonactionable under the circumstances of the particular family, even though the same conduct between strangers would be unreasonable and tortious. Within this analytical framework, the existence of an in loco parentis relationship in the stepfamily, like the existence of a biologic parent-child relationship, would certainly influence judgments about what conduct within the family is reasonable.

In summary, stepfamilies in which in loco parentis ties have been established are generally treated like natural families under the laws regulating parent-child tort immunity. There is, however, wide disparity among the state laws defining liability for personal injuries within the family. Indeed, the modern law in this field has been described as a "mosaic of different shades and variations on [the] theme of parental tort immunity."[42] Current state standards range from full recognition to total abrogation of the common law immunity doctrine, with many variations in between. The merits of each approach, for stepfamilies as well as for other families, are best assessed in terms of the balance achieved between the interests of family privacy and autonomy and the goal of compensating tort victims for their personal injuries.[43]

III. Loss of Consortium

The doctrine of tort immunity, described in the previous section, defines rights and duties between family members who injure each other. The tort doctrines of consortium and vicarious liability, the subjects of the next two

---

41. *See* Hollister, *supra* note 5, at 526 n.228 ("There is some doubt whether California, in abrogating the immunity, gave parents some protection not provided other defendants."); Rooney & Rooney, *supra* note 2, at 1174 ("A cursory review of the California 'alternative standard' and the general negligence standard clearly reveals that the difference between the two standards is purely semantic."). In a number of other states, a general negligence standard is clearly the controlling principle for determining when conduct in the family gives rise to tort liability. *See* Rooney & Rooney, *supra* note 2, at 1173 (listing "states where parental tort immunity has been completely abolished and no explicit or specific alternative thereto has been adopted, and . . . states where parental immunity was never adopted in the first place.").

42. Andrews, *supra* note 26, at 116.

43. According to Professor Homer Clark, the best approach to balancing the competing interests in the area of parent-child tort immunity is a straightforward one. He has proposed that the courts balance family privacy against the interests of injured victims on a case-by-case basis, without reference to any other standard. *See* CLARK, *supra* note 3, at 379.

sections, bring a third party into the picture. These doctrines address the significance of family relationships when a family member injures or is injured by a person outside the family circle.

People assign great value to many aspects, both financial and nonfinancial, of their family relationships. If a third party disrupts or destroys a family relationship by injuring one member, the other may seek compensation for his or her indirect losses. Consortium is the term used to describe the nonfinancial, intangible aspects of family life, including affection and companionship, that may be harmed or destroyed in this situation. While acknowledging that such noneconomic losses are real and devastating, lawmakers have routinely taken a cautious approach to allowing family members to recover damages. Indeed, only a handful of states recognize a cause of action based on noneconomic injury to the parent-child relationship resulting from the negligent behavior of a third party.[44] As discussed in this section, the same type of relief has not been extended to stepparents and stepchildren.

Like the tort immunity doctrine, the family consortium doctrine developed first in the context of marital relationships. Initially, the cause of action for loss of spousal consortium was defined narrowly, to permit recovery by a husband for the loss of his injured wife's services. Gradually, the courts expanded the theory of spousal compensation in two ways: first, by acknowledging that a husband's losses might include spousal companionship and society; and second, by extending the theory of recovery to wives when

---

44. *See generally* CLARK, *supra* note 3, at 398–404 (discussing limitations on recovery for lost consortium between parent and child); Mark L. Johnson, Note, *Compensating Parents for the Loss of Their Nonfatally Injured Child's Society: Extending the Notion of Consortium to the Filial Relationship*, 1989 U. ILL. L. REV. 761 (proposing change in the law to permit compensation for lost consortium). The consortium doctrine discussed in the text involves compensation for harm to nonfinancial interests in cases where a family member is injured by the negligent act of a third party and survives the injury. Where the third party *intentionally* interferes with family relationships, for example, by abducting a child, compensation for all of the resulting losses within the family is generally available. *See* CLARK, *supra* note 3, at 384–90 (discussing remedies for intentional torts that harm family interests).

Furthermore, recovery for lost consortium is more widely available under the wrongful death statutes in cases where the injury to a parent or child results in death. *See, e.g.*, HAW. REV. STAT. § 663–3 (1985) (defining damages "with reference to the pecuniary injury and loss of love and affection, including . . . loss of society, companionship, comfort, consortium, or protection"); Sanchez v. Schindler, 651 S.W.2d 249, 251 (Tex. 1983) (expanding recovery in lawsuit for child's wrongful death "beyond the antiquated and inequitable pecuniary loss rule"). *But see* Nelson v. Dolan, 434 N.W.2d 25, 29 (Neb. 1989) (limiting wrongful death damages to pecuniary losses in the absence of contrary legislative amendment). For the most part, as discussed in chapter 5, stepparents and stepchildren are not included as beneficiaries under the state wrongful death statutes.

their husbands were injured.[45] Currently, when a third party injures a married victim, the injured spouse is entitled to recover for his or her own personal and economic losses; simultaneously, the noninjured spouse is generally entitled to recover consortium damages for the harm inflicted on the marital relationship.[46]

In the early common law framework, just as husbands were entitled to the value of their wives' services, fathers were also entitled to their minor children's services and wages. Thus, a father could sue the third party who injured his child, if the injury prevented the child from providing valuable services in the family or earning wages.[47] In the modern context, two obvious deficiencies in this theory of recovery became readily apparent. First, the exclusion of mothers as potential plaintiffs violated the legal principle of gender neutrality. And second, the economic value of the child's lost services became a meaningless measure of parental loss in a society where healthy children are an economic liability to their parents; the primary value of such relationships now is the intangible affection between the parties.

In 1975, the Wisconsin Supreme Court became the first to articulate a cause of action for parents that transcended these limitations.[48] The rule of *Shockley v. Prier* recognizes and compensates both fathers and mothers for the loss of society and companionship of their injured children, in much the same way that the spousal consortium doctrine compensates one spouse for relational losses resulting from the partner's injuries. In expanding the former rule, which had limited recovery to the value of the child's services, the Wisconsin Supreme Court emphasized the altered status of children in modern society.

> The "remedy" of loss of minor's earning capacity during minority is of diminishing significance. . . . Society and companionship between parents and their children are closer to our present day family ideal than the right of the parents to the "earning capacity during minority," which once seemed so important when the common law was originally established.[49]

---

45. *See* PROSSER AND KEETON, *supra* note 1, at 931–34 (discussing evolution of the law regarding recovery by husbands and wives for loss of consortium).

46. *See* CLARK, *supra* note 3, at 390–92 (collecting cases that recognize the cause of action by spouses for loss of consortium).

47. *See* PROSSER AND KEETON, *supra* note 1, at 934. For a general discussion of the reciprocal duties of support and services between parents and children, see chapter 2.

48. *See* Shockley v. Prier, 225 N.W.2d 495 (Wis. 1975), *discussed in* Jean C. Love, *Tortious Interference with the Parent-Child Relationship: Loss of an Injured Person's Society and Companionship*, 51 IND. L.J. 590 (1976).

49. *Id.* at 499.

Shockley involved the alleged negligence of doctors who treated a newborn child, causing his permanent blindness and disfigurement. The child's representative sued the physicians for the damages sustained by the child in his own right. Concurrently, the Wisconsin Supreme Court permitted the parents to pursue a claim based on their additional injuries, which the court described in the following manner.

[O]ne needs little imagination to see the shattering effect that [the child's] blindness will have on the relationship between him and his parents. The loss of the enjoyment of those experiences normally shared by parents and children need [*sic*] no enumeration here.[50]

It is obvious that parents suffer a genuine and substantial loss "when the child suffers a severe, permanent, and disabling injury that substantially interferes with the child's capacity to interact with his parents in a normally gratifying way."[51] Nevertheless, only a handful of states actually authorize any compensation for such losses,[52] either by judicial decision or legislative enactment.[53] Indeed, the vast majority of states have expressly rejected the doctrine of *Shockley v. Prier*.[54] This result is based on a belief that the desirability of compensating parents is outweighed by competing policy considerations relating to judicial economy, fairness to defendants, and fiscal responsibility. For example, the New Hampshire Supreme Court summarized its reservations about the proposed recovery for loss of a child's consortium as follows.

The emotional nature of the loss makes defining and quantifying damages difficult, which may lead to disproportionate awards. We also note the probability of increased litigation and multiple claims, which will hinder settlements and increase expenses. . . . Addi-

---

50. *Id.*

51. Pierce v. Casas Adobes Baptist Church, 782 P.2d 1162, 1165 (Ariz. 1989) (recognizing cause of action for loss of child's consortium).

52. *See* Todd R. Smyth, Annotation, *Parent's Right to Recover for Loss of Consortium in Connection with Injury to Child*, 54 A.L.R. 4th 112, § 4 (1987 & Supp. 1991) (listing states that allow recovery for loss of child's consortium).

53. *See, e.g.*, MASS. GEN. LAWS ANN. ch. 231, § 85X (West Supp. 1993) (creating "cause of action for loss of consortium of the child who has been seriously injured"); WASH. REV. CODE ANN. § 4.24.010 (West 1988) (allowing "damages . . . for the loss of love and companionship of the child and for injury to or destruction of the parent-child relationship").

54. *See* RESTATEMENT, *supra* note 3, § 703 comment h (1977) (limiting parent's recovery to medical expenses and value of child's lost services); Smyth, *supra* note 52, § 3 (listing states that deny "recover[y] for loss of filial consortium"). The rule denying consortium damages for parents and children has been the subject of scholarly criticism. *See, e.g.*, Love, *supra* note 48.

tionally, the social burden of providing damages for this loss will ultimately be borne by the public through increased insurance premiums . . . .[55]

A related rationale for denying consortium damages emphasizes the potential scope of liability involved in the economic protection of personal relationships. According to this analysis, the protection of relationships other than marriage would open the door to future claims by any person who is harmed or inconvenienced by a victim's tortious injury. For example, the Tennessee Court of Appeals observed that, if parent-child relationships were protected for this purpose, "it would be difficult to deny the equally compelling logic and justice of allowing other relatives, friends, and even employees to recover damages on the same grounds."[56] Of course, since the consortium doctrine is a creature of state law, courts and legislatures are free to draw the line on protected relationships wherever they choose. Most, including the Tennessee Court of Appeals, have drawn the line to permit spousal claims only.

Even in the small number of states, including Wisconsin, that have overcome these objections to compensating parents when their children are seriously injured, the consortium doctrine has not been extended to stepfamilies.[57] For example, in *Garrett v. City of New Berlin*,[58] the Wisconsin Supreme Court dismissed the claim of a stepfather, Paul Helders, based on the "loss of services, society and companionship" of his thirteen-year-old stepson, Raymond Garrett, who had been permanently and seriously injured due to the negligence of a police officer. Raymond's injuries occurred when the officer, who was chasing several other children through the premises of a drive-in movie theater in a police car with its headlights off, accidentally ran over Raymond as he lay on the ground watching the movie. At the time of the accident, Paul Helders had stood in loco parentis to his stepson for more than ten years. Despite this significant and longstanding relationship in the stepfamily, the Wisconsin Supreme Court "declin[ed] to . . . extend the rule set forth in *Shockley*"[59] to permit recovery by Paul Helders for the lost society and companionship of his stepson.

In reaching this result, the *Garrett* court emphasized two aspects of the common law in loco parentis doctrine: the absence of any enforceable stepparent support obligation and the stepfather's ability to terminate his in

55. Siciliano v. Capitol City Shows, Inc., 475 A.2d 19, 22 (N.H. 1984) (citations omitted).

56. Still v. Baptist Hospital, Inc., 755 S.W.2d 807, 813 (Tenn. Ct. App. 1988) (denying child's claim for loss of parental consortium).

57. *See* Smyth, *supra* note 52, § 11 (discussing "[r]ecovery by persons standing in loco parentis" under doctrines that compensate for lost consortium).

58. Garrett v. City of New Berlin, 362 N.W.2d 137 (Wis. 1985).

59. *Id.* at 145.

loco parentis status at will.[60] The court's brief analysis did not, however, explain why these two factors were relevant in determining the appropriateness of the consortium remedy for stepfamilies. Indeed, as discussed previously, in establishing the consortium doctrine in *Shockley v. Prier*, the Wisconsin Supreme Court had emphasized the *noneconomic* aspects of parent-child relationships. These aspects of family life, involving affection and companionship between the parties, are often present where an in loco parentis relationship of many years has been established between stepparent and child, as in *Garrett*. Nevertheless, the Wisconsin Supreme Court refused to recognize and protect this type of relational interest outside of the traditional nuclear family.

The development of the corollary doctrine, which compensates children for their losses when a parent is injured, has followed the same pattern. Thus, claims for the loss of parental consortium are recognized in only a small number of states. Furthermore, even in these jurisdictions, stepchildren are not permitted to recover damages when a stepparent is wrongfully injured.

The Massachusetts Supreme Court became the first to authorize recovery by children for the loss of parental consortium, in the 1980 case of *Ferriter v. Daniel O'Connell's Sons, Inc.*[61] The nature of the child's loss in this situation was later described by the West Virginia Supreme Court in an opinion that adopted the rule of the *Ferriter* case.

> It is common knowledge that a parent who suffers serious physical or mental injury is unable to give his (or her) minor children the parental care, training, love and companionship in the same degree as he (or she) might have but for the injury. . . . When the vitally important parent-child relationship is impaired and the child loses the love, guidance and close companionship of a parent, the child is deprived of something that is indeed valuable and precious.[62]

In spite of the undeniable interests at stake for children in this situation, and the small but notable trend toward allowing recovery,[63] the

---

60. *Id.* The absence of enforceable support obligations under the in loco parentis doctrine is discussed at length in chapter 2.

61. Ferriter v. Daniel O'Connell's Sons, Inc., 413 N.E.2d 690 (Mass. 1980), *discussed in* PROSSER AND KEETON, *supra* note 1, at 936.

62. Belcher v. Goins, 400 S.E.2d 830, 836 (W. Va. 1990).

63. *See* Annotation, *Child's Right of Action for Loss of Support, Training, Parental Attention, or the Like, Against a Third Person Negligently Injuring Parent*, 11 A.L.R.4th 549, § 3 (1982 & Supp. 1991) (listing states that allow damages for loss of parental consortium).

majority of states continue to deny any cause of action based on a parent's permanent injury.[64] The primary justifications for this result involve administrative and fiscal concerns about widening the circle of individuals who are entitled to recover when one person tortiously injures another. Of course, these are the same policies relied upon by the courts that have refused to compensate parents for loss of consortium when their children are injured.[65]

Even in the handful of states that recognize a cause of action for children, including Massachusetts and West Virginia, the consortium doctrine has not been extended to stepfamilies. In *Mendoza v. B.L.H. Electronics*,[66] the Massachusetts Supreme Court refused to apply the rule of the *Ferriter* case to allow recovery of consortium damages by an eighteen-year-old stepson when his stepmother was injured. The opinion of the court apparently relied in part upon the age of the plaintiff as a basis for denying the claim. However, the following analysis in a concurring opinion relied exclusively

---

64. *See* RESTATEMENT, *supra* note 3, § 707A (1977) (denying cause of action for loss of parental consortium); Annotation, *supra* note 63, § 4 (listing states that do not compensate children for loss of parental consortium).

65. The same public policies, relating to administrative and fiscal responsibility, have limited recovery for family members under another tort theory, the doctrine of emotional distress. The classic case involves the parent whose child is run over by a negligent driver while parent and child are crossing the street together. Although the parent may suffer severe mental and emotional injury by virtue of witnessing the accident, the standards developed by the courts have imposed numerous restrictions on so-called bystander recovery. *See* PROSSER AND KEETON, *supra* note 1, at 359–67; Douglas B. Marlowe, Comment, *Negligent Infliction of Mental Distress: A Jurisdictional Survey of Existing Limitation Devices and Proposal Based on an Analysis of Objective Versus Subjective Indices of Distress*, 33 VILL. L. REV. 781 (1988). The existence of a close family relationship between the injured person and the bystander is frequently an important factor in determining whether recovery is available. *See generally* John S. Herbrand, Annotation, *Relationship Between Victim and Plaintiff-Witness as Affecting Right to Recover Damages in Negligence for Shock or Mental Anguish at Witnessing Victim's Injury or Death*, 94 A.L.R.3d 486 (1979 & Supp. 1992). Unlike their treatment in the law of parent-child consortium, detailed in the text, stepfamily relationships have frequently been recognized as legally significant family relationships in the law of emotional distress. *See, e.g.,* Grandstaff v. City of Borger, Tex., 767 F.2d 161, 172 (5th Cir. 1985) (ruling that stepsons and stepfather "stood in the close relationship required by Texas law"); Kriventsov v. San Rafael Taxicabs, Inc., 229 Cal. Rptr. 768, 770 (Ct. App. 1986) ("The membership of many family units extends beyond parents and children to grandparents, stepparents, aunts and uncles."); Leong v. Takasaki, 520 P.2d 758, 766 (Haw. 1974) ("[T]he absence of a blood relationship between victim and plaintiff-witness [should not] foreclose recovery."); Barnhill v. Davis, 300 N.W.2d 104, 108 (Iowa 1981) (recognizing relationships of affinity); Ramirez v. Armstrong, 673 P.2d 822, 825 (N.M. 1983) (recognizing in loco parentis relationships).

66. Mendoza v. B.L.H. Elecs., 530 N.E.2d 349 (Mass. 1988).

upon the distinction between stepfamilies and biologic families to justify the outcome.

> [T]here was no legally cognizable relationship between the step-parent and the stepchild. Unlike the . . . parent-child relationship in *Ferriter* . . . the stepparent-stepchild relationship does not trigger certain well-established rights and duties under Massachusetts law. . . .
>
> . . . Limiting loss of consortium claims to members of legally cognizable relationships provides a clear, principled, easily ascertainable standard which adequately distinguishes those entitled to recover from those involved in the "myriad relationships" which exist in society.[67]

This type of reasoning is circular; the stepparent-child relationship does not "trigger . . . legal rights" precisely because the courts refuse to recognize them. A more meaningful analysis would ask whether losses in the step-family are like those already compensated in the biologic family, and whether the benefits derived by compensating such losses would outweigh the resulting administrative and economic costs to the courts and the compensation system.[68]

The decision of the Massachusetts Supreme Court in *Mendoza*, refusing to extend the parental consortium doctrine to stepfamilies, is a counterpart to the decision of the Wisconsin Supreme Court in *Garrett v. City of New Berlin*, discussed earlier, that similarly denied stepparent claims for loss of a stepchild's consortium. These decisions may reflect a continuing ambivalence about the basic wisdom of recognizing consortium claims outside the marital relationship. In deciding where to draw the line on protected relationships, these courts emphasized the goals of fiscal and administrative integrity, without considering the nature of the affected stepfamily relationships. The analysis and result here stand in sharp contrast to the corresponding treatment of stepparents and stepchildren under the immunity doctrine, discussed in the previous section. There, the primary goals

---

67. *Id.* at 350–51 (concurring opinion).

68. For example, Professor Jean Love assessed the issue of consortium damages in the stepfamily, as well as other families where in loco parentis ties have been established, in the following manner.

> A cogent argument can be made that recovery should be allowed because the loss of society and companionship will often be as great in this type of situation as in the case of an injury to a natural parent or child. The principle counter argument would be that subjecting the defendant to suit both by the parties to the in loco parentis relationship and by the natural parents or children would compound the danger of a multiplicity of suits.

Love, *supra* note 48, at 622.

tended to be the protection of family interests and the compensation of victims, with the result that in loco parentis relationships between stepparents and stepchildren were protected. This approach to various stepfamily issues, emphasizing the general purposes of each legal doctrine, has led to the inconsistent treatment of stepfamily members in the field of tort law.

IV. Liability for Damage Caused by Stepchildren

It is a general principle in the law of torts that children are recognized as independent actors, responsible for their own conduct.[69] Whenever a child's negligent or intentional behavior causes injury to another, the victim's primary avenue of recovery is against the child. Nevertheless, the victims of children frequently seek compensation from parents or other responsible adults, especially when the children lack resources of their own. Two theories of recovery have emerged. First, under common law tort principles, parents may be negligent in their own right for the failure to properly supervise the children who cause harm. Second, family responsibility statutes sometimes impose liability upon parents for the misconduct of their children. This section discusses the application of these two theories of adult responsibility in the stepfamily.

Well-established common law principles require parents to exercise supervisory authority over their children in a manner that reasonably protects the interests of others. If a parent's negligence in this regard enables the child to injure another, then the victim has a cause of action against the parent.[70] This theory of negligent supervision is not intended to make parents responsible for the actions of their children; rather, parents are accountable for their own actions when they undertake the important role of custodian.[71]

---

69. *See generally* PROSSER AND KEETON, *supra* note 1, at 1071–72 (discussing treatment of minors in the law of torts).

70. In addition to this civil liability, laws were enacted in several states during the 1980s to establish criminal liability for the parental failure to supervise children who commit antisocial acts. These statutes are discussed in S. Randall Humm, *Criminalizing Poor Parenting Skills as a Means to Contain Violence By and Against Children*, 139 U. PA. L. REV. 1123 (1991); Toni Weinstein, *Visiting the Sins of the Child on the Parent: The Legality of Criminal Parental Liability Statutes*, 64 S. CAL. L. REV. 859 (1991).

71. The specific duty of parents to supervise children is one application of the more general duty imposed upon any person who has control over another to exercise that control in a reasonable fashion. Others who have incurred liability for breach of such duties include employers, bartenders, and those who have responsibility for dangerous criminals. *See* RESTATEMENT, *supra* note 3, § 319 (1965); PROSSER AND KEETON, *supra* note 1, at 383–85.

This doctrine of negligent supervision has been applied to other adults, including stepparents, who informally assume the custodial responsibility for children. For example, the Florida courts have invoked the common law in loco parentis doctrine as the basis for identifying responsible adults in this situation.[72] Under this application of the doctrine, the stepparent who "stands in the place of a parent" in the family owes the same duty as a natural parent to exercise reasonable control over a stepchild.

The scope of the common law duty to supervise children has generally been defined quite narrowly. According to a leading treatise, "the effect of the decided cases is that there is no liability upon the parent unless he has notice of a specific type of harmful conduct, and an opportunity to interfere with it."[73] The duty imposed upon stepparents, with respect to the step-children in their care, is certainly no broader than the duty that has been defined in this restrictive manner for natural parents.

For example, the Supreme Court of Maine recently applied the parental supervision doctrine to a stepfather and concluded that he had not behaved in a negligent manner. The plaintiff in *Merchant v. Mansir*,[74] who was injured when she borrowed a defective bicycle from her friend, sued the friend's stepfather for failing to supervise his eleven-year-old stepdaughter. Employing the narrow definition of parental supervision, the *Merchant* court ruled that the stepfather had no duty to control the behavior of his stepdaughter in these circumstances, because he had no actual knowledge of the activities that resulted in the plaintiff's injuries. Regarding the impact of the stepfather's status in the family, the court found it unnecessary to "decide whether the [stepfather] had any reduced obligation as a stepparent,"[75] because his conduct in this case clearly satisfied the minimal standard of supervision generally imposed upon parents.

Apart from the parent's own negligent failure to supervise a child, the common law has never imputed liability to the parent for a child's tortious conduct. This result is consistent with the basic tort law principle of individual responsibility. However, beginning in the 1950s, the legislatures in all

---

72. *See* Wyatt v. McMullen, 350 So. 2d 1115, 1117 (Fla. Dist. Ct. App. 1977) ("There is no difference, so far as common law tort liability is concerned, between one in loco parentis and a natural parent."); Weigl v. Ombres, 106 So. 2d 614 (Fla. Dist. Ct. App. 1958) (denying liability of uncle under negligent supervision theory because he did not stand in loco parentis to the nephew who shot another child). Courts in other states have imposed supervisory duties on de facto custodians without requiring proof of an in loco parentis relationship. *See* Poncher v. Brackett, 55 Cal. Rptr. 59 (Ct. App. 1966) (grandparents); Carey v. Reeve, 781 P.2d 904 (Wash. Ct. App. 1989) (grandparents).

73. PROSSER AND KEETON, *supra* note 1, at 915; *see also* RESTATEMENT, *supra* note 3, § 316 (1965).

74. Merchant v. Mansir, 572 A.2d 493 (Me. 1990).

75. *Id.* at 494.

states carved out discrete exceptions to this common law rule by enacting parental responsibility statutes.[76]

The statutes do not make parents vicariously liable for all of their children's torts. For example, many states limit recovery to amounts ranging from several hundred dollars to several thousand dollars.[77] Furthermore, the statutes in many jurisdictions are aimed at juvenile vandalism, permitting recovery only if the minor's conduct was intentional, rather than negligent,[78] or limiting coverage to property damage, rather than personal injury.[79] Even with these limitations, the creation of parental liability for the torts of minor children was intended to serve two purposes: to establish a meaningful source of compensation for the victims of children and to motivate parents to control the behavior of their children.[80]

The dual purposes of the vicarious liability statutes have not been implemented in the stepfamily. In identifying the adults to whom a child's misconduct may be imputed, the various state laws employ the terms "parent," "father," "mother," "guardian," and "tutor."[81] Not a single statute expressly includes stepparents or persons in loco parentis in the category of responsible adults.[82] Furthermore, these statutory terms have been consistently construed by the courts in a manner that excludes stepparents.

For example, in *Gosnell v. Middlebrook*,[83] an appellate court in Ohio

---

76. *See* Robert C. Levine, Note, *Parental Liability for the Torts of Their Minor Children: Limits, Logic and Legality*, 9 Nova L.J. 205, 220 n.115 (1984) (collecting statutes from all fifty states). Although liability under the parental responsibility statutes is generally strict liability, a few states absolve parents who make reasonable efforts to control their children. *See, e.g.,* Utah Code Ann. § 78–11–21 (1992).

77. *See, e.g.,* N.Y. Gen. Oblig. Law § 3–112 (McKinney 1989) (upper limit of $2,500 with judicial discretion to adjust awards downward based on parent's ability to pay).

78. *See, e.g.,* Cal. Civ. Code § 1714.1 (West 1985) (willful misconduct).

79. *See, e.g.,* Del. Code Ann. tit. 10, § 3922 (Supp. 1992) (intentional or reckless destruction of property).

80. *See* Buie v. Longspaugh, 598 S.W.2d 673, 676 (Tex. Ct. App. 1980) ("The provisions [of the Texas vicarious liability statute] . . . protect property owners by both compensating the owners for damages incurred, and by encouraging parents to train and discipline their children."); Note, *The Iowa Parental Responsibility Act*, 55 Iowa L. Rev. 1037, 1037 (1970).

81. The status of "tutor" is created by statute in Louisiana and entails many of the same legal rights and duties involved in the guardianship status in the common law states. *See* Leonard Oppenheim, *The Basic Elements of Tutorship in Louisiana*, 44 Tul. L. Rev. 452 (1970).

82. For a relatively brief period, from 1966 until 1982, the parental responsibility statute in Georgia included in loco parentis relationships. *See* Ga. Code Ann. § 51–2–3 legislative note (Supp. 1993).

83. Gosnell v. Middlebrook, 563 N.E.2d 32 (Ohio Ct. App. 1988).

refused to permit recovery against a stepfather under the following parental responsibility statute.

> Any person is entitled to maintain an action to recover compensatory damages in a civil action, in an amount not to exceed two thousand dollars . . . , from *the parents who have the custody and control of a child* under the age of eighteen, who willfully and maliciously assaults the person by a means or force likely to produce great bodily harm.[84]

In *Gosnell*, both the custodial mother and stepfather of the child, whose willful conduct caused the plaintiffs' injuries, were named as defendants. While acknowledging that the complaint stated a proper cause of action as to the mother, the court ruled that "strict construction of [the statute] requires that the word 'parents'. . . be limited in its application to the natural parents of the minor child whose tort is involved."[85] Accordingly, under Ohio law, the stepfather could not be considered vicariously liable for the intentional wrongdoing of his stepson.

The same conservative approach to identifying responsible adults under the parental responsibility statutes has been taken by the courts in other jurisdictions,[86] including Louisiana. The origins of Louisiana law are in the civil law tradition, which historically imposed greater responsibility upon parents for the acts of their children. For example, while most states first enacted vicarious parental responsibility laws in the 1950s, the Louisiana statute dates back to 1800.[87] In spite of this strong tradition of imputed responsibility within the family, statutory liability in Louisiana has not been extended to stepparents.[88]

For example, in *Hay v. American Motorists Insurance Co.*,[89] an appel-

---

84. *Id.* at 33 (emphasis added). This parental responsibility statute is currently codified in Ohio Rev. Code Ann. § 3109.10 (Supp. 1991).

85. *Gosnell*, 563 N.E.2d at 34.

86. *See* Landers v. Medford, 133 S.E.2d 403 (Ga. Ct. App. 1963) (stepparent was not responsible under parental responsibility statute); *In re* Ramont K., 505 A.2d 507 (Md. 1986) (grandmother was not responsible under state statute requiring restitution from parents for damage caused by juvenile).

87. *See* La. Civ. Code Ann. art. 2318 comment regarding history and text of former codes (West 1979). *See generally* F.H. Lawson, A Common Lawyer Looks at the Civil Law 179–83 (1955) (discussing strength of legal family ties in civil law societies).

88. *See* B.C. Ricketts, Annotation, *Validity and Construction of Statutes Making Parents Liable for Torts Committed by Their Minor Children*, 8 A.L.R.3d 612, § 5(c) (1966 & Supp. 1991).

89. Hay v. American Motorists Ins. Co., 66 So. 2d 371 (La. Ct. App. 1953).

late court in Louisiana construed the following statute to exclude a stepfather, who stood in loco parentis to the stepson whose negligence caused an automobile accident.

> The father, or after his decease, the mother, are responsible for the damage occasioned by their minor or unemancipated children, residing with them. . . . The same responsibility attaches to the tutors of minors.[90]

The plaintiff in *Hay* emphasized the stepfather's familial relationship with his stepson, which involved custody and "control over the said minor's action and conduct."[91] According to this line of analysis, the allocation of legal responsibility to the family member who had actual control over the child would effectively achieve the purposes of the vicarious liability law. The *Hay* court rejected this reasoning and narrowly construed the language of the parental responsibility statute as follows.

> The [statute] does not establish the factors urged by counsel as the . . . measures or standards for the imputation of liability. The only relationships carrying such imputation . . . are the father, the mother, [and] tutors of minors.[92]

The line of reasoning proposed by the plaintiff in *Hay*, which leads to an expanded list of persons responsible for the misconduct of children in their care, appears also in the legislative history of the Pennsylvania vicarious liability statute. During the floor debate regarding the proposed parental responsibility law, which expressly defined "parent[s]" to mean "natural or adoptive parents," one state legislator proposed a broader class of responsible adults.

> If the purpose of this bill be to check juvenile delinquency by having parents pull the rein tighter on the conduct of their children, . . . then why did we limit the provisions of this bill to only the natural or adopt[ive] parents? . . . Is there not just as much justification for

---

90. *Id.* at 373. The quoted statute is currently codified in LA. CIV. CODE ANN. art. 2318 (West Supp. 1992).

91. *Hay*, 66 So. 2d at 373.

92. *Id. See also* Liddell v. Hanover Ins., 252 So. 2d 762, 764 (La. Ct. App. 1971) ("Since [stepson] was not [stepfather's] . . . child or ward, [stepfather] is not responsible for any tort which [stepson] may have committed."); Gustafson v. Koch, 460 So. 2d 655 (La. Ct. App. 1984) (same); *cf.* Quintano v. Ibos, 128 So. 186 (La. Ct. App. 1930) (holding stepfather, who had been appointed cotutor of child, responsible for the child's torts).

holding . . . any other relative who is similarly situated just as responsible as we would hold the natural or adopted parent?[93]

The Pennsylvania law was subsequently enacted with the original, limited definition of "parent." The state legislator's suggestion regarding a functional definition of parental responsibility, which would have included stepparents in appropriate cases, was not implemented.[94]

The likely explanation for the restricted definition of responsible adults, illustrated in *Gosnell, Hay,* and the Pennsylvania statute, relates to the manner in which the law of parental responsibility evolved. As a legislative exception to the well-established common law premise that every person is solely responsible for his or her own actions, statutory liability has been imposed with caution. The Ohio court in the *Gosnell* case summarized this viewpoint and highlighted its impact for stepfamily responsibility as follows.

[W]e believe it to be the general view that these laws having been enacted in derogation of the common law, and having not been enacted primarily as a remedial measure, but equally as a form of penalty, courts should construe the liability to be imposed upon the parents in a strict, rather than a liberal, manner. . . . In our opinion strict construction of [the parental responsibility statute] requires that the word "parents" . . . be limited in its application to the natural parents . . . .[95]

Thus, the significance of the vicarious liability doctrine for stepfamilies has been determined by reference to the limitations of the doctrine itself, rather than through any analysis of the stepparent-child relationship. The same is true for the other family-related tort rules explored in this chapter— immunity, consortium, and negligent supervision. The overall result for stepfamilies has been inconsistent treatment and selective recognition in the field of tort law.

---

93. Pennsylvania Legislative Journal-House Report of the Gen. Assembly of 1967, at 459 (May 2, 1967) (statement of Mr. Fineman).

94. *See* 23 Pa. Cons. Stat. Ann. § 5501 (1991).

95. *Gosnell,* 563 N.E.2d at 34.

CHAPTER 5

Wrongful Death

I. Introduction

As described in chapter 4, the law of torts creates a cause of action for victims who suffer personal injuries due to the negligent or willful conduct of another person. The laws in this field are designed to compensate victims and to deter injurious behavior in the future. These same purposes are accomplished, when the victim dies, by permitting a lawsuit by the victim's survivors. Nevertheless, during the nineteenth century, the courts in England and the United States developed a universal rule that no common law cause of action existed in this situation. The resulting deficiency in the system of compensation was poignantly described by the authors of a leading treatise, in the following manner.

> [I]t was cheaper for the defendant to kill the plaintiff than to injure him, and . . . the most grievous of all injuries left the bereaved family of the victim, who frequently were destitute, without a remedy.[1]

In response to this deficiency, in 1846 the English Parliament enacted Lord Campbell's Act,[2] which authorized the representative of a deceased tort victim's estate to sue the wrongdoer on behalf of certain surviving relatives. Similar legislation was enacted in each of the states,[3] although the statutes vary as to the types of losses compensated[4] and the persons entitled

---

1. W. PAGE KEETON ET AL., PROSSER AND KEETON ON THE LAW OF TORTS 945 (5th ed. 1984) [hereinafter PROSSER AND KEETON].
2. Lord Campbell's Act (Fatal Accidents Act), 1846, 9 & 10 Vict., ch. 93 (Eng.) [hereinafter Lord Campbell's Act].
3. A listing of the state wrongful death statutes can be found in 2 STUART M. SPEISER, RECOVERY FOR WRONGFUL DEATH at 649–787 (2d ed. 1975 and Supp. 1990).
4. The types of damages available under the wrongful death statutes include recovery for economic losses and, in a number of jurisdictions, recovery for non-economic losses as well. Recovery for loss of consortium between parent and child, which is generally not permitted in tort actions when the victim survives, *see* chapter 4, is available in a number of states when the action is for wrongful death. *See generally* PROSSER AND KEETON, *supra* note 1, at 949–54 (discussing damages in wrongful death actions).

to recover. This chapter examines the eligibility of surviving stepparents and stepchildren as claimants under the wrongful death laws.

For the purpose of evaluating the rights of surviving stepfamily members, the wrongful death statutes can be classified into three categories. First, a handful of state laws, discussed in section II, include certain step-relatives, usually stepchildren, in the list of wrongful death claimants. The second category of statutes, enacted in just three states, departs from the usual limitation of claimants to specified relatives, and opens eligibility to any person who can prove financial dependency upon the decedent. Section III summarizes the success achieved by stepfamily claimants under this broader definition of wrongful death beneficiaries. The third category of statutes, and by far the largest, confers rights upon a list of relatives that does not include stepparents or stepchildren. As discussed fully in section IV, the courts have uniformly construed statutory language relating to "heirs," "parents," and "children" in this context to exclude stepfamily members.

Thus, the law of wrongful death is governed by state statutes that overruled the common law prohibition against recovery when a tort victim dies. Nationwide, no uniform approach has been taken to the issue of recovery within the stepfamily. In the large majority of states, however, the stepparent-child relationship receives no legal recognition in the wrongful death context.[5]

II. Statutes That Include Stepfamily Members

When the English Parliament enacted Lord Campbell's Act in 1846, step-parents and stepchildren were expressly included as wrongful death beneficiaries. The Act provided that "every such action shall be for the benefit of the wife, husband, *parent*, and *child* of the person whose death shall have been [wrongfully] caused, and . . . the Jury may give such damages as they may think proportioned to the injury resulting from such death." Parliament further defined "parent" and "child" as follows: "The word 'parent' shall include father and mother, and grandfather and grandmother, and *stepfather* and *stepmother*; and the word 'child' shall include son and daughter, and grandson and granddaughter, and *stepson* and *stepdaughter*."[6] The current English wrongful death statute continues in this same manner to recognize a cause of action for stepparents and stepchildren.[7]

Although modeled after Lord Campbell's Act in many other respects,

---

5. *See generally* Daniel E. Feld, Annotation, *Action for Death of Stepparent by or for Benefit of Stepchild*, 68 A.L.R.3d 1220 (1976 and Supp. 1992) (collecting cases).

6. Lord Campbell's Act, *supra* note 2 (emphasis added).

7. *See* Fatal Accidents Act 1976, ch. 30, § 1, *reprinted in* 31 HALSBURY's STATUTES OF ENGLAND AND WALES 202–03 (4th ed. 1987).

most of the wrongful death statutes in the United States do not mention stepfamily members. California, Idaho, Michigan, and Washington are exceptional, because they expressly include stepchildren as beneficiaries.[8] Accordingly, in these states, the stepchild who depended upon a stepparent for financial support is entitled to recover damages from the person who caused the stepparent's wrongful death.

Two additional states, Delaware and Maryland, list "any person related to the deceased person by blood or marriage" as a second tier of beneficiaries who are eligible to recover, but only if the decedent left no surviving "wife, husband, parent [or] child."[9] The phrase "person related . . . by marriage" in the Delaware and Maryland legislation broadly includes steprelatives and relatives-in-law who suffer economic loss as a result of a family member's wrongful death. However, the secondary status of these claimants was reaffirmed by the Maryland Court of Special Appeals in *Flores v. King*.[10] There, the court rejected the claim of a dependent surviving stepdaughter whose actual damages were similar in kind to those of the decedent's surviving wife and children. The court reaffirmed the legislative intent to permit recovery by steprelatives only if no primary beneficiaries survived the wrongful death victim.

Thus, the legislatures in only a handful of states have expressly provided relief for surviving stepfamily members. The remaining statutes make no reference to stepfamily members or to "relatives by marriage" as wrongful death beneficiaries.

III. Eligibility Based on Dependency

The statutes in just three states—Alaska, Arkansas, and Hawaii—permit wrongful death awards to individuals who were financially dependent upon the decedent without regard to any other relationship by blood or affinity. For example, the Hawaii statute authorizes wrongful death claims by "any person wholly or partly dependent upon the deceased person," in addition to the "surviving spouse, children, father, mother."[11] Not surprisingly, stepfamily members who form relationships of economic interdependence have been successful in asserting claims under this second category of wrongful death statutes.

---

8. *See* CAL. CIV. PROC. CODE § 377 (West Supp. 1993) (authorizing claims by stepchildren); IDAHO CODE § 5–311 (1990) (same); MICH. COMP. LAWS ANN. § 600.2922 (West 1986) (authorizing claims by "[t]he children of the deceased's spouse"); WASH. REV. CODE ANN. § 4.20.020 (West 1988) (authorizing claims by stepchildren).

9. *See* DEL. CODE ANN. tit. 10, § 3724 (Supp. 1992); MD. CODE ANN., CTS. & JUD. PROC. § 3–904 (1989).

10. Flores v. King, 282 A.2d 521 (Md. Ct. Spec. App. 1971).

11. *See* HAWAII REV. STAT. § 663–3 (1985).

In *Greer Tank & Welding, Inc. v. Boettger*,[12] the Alaska Supreme Court applied this type of statute in the stepfamily setting. The Alaska wrongful death statute adds a category of "other dependents" to the specified relatives (spouse and children) who are permitted to recover damages.[13] The *Boettger* court applied the "other dependents" provision to a stepfamily in which the stepfather and the custodial mother had been divorced prior to the stepfather's wrongful death. Following the divorce, the stepfather had maintained real family ties with his former wife and stepson, including the payment of support. Based on this record, the *Boettger* court affirmed an award of wrongful death benefits to the former wife and stepchild as "other dependents" of the decedent.

In reaching this result, the Alaska Supreme Court dismissed the defendant's contention that recognizing these plaintiffs would open the door to an unacceptably large number of potential claimants in wrongful death cases. The defendant in *Boettger* urged the court to limit the meaning of "other dependents" by requiring proof that the decedent was legally obligated to support the claimant at the time of death. Because the stepfather had no child support duty under state law, this requirement would have automatically excluded the stepson from eligibility. The Alaska Supreme Court acknowledged the need for clarity and fair limits on recovery under the "other dependents" provision, but refused to restrict recovery to situations where legal support obligations existed. Rather, the *Boettger* court authorized compensation in cases where the decedent had actually assumed the financial responsibility for another person.

> [T]he legislature, by adding "other dependents" to the categories of spouse and children, intended to embrace those who occupy a position similar to those in the specified classes and who were actually dependent upon the decedent for support at the time of his death. A showing must be made of actual dependency for significant contributions of support over a sufficient period of time to justify the assumption that such contribution would have continued.[14]

According to the court, this standard satisfied the requirements of clarity and fair limits on the number of claimants under the wrongful death act. The former wife and stepson in *Boettger* clearly met this test for "actual dependency," as would the members of many established stepfamilies.[15]

The Arkansas wrongful death provision similarly permits recovery

---

12. Greer Tank & Welding, Inc. v. Boettger, 609 P.2d 548 (Alaska 1980). *Contra* Jones v. Jones, 530 P.2d 34 (Or. 1974) (narrowly construing "dependents" in the applicable Oregon wrongful death act, since repealed, to exclude dependent stepchildren).

13. *See* ALASKA STAT. § 09.55.580 (Supp. 1992).

14. *Boettger*, 609 P.2d at 551.

15. In *Boettger*, the surviving stepson, spouse, and child all recovered damages. Thus, the court rejected an argument that had been accepted by the trial court in an

when financial dependency has been established outside formal family relationships. The Arkansas statute invokes the common law in loco parentis doctrine in order to identify eligible beneficiaries, as follows.

> The beneficiaries of the action created in this section are the surviving spouse, children, father and mother, brothers and sisters of the deceased person, *persons standing in loco parentis to the deceased person, and persons to whom the deceased stood in loco parentis.*[16]

The benefit of the in loco parentis doctrine, as it pertains to stepfamilies, is highlighted in the opinion of the Arkansas Supreme Court in *Moon Distributors v. White.*[17] There, the court upheld an award of $194,000 to the deceased stepmother's surviving husband, adopted child, and stepchild, including the award of $50,000 to the stepdaughter.

The stepmother in *White* died as a result of the negligence of defendant's employee when the defendant's dump truck became unhitched, crossed the median of a divided highway, and ran over her car. The defendant challenged the subsequent award of damages to the decedent's ten-year-old stepdaughter on the grounds that she was not an eligible beneficiary and that the award was excessive. In affirming the award of damages, the *White* court relied upon the following evidence of strong family ties between the stepmother and daughter.

> Wandasue White, according to the proof, was a truly exceptional wife and mother. When she married, [her husband's] daughter Karen was four years old and was living with his parents rather than with her divorced mother. Wandasue took Karen into her home and could not have treated her with greater affection had the child been her own daughter . . . . Considering what [the child] lost by Wandasue's death, we cannot say that [the award] is excessive.[18]

Thus, the provision for in loco parentis relationships in the Arkansas statute enabled the court to consider the actual loss to the stepchild resulting from her stepmother's death.

This feature of the Arkansas wrongful death statute is unique. As discussed fully in the next section, stepfamily members have tried, without success, to establish their in loco parentis eligibility in other states, where the legislatures have named only "heirs," "parents," and "children" as beneficiaries. The courts have consistently refused to recognize and compensate surviving stepfamily members, absent express statutory language authoriz-

---

earlier case, Brown v. Estate of Jonz, 591 P.2d 532 (Alaska 1979), that "other dependents" were entitled to recover only if no spouse or children survived the decedent.

16. ARK. CODE ANN. § 16–62–102(d) (Michie 1987) (emphasis added).

17. Moon Distribs. v. White, 434 S.W.2d 56 (Ark. 1968).

18. *Id.* at 60.

ing such a recovery. Under the wrongful death acts in the majority of states, the stepdaughter in the *White* case would have been left without any remedy following her stepmother's death.

IV. Statutes Limited to "Heirs," "Parents," and Children"

The wrongful death acts in most states list specific categories of relatives of the victim, such as the spouse, parents, children, and heirs, as eligible beneficiaries. These laws do not include any additional categories of step-relatives, persons standing in loco parentis, or dependent survivors. Because the courts narrowly construe the family terminology in these provisions, stepfamily members are generally unable to recover wrongful death damages.

For example, in *Steed v. Imperial Airlines*,[19] the California Supreme Court narrowly construed the state wrongful death statute, which authorized recovery by the decedent's "heirs and dependent parents." The claimant in *Steed* was the nine-year-old stepdaughter, Elizabeth Steed, toward whom the decedent, Robert Steed, had "assume[d] the full obligation of father and parent" during his lifetime. Indeed, the stepfather had "held out the [child] to all the world as his daughter . . . leading the said minor to believe to [the date of the lawsuit] that he was in fact her father."[20] In spite of this evidence of strong family ties and the stepdaughter's financial dependence on the decedent, the California Supreme Court refused to construe "heirs" in the wrongful death statute to include Elizabeth Steed.

In reaching this result, the California Supreme Court relied upon the commonly accepted legal definition of "heirs," which is those individuals who would inherit the decedent's property under the law of intestate succession. As a general rule in the United States, and in California at that time, stepchildren were not designated as heirs under state intestacy statutes.[21] Therefore, the court's reference to the California intestacy statute foreclosed any wrongful death claim by Elizabeth Steed in spite of her actual dependence upon and family connection with her stepfather.[22]

The three dissenting justices of the California Supreme Court believed

---

19. Steed v. Imperial Airlines, 524 P.2d 801, 803 (Cal. 1974).

20. *Id.* at 803 n.2.

21. The treatment of stepfamily members under the law of intestate succession is discussed fully in chapter 3. A current California law, which permits stepchildren to inherit in certain limited situations, had not been enacted at the time of the *Steed* decision. *See* CAL. PROB. CODE § 6408(3) (West 1991).

22. *Accord* Versland v. Caron Transport, 671 P.2d 583 (Mont. 1983) (construing "heirs" in Montana wrongful death act to exclude victim's two minor stepdaughters); *In re* Estate of Gorman, 15 Ohio Op. 253 (P. Ct. 1939) (construing "next of kin" in Ohio wrongful death statute to exclude victim's stepson).

that a less technical construction of the word "heirs" would have better accomplished the purpose of the wrongful death legislation in the *Steed* case. According to the dissent, the legislative purpose was to compensate those survivors who were dependent on the tort victim and therefore suffered economic loss as a result of his wrongful death. The opinion concluded "that the inclusion of dependent children such as [the stepdaughter] promotes, rather than frustrates, existing legislative policy to allow a wrongful death recovery by the heirs and relatives of the decedent."[23]

Shortly after the decision in *Steed*, the California legislature confirmed the view of the dissenting justices, that the exclusion of stepchildren was inconsistent with the purpose of the wrongful death act. A 1975 amendment to the act expressly defined "heirs" to include stepchildren for this purpose.[24] Subsequently, the state legislature abandoned its primary emphasis on heirship in defining wrongful death beneficiaries; a new statute, enacted in 1992, lists categories of surviving relatives who may recover damages, including "stepchildren" who "were dependent on the decedent."[25]

Like the 1975 amendment to the California law, the current Idaho wrongful death act expressly waives the technical definition of "heirs." The Idaho statute defines "heirs" to include stepchildren,[26] even though stepchildren are not considered to be heirs under the state law of intestate succession. Absent this type of legislative redefinition of "heirs" in the wrongful death context, however, the courts have consistently excluded stepchildren from recovery as the "heirs" of wrongful death victims.

As revealed in the opinion of the California Supreme Court in *Steed*, "heirs" has a widely accepted, technical definition that excludes stepchildren and other relatives by marriage. In contrast, the words "parent" and "child," which appear in a number of other wrongful death statutes, have no single legal referent. Thus, stepfamily members have attempted to rely upon numerous theories, including the common law in loco parentis doctrine and the doctrine of equitable adoption, to support their claims as the surviving "parents" and "children" of wrongful death victims. The courts construing these statutory terms, however, have uniformly rejected the claims of stepfamily members.[27]

---

23. *Steed*, 524 P.2d at 809 (dissenting opinion).

24. *See* CAL. CIV. PROC. CODE § 377 (West Supp. 1993), *repealed by* Act of July 11, 1992, ch. 178, § 377.60, 1992 Cal. Legis. Serv. 716, 727 (West).

25. *See* Act of July 11, 1992, ch. 178, § 377.60, 1992 Cal. Legis. Serv. 716, 727 (West) (to be codified in CAL. CIV. PROC. CODE § 377.60).

26. *See* IDAHO CODE § 5–311 (1990).

27. The equitable adoption doctrine was first established by the courts in the context of intestate succession law. Most jurisdictions that recognize the doctrine have refused to extend it to the wrongful death context, and the equitable theory has provided no relief for stepchildren from their exclusion under the wrongful death acts. *See* George A. Locke, Annotation, *Modern Status of the Law as to Equitable*

Two themes emerge from the judicial opinions that narrowly construe the "parent" and "child" terminology in the wrongful death statutes. First, the courts have applied a rule of statutory construction, which generally requires the courts to narrowly construe statutes that were enacted in derogation of the common law. Second, the courts have relied upon their own limited views about the "ordinary meaning" of family terminology.

The first theme focuses on the historical development in this field, where state statutes were first enacted in response to a clear refusal by the courts to recognize any cause of action for the survivors of tort victims. A basic rule of statutory construction, relied upon by many judges at the time of the early wrongful death acts, requires the narrow application of any statute enacted in this manner. Thus, in construing the state wrongful death statute in 1898, the Georgia Supreme Court reasoned that "child" did not include stepchildren.

> This statute is . . . in derogation of the common law, and, applying to it the universal rule of strict construction, we cannot see how there is any escape from the conclusion that the legislature never contemplated giving a child any right of action for the homicide of a stepparent.[28]

In more recent decades, the general premise that wrongful death legislation must be narrowly construed has sometimes been rejected, based in part on the competing mandate that remedial and compensatory statutes should be construed broadly.[29] Even without the aid of rules requiring the

---

Adoption or Adoption by Estoppel, 97 A.L.R.3d 347 §§ 8, 15 (1980 & Supp. 1992) (collecting cases). Similarly, the common law in loco parentis doctrine, which provides a legal basis for recognizing the stepparent-child relationship in other legal settings, has not been incorporated by the courts into wrongful death law. *See* Marshall v. Macon Sash, Door & Lumber Co., 30 S.E. 571 (Ga. 1898); St. Paul Fire & Marine Ins. Co. v. Miniweather, 168 S.E.2d 341 (Ga. Ct. App. 1969); Thornburg v. American Strawboard Co., 40 N.E. 1062 (Ind. 1895); Aymond v. State Dep't of Highways, 333 So. 2d 380 (La. Ct. App. 1976); Palmer v. American Gen. Ins. Co., 126 So. 2d 777 (La. Ct. App. 1961); Flores v. King, 282 A.2d 521 (Md. 1971); Seachrist v. Kreider, 38 Lancaster L.R. 135 (Pa. C.P. 1921); Boudreaux v. Texas & N.O.R. Co., 78 S.W.2d 641 (Tex. Civ. App. 1935); Brown v. Brown, 309 S.E.2d 586 (Va. 1983).

28. Marshall v. Macon Sash, Door & Lumber Co., 30 S.E. 571, 572 (Ga. 1898); *see also* Thornburg v. American Strawboard Co., 40 N.E. 1062, 1063 (Ind. 1895); Boudreaux v. Texas & N.O.R. Co., 78 S.W.2d 641, 643 (Tex. Civ. App. 1935).

29. The author of a leading treatise in the area of wrongful death law has summarized the results of the conflicting rules of statutory construction in this area as follows.

> [T]here is considerable disagreement among judicial pronouncements as to whether death statutes should be strictly or liberally construed. Some take the position that since such statutes are remedial in nature, they should be liberally construed and given a practical construction so as to promote justice.

strict construction of wrongful death statutes, however, the courts have continued to exclude stepparents and stepchildren from recovery. An additional rationale for narrowly construing the statutory terms "parent" and "child" has focused on judicial views about the "ordinary meaning" of family relationships.

For example, prior to its decision in *Klossner v. San Juan County*,[30] the Washington Supreme Court had determined that the state wrongful death act should, as a general rule, be liberally construed in order to accomplish its compensatory purpose.[31] Nevertheless, the *Klossner* court refused to interpret "child" to embrace stepchildren, because this result would require the court to "read into the statute matters which are not there."[32] The court relied upon the "general rule of construction that words in a statute, unless otherwise defined, must be given their usual and ordinary meaning."[33] In a perfunctory fashion, the court concluded that the ordinary meaning of "child" did not include stepchildren, apparently based on the court's own understanding about the meaning of parent-child relationships.[34]

The lack of any consensus on the "ordinary meaning" of the word "child" was reflected in the dissenting opinion in *Klossner*, which observed that "the narrow view might well have fitted the outlook and mores of Victoria's England, [but] it hardly comports with either the realities of or the appropriate value systems of today."[35] According to this alternative view, the "ordinary meaning" of family relationships would properly include stepfamily members. The Washington legislature subsequently adopted this broader definition by joining the handful of states that expressly include stepfamilies in their wrongful death acts. Amended in 1985, the current statute authorizes recovery "for the benefit of the wife, husband, child or children, including *stepchildren*, of the person whose death shall have been [wrongfully] caused."[36]

---

1 SPEISER, *supra* note 3, § 1:12, at 32. *See generally* NORMAN J. SINGER, SUTHERLAND STATUTORY CONSTRUCTION § 61.04, at 101, § 61.05, at 103 (5th ed. 1992) (noting that no modern consensus exists regarding the rule of strict statutory construction).

30. *See* Klossner v. San Juan County, 605 P.2d 330 (Wash. 1980).

31. *See id.* at 332–33; Celia E. Holuk, Note, *The Washington Wrongful Death and Survival Statutes Do Not Allow Recovery By the Unadopted Stepchildren of a Decedent*, 16 GONZ. L. REV. 509, 514–15 (1981) (discussing development of the rule of broad construction of the Washington wrongful death act in cases prior to *Klossner*).

32. *Klossner*, 605 P.2d at 333.

33. *Id.* at 332.

34. *See also* Boudreaux v. Texas & N.O.R. Co., 78 S.W.2d 641, 644 (Tex. Civ. App. 1935) ("[W]e must say that the Legislature used the word 'parent' in its ordinary meaning, unless it affirmatively appears that a peculiar meaning was intended which would include stepmothers.").

35. *Klossner*, 605 P.2d at 334 (dissenting opinion).

36. WASH. REV. CODE ANN. § 4.20.020 (West 1988) (emphasis added).

The dissenting opinion in *Klossner* represents the minority view of state court judges regarding the proper construction of family terminology in wrongful death legislation.[37] Another example of this viewpoint appears in the federal court decisions interpreting the federal laws that apply in certain wrongful death situations.[38] For example, the United States Court of Appeals construed the Death on the High Seas Act,[39] which created a cause of action "for the exclusive benefit of the decedent's wife, husband, parent, child, *or dependent relative*," to include a stepchild who was financially dependent upon the decedent. In *In re United States*, the Court of Appeals ruled that Congress intended to include stepchildren in the definition of "dependent relative," with the following explanation:

> Statutory language is to be given its natural and ordinary meaning absent a manifest legislative expression to the contrary. . . . "Relative" is ordinarily understood to include persons connected with another by affinity as well as blood. . . . A distinction between affines and consanguines would not be well-founded, since the Act is intended to benefit persons suffering pecuniary loss by reason of a death within its scope. Whether such a loss is suffered has nothing to do with whether the relationship is one of blood or of affinity.[40]

Thus, the court's reference to remedial and compensatory purposes in the federal wrongful death context, along with a broader understanding of the "ordinary" meaning of family relationships, led to an outcome that is inconsistent with the prevailing state law in this area.

The state laws that exclude stepfamily members from wrongful death recovery, as in the *Steed* and *Klossner* opinions, have survived constitutional challenge under the Equal Protection Clause of the Fourteenth Amend-

---

37. A notable exception to the state court decisions that narrowly construe family terminology in the wrongful death statutes appears in the recent opinion of the Ohio Supreme Court in Lawson v. Atwood, 536 N.E.2d 1167 (Ohio 1989), which involved a wrongful death claim by foster parents. The expanded definition of parent set forth in the *Lawson* opinion is still likely to exclude stepparents in most cases, because other adults are permitted to recover as "parents" only if "[t]he natural parents of the child have disclaimed or abandoned [their] parental rights." *Id.* at 1170. This condition is not likely to be satisfied in most stepfamilies.

38. *See generally* 1 SPEISER, *supra* note 3, § 1:17, at 43 (discussing federal laws that govern certain types of wrongful death claims).

39. *See* Death on the High Seas Act, 46 U.S.C. § 761 (1988) (authorizing recovery "against the vessel, person, or corporation which would have been liable if death had not ensued" as a result of the defendant's wrongful act).

40. *In re* United States, 418 F.2d 264, 270–71 (1st Cir. 1969); *see also* Stissi v. Interstate and Ocean Transp. Co., 590 F. Supp. 1043, 1046 (E.D.N.Y. 1984) (ruling that stepchildren were entitled to wrongful death damages under federal common law maritime principles).

ment.[41] The constitutional standard employed to review the classifications drawn by wrongful death legislation is the lenient standard of reasonableness. Although the automatic exclusion of stepfamilies clearly produces results in some cases that are inconsistent with the legislative purpose of compensating the dependent survivors of wrongful death victims, this element of underinclusiveness has not been regarded as unreasonable in the constitutional sense. As discussed in this section, the large majority of state lawmakers have exercised their discretion under this broad constitutional standard to exclude stepparents and stepchildren from wrongful death recoveries.

---

41. *See, e.g.,* Steed v. Imperial Airlines, 524 P.2d 801, 806–07 (Cal. 1974) (upholding constitutionality of California wrongful death statute); Dickerson v. Continental Ohio Co., 449 F.2d 1209, 1217 (5th Cir. 1971) (upholding constitutionality of Louisiana wrongful death statute).

CHAPTER 6

Workers' Compensation

I. Introduction

Like the wrongful death acts, state workers' compensation statutes were enacted to fill a critical gap in the common law system of compensation for personal injuries. Prior to their enactment, the application of general tort law principles to the workplace had created an almost insurmountable burden for workers and their survivors who sued employers for damages arising from workplace accidents. As a result, according to a leading treatise, "by far the greater proportion of industrial accidents remained uncompensated."[1] Besides the problem of uncompensated injuries, the system contributed to another social problem by removing the financial incentive for employers to improve safety standards. The first workers' compensation statutes were enacted around the turn of the century to address these concerns. Indeed, "[i]t has been said that no subject of labor legislation ever has made such progress or received such general acceptance of its principles in so brief a period."[2]

The remedial statutes enacted in every state substituted the workers' compensation claim for traditional tort law remedies. This compensation system shifted the cost of worker injury to the employer by replacing the principle of fault with a rule of strict employer liability. The worker is guaranteed a quick and certain recovery for job-related injuries, although state statutes ordinarily limit compensation to amounts related to medical expenses and lost earning capacity.[3]

In the event that an injured worker dies, the compensation statutes in every state authorize awards to surviving family members.[4] The question

---

1. W. PAGE KEETON ET AL., PROSSER AND KEETON ON THE LAW OF TORTS 572 (5th ed. 1984).

2. *Id.* at 573.

3. *See* 1 ARTHUR LARSON, THE LAW OF WORKMEN'S COMPENSATION §§ 1–5 (1992) (describing the origins and basic features of the compensation system).

4. *See id.* §§ 62–64 (describing dependency and death benefits under state workers' compensation laws). The following statutes create survivors' rights: ALA. CODE §§ 25–5–1, –61 (1992); ALASKA STAT. §§ 23.30.215, .265 (1990 & Supp. 1992); ARIZ. REV. STAT. ANN. §§ 23–1046, –1064 (Supp. 1993); ARK. CODE ANN. §§ 11–9–102, –527 (Michie 1987); CAL. LAB. CODE §§ 3501 to 3503 (West 1989 & Supp. 1993); COLO. REV. STAT. §§ 8–41–501, 8–42–114 (Supp. 1992); CONN. GEN.

explored in this chapter is the eligibility of stepfamily members for survivors' benefits. The exploration reveals that the workers' compensation system is one of the rare legal settings in which stepfamilies receive fairly uniform recognition.

The unusually benevolent approach to stepfamilies in this area of law is explained, at least in part, by both history and the limited nature of the workers' compensation remedy. As part of a larger historical movement to change the balance of economic power between workers and employers, workers' compensation legislation has been drafted and construed broadly by legislatures and courts. Broad coverage for families is consistent with this expansive purpose.[5]

Furthermore, the special nature of the workers' compensation system enabled lawmakers to extend coverage to numerous beneficiaries without

Stat. Ann. §§ 31–275, –306 (West Supp. 1993); Del. Code Ann. tit. 19, §§ 2301, 2330 (1985 & Supp. 1992); D.C. Code Ann. §§ 36–301, –309 (1988 & Supp. 1992); Fla. Stat. Ann. §§ 440.02, .16 (West 1991); Ga. Code Ann. § 34–9–13 (1992); Haw. Rev. Stat. §§ 386–2, –42 (1985); Idaho Code §§ 72–102, –410 (1989 & Supp. 1993); Ill. Ann. Stat. ch. 48, para. 138.7 (Smith-Hurd Supp. 1992); Ind. Code Ann. § 22–3–3–19 (Burns 1992); Iowa Code Ann. §§ 85.31, .42, .44 (West 1984 & Supp. 1993); Kan. Stat. Ann. §§ 44–508, –510b (Supp. 1992); Ky. Rev. Stat. Ann. §§ 342.075, .085 (Baldwin 1986); La. Rev. Stat. Ann. §§ 23:1021, :1231 (West 1985 & Supp. 1993); Me. Rev. Stat. Ann. tit. 39, § 2 (West 1989 & Supp. 1992); Md. Code Ann., Lab. & Employment §§ 9–101, –681 (1991); Mass. Gen. Laws Ann. ch. 152, §§ 31, 32 (West 1988 & Supp. 1993); Mich. Comp. Laws Ann. §§ 418.321, .331 (West Supp. 1993); Minn. Stat. Ann. §§ 176.011, .111 (West 1993); Miss. Code Ann. §§ 71–3–3, –25 (1989 & Supp. 1992); Mo. Ann. Stat. § 287.240 (Vernon 1993); Mont. Code Ann. §§ 39–71–116, –721 (1991); Neb. Rev. Stat. § 48–124 (Supp. 1992); Nev. Rev. Stat. Ann. § 616.510 (Michie 1992); N.H. Rev. Stat. Ann. §§ 281–A:2, :26 (Supp. 1992); N.J. Stat. Ann. § 34.15–13 (West Supp. 1993); N.M. Stat. Ann. § 52–1–46 (Michie 1991); N.Y. Work. Comp. Law §§ 2, 16 (McKinney 1992 & Supp. 1993); N.C. Gen. Stat. §§ 97–2, –39 (1991); N.D. Cent. Code §§ 65–01–02, 65–05–17 (Supp. 1991); Ohio Rev. Code Ann. § 4123.59 (Baldwin 1990); Okla. Stat. Ann. tit. 85, § 3.1 (West 1992); Or. Rev. Stat. §§ 656.005, .204 (Supp. 1992); Pa. Stat. Ann. tit. 77, §§ 561, 562 (1992); R.I. Gen. Laws § 28–33–12, –13 (1986 & Supp. 1993); S.C. Code Ann. §§ 42–1–70, –170, 42–9–110, (Law. Co-op. 1985); S.D. Codified Laws Ann. §§ 62–4–8, –12, –13 (1978); Tenn. Code Ann. § 50–6–210 (1991); Tex. Rev. Civ. Stat. Ann. arts. 8308–1.03, –4.42 (West Supp. 1993); Utah Code Ann. §§ 35–1–68, –71 (1988 & Supp. 1993); Vt. Stat. Ann. tit. 21, §§ 601, 634 (1987 & Supp. 1992); Va. Code Ann. §§ 65.2–512, –515 (Michie 1991 & Supp. 1993); Wash. Rev. Code Ann. §§ 51.32.010, .020 (West 1990); W. Va. Code §§ 23–4–10, –11 (1985); Wis. Stat. Ann. §§ 102.49, .51 (West 1988); Wyo. Stat. §§ 27–14–102, –403 (1991).

5. The stepparent-child relationship has also been recognized in the system of compensation for workers and their surviving family members established by Congress under the Social Security Act. *See* Margaret M. Mahoney, *Stepfamilies in the Federal Law*, 48 U. Pitt. L. Rev. 491, 496–514 (1987) (describing eligibility of stepchildren under the Old-Age, Survivors, and Disability Insurance Program).

creating difficult administrative and financial burdens. The forum for workers' compensation claims is typically an administrative body that has specialized expertise in the field, and recoveries are limited by statutory schedules to relatively modest amounts. These administrative and economic factors have contributed to the willingness of lawmakers to open the doors to a broad range of beneficiaries in workers' compensation cases.

Two issues affect the eligibility of every claimant under the workers' compensation survivors' statutes. First, the statutes limit recovery to those individuals who enjoyed designated relationships with the worker, such as a family or household relationship. In addition, the claimant must establish that he or she was dependent upon the deceased worker. As described in sections II and III, stepfamily members have been able to satisfy these dual relationship and dependency requirements under a variety of state workers' compensation laws.

II. The Relationship Requirement

Survivors are included as beneficiaries in the workers' compensation system, because a worker's death usually causes real, compensable losses for those individuals who were supported by the worker's wages. As described in the next section, the survivors' statutes directly address the issue of economic loss by requiring that each claimant establish his or her dependency upon the deceased worker. As a threshold matter, before reaching the issue of dependency, the claimant must also prove that he or she stood in a recognized relationship to the worker.

Workers' compensation laws usually designate certain qualifying relatives, such as the spouse, child, parent, brother, and sister, as the eligible survivors of a deceased worker. Steprelatives are expressly included in many of the state statutes. The California Code, for example, includes stepchildren in the following provision.

> No person is a dependent of any deceased employee unless . . . the person bears to the employee the relation of husband or wife, child . . . or *stepchild*, grandchild, father or mother, father-in-law or mother-in-law, grandfather or grandmother, brother or sister, uncle or aunt, brother-in-law or sister-in-law, nephew or niece.[6]

Stepchildren have also qualified for survivors' benefits under state statutes that recognize in loco parentis relationships for this purpose.[7] While step-

---

6. Cal. Lab. Code § 3503 (West 1989) (emphasis added).

7. *See, e.g.*, Alaska Stat. § 23.30.265(6) (Supp. 1992) (establishing eligibility based on the existence of an in loco parentis relationship for at least one year prior to the time of injury); Del. Code Ann. tit. 19, § 2301(2) (1985); D.C. Code Ann. § 36–

children are the most common stepfamily beneficiaries, several state workers' compensation acts also extend eligibility to dependent stepparents, stepsiblings, and stepgrandchildren.[8]

In addition to the designated family and stepfamily relationships, eligibility under many workers' compensation laws may be established by proof that the claimant was a member of the deceased worker's household. The California Code, for example, includes the list of relatives quoted above, then adds that "[n]o person is a dependent of any deceased employee unless in good faith a member of the family or household of the employee, or unless [one of the designated relatives]."[9] The "household member" status is important in this context, because individuals who share a household often establish de facto family ties and economic interdependence. For example, an Ohio trial court approved the claims of four stepchildren as "members of the [deceased worker's] family entitled to participate in the workmen's compensation fund," based on evidence that they "lived in the same house with the deceased and their mother [and] ate at the table of the deceased."[10]

The workers' compensation statutes in several states contain neither the specific reference to steprelatives nor the broad reference to household members that appear in the California Code. Nevertheless, courts have

---

301(4) (1988); ILL. ANN. STAT. ch. 48, para. 138.7(a) (Smith-Hurd Supp. 1992); NEB. REV. STAT. § 48–124 (Supp. 1992); OR. REV. STAT. § 656.005(5) (Supp. 1992); PA. STAT. ANN. tit. 77, § 562 (1992); WIS. STAT. ANN. § 102.49(2) (West 1988 & Supp. 1992); cf. MISS. CODE ANN. § 71–3–3(m) (Supp. 1992) (establishing eligibility for person who stood in the place of a parent to the deceased employee).

8. See Alabama (stepchild); Alaska (stepchild, stepsibling); Arizona (stepchild, stepparent); Arkansas (stepchild, stepsibling); California (stepchild); Delaware (stepchild); District of Columbia (stepchild, stepparent, stepsibling); Florida (stepchild, stepgrandchild, stepsibling, stepparent); Georgia (stepchild, stepparent); Hawaii (stepchild, child of a stepchild, stepsibling, stepparent); Idaho (stepchild, child of stepchild, stepsibling, stepparent); Indiana (stepchild, stepparent); Iowa (stepchild); Kansas (stepchild, stepgrandchild, stepsibling, stepparent); Kentucky (stepchild, stepsibling, stepparent); Louisiana (stepchild, stepsibling); Maine (stepchild); Maryland (stepchild); Minnesota (stepchild); Mississippi (stepchild, stepsibling, stepparent); Montana (stepchild); Nebraska (stepchild, stepchild of a child, stepsibling, stepparent); Nevada (stepchild, stepparent); New Jersey (stepchild, stepparent); New York (stepchild); North Carolina (stepchild, stepparent, stepsibling); North Dakota (stepchild, stepsibling, stepparent); Oklahoma (stepchild, stepparent); Oregon (stepchild, stepparent); Pennsylvania (stepchild); Rhode Island (stepchild); South Carolina (stepchild, stepsibling, stepparent); Texas (stepchild); Vermont (stepchild, child of a stepchild, stepparent, stepsibling); Virginia (stepchild, stepparent); Washington (stepchild, stepparent); West Virginia (stepchild); Wyoming (stepchild).

9. CAL. LAB. CODE § 3503 (West 1989).

10. Blair v. Keller, 241 N.E.2d 767, 768 (Ohio C.P. 1968); see also Duluth-Superior Milling Co. v. Industrial Comm'n, 275 N.W. 515, 519 (Wis. 1937) (holding that a deceased worker's adult stepdaughter, who was a member of his household, was entitled to prove her actual dependence on him).

construed the words "parent" and "child" in these statutes broadly, to include nonbiologic and nontraditional family members. One noted scholar has summarized the liberal approach to defining family terminology in this field as follows.

> [P]robably the most that can be said about the application of domestic relations law to compensation claims is that, because of the beneficent character of the legislation, established definitions and rules will usually be stretched as far as precedents will allow, to take care of meritorious cases of dependency.[11]

For example, the in loco parentis doctrine has been judicially incorporated into the workers' compensation laws.[12] Of course, stepfamily members frequently benefit as "parents" and "children" under this doctrine, which acknowledges the de facto family relationships established when an adult voluntarily assumes responsibility for a child.

A notable exception to the rule that legislatures and courts have found a place for stepfamilies in the workers' compensation system appears in the 1984 decision of the Colorado Court of Appeals in *Tri-State Commodities, Inc. v. Stewart*.[13] There, the court refused to construe "child" in the Colorado statute to include the minor stepsons of a worker who died in an industrial accident. On the day of the accident, Mr. Stewart, who worked as a truck driver for Tri-State, allowed his two minor stepsons to accompany him as he delivered a truckload of a granular chemical called urea. As the urea was being deposited from the truck into bins, one stepson slipped and fell into the cascading chemical. Although the boy survived the accident, his stepfather suffocated while attempting to rescue him. The Colorado workers' compensation statute did not expressly include stepchildren, and the court in *Stewart* ruled that the provision for "children" did not include stepchildren or the children to whom a deceased worker had stood in loco parentis. Accordingly, the two stepsons had no opportunity to prove their actual dependence on the deceased worker as the basis for recovering survivors' benefits.

As discussed fully in this section, the result in the *Stewart* case is an

---

11. 2 LARSON, *supra* note 3, § 62.21(c), at 11–9 to 11–10.

12. *See* Gonzalez v. Workmen's Compensation Appeals Bd., 122 Cal. Rptr. 515, 517 (Ct. App. 1975) ("dependent minor children" included "all minors who are dependent members of decedent's household regardless of the relationship to the deceased"); Faber v. Industrial Comm'n, 185 N.E. 255 (Ill. 1933) (foster mother qualified as mother); MacArthur v. Nashua Corp., 493 A.2d 1126 (N.H. 1985) (foster child qualified as child of decedent); Custer v. Reitz Coal Co., 101 A.2d 433 (Pa. Super. Ct. 1953) (grandmother qualified as mother). *But see* Miles v. Theobald Indus., 366 A.2d 710 (N.J. Super. Ct. App. Div. 1976) (woman standing in loco parentis to deceased worker did not qualify as his surviving mother).

13. Tri-State Commodities, Inc. v. Stewart, 689 P.2d 712 (Colo. Ct. App. 1984).

exception to the general rule nationwide that stepfamily members are regarded as survivors of a deceased worker under various state workers' compensation laws. Once a qualifying relationship is established, the surviving family members must proceed to establish their dependency upon the deceased worker. This additional requirement is explored in the next section.

III. The Dependency Requirement

The workers' compensation statutes uniformly focus on dependency as the second criterion for the recovery of survivors' benefits, although the definition of dependency varies from state to state. The most liberal statutes create a conclusive presumption of dependency for certain categories of claimants, if the first requirement regarding relationship to the decedent has been met. The Virginia Code extends this presumption of dependency to stepchildren.

> The following persons shall be conclusively presumed to be dependents wholly dependent for support upon the deceased employee:
> . . . [a] child under the age of eighteen upon a parent . . . . As used in this section, the term 'child' shall include a stepchild . . . .[14]

Under this provision, proof of the stepparent-child relationship alone would establish the stepchild's eligibility for survivors' benefits.

The automatic eligibility resulting from this type of conclusive presumption of dependency has been limited in a number of states to biologic relatives. For example, the Idaho statute establishes a conclusive presumption of dependency in favor of the deceased worker's minor children, and adds that "children . . . does not include stepchildren unless actually dependent" upon the worker.[15] The distinction drawn here between children and stepchildren reveals a legislative judgment that the overbreadth inherent in such a presumption is justified as to natural children only. Certainly, there are children of deceased workers who will benefit under the Idaho statute even though they did not, in fact, depend upon the decedent for support. The legislature has resolved that the number of cases in this category is small enough to justify the conclusive presumption. On the other hand, the exclusion of stepchildren reflects a contrary view about the likely number of stepfamily cases in which an actual determination of dependency will yield negative results.

In *Flint River Mills v. Henry*,[16] the Georgia Supreme Court rejected

---

14. Va. Code Ann. § 65.2–515 (Michie 1991); *see also* Ind. Code Ann. § 22–3–3–19 (Burns 1992).

15. Idaho Code §§ 72–102(8)(c), –410 (1989 & Supp. 1993).

16. Flint River Mills v. Henry, 236 S.E.2d 583 (Ga. 1977).

the theory that the exclusion of steprelatives from the conclusive presumption of dependency, as in the Idaho statute, is constitutionally required. In *Henry*, the workers' compensation board awarded compensation to Curtis Henry's children and stepchildren under a Georgia statute creating a conclusive presumption in favor of both. Mr. Henry had been the sole source of support for the six children of his first marriage, who resided with their grandmother at the time of his death. In contrast, he had provided no support to the stepchildren, who resided with Mr. Henry and their mother. In an attempt to exclude the stepchildren from sharing in the survivors' benefits that had accrued as a result of Mr. Henry's death, his children alleged that the statutory presumption in favor of stepchildren violated the Due Process Clause. The children argued that the conclusive presumption was unconstitutionally arbitrary in light of the legislative purpose of compensating dependent family members, because stepparents owed no support duty to stepchildren under Georgia law. The Georgia Supreme Court dismissed the constitutional claim, upholding the authority of the legislature to establish the eligibility of stepchildren "without regard to their actual dependency on the [decedent]."[17]

Although the *Henry* case established the constitutional authority of the state legislature to extend the conclusive presumption of dependency to stepchildren, the Georgia legislature subsequently amended the workers' compensation statute to exclude stepchildren from the statutory presumption.[18] Indeed, the statutes in most states resemble the current Georgia provision, requiring steprelatives to prove actual dependency in order to qualify for survivors' benefits.

The courts have been quite liberal in making determinations about actual dependency in individual stepfamily cases. For example, the three stepchildren in *Housley v. Everts' Commercial Transport, Inc.*[19] were awarded survivors' benefits even though they had never received a single dollar of support from their stepfather during his lifetime. The Oregon Court of Appeals relied upon evidence that the stepfamily had been created with the intention that the stepfather, who died just days after his marriage, would support his wife's children in the future. Not only did the surviving wife have no income at the time of her husband's death, but public assistance benefits for the children had been terminated at the time of the marriage. Based on this record, the court reached the following affirmative conclusion regarding the dependency of the stepchildren.

---

17. *Id.* at 585; *see also* Shahan v. Beasley Hot Shot Serv., Inc., 575 P.2d 1347 (N.M. Ct. App. 1978) (upholding constitutionality of workers' compensation law that created conclusive presumption of dependence for children and stepchildren).

18. *See* GA. CODE ANN. § 34–9–13 (1992).

19. Housley v. Everts' Commercial Transp., Inc., 475 P.2d 977 (Or. Ct. App. 1970).

[T]he tragic brevity of the marriage [should] not alone operate to deprive these three stepchildren of the support normally to be anticipated when, as here, the stepfather has clearly assumed an ongoing responsibility for their support . . . .[20]

The employer in *Housley* raised an additional objection to the stepchildren's claim, relating to their natural father's court-ordered obligation to make monthly child support payments. In response, the court emphasized that surviving dependents under the workers' compensation program are entitled to a level of support commensurate with the level they would have enjoyed if the industrial accident never occurred. Thus, "the three minor children were indeed substantially dependent upon the [stepfather] for support at the time he was killed,"[21] despite the financial role played by their father.

As in *Housley*, the presence of a noncustodial parent who is legally obligated to support the children frequently complicates the assessment of their dependence on a stepparent. Most courts take the same approach, looking to the facts of each case to determine whether the natural parent's contributions actually eliminated the children's dependency on the stepparent. In *Employers Liability Assurance Corporation v. Dull*,[22] for example, the Supreme Court of Alaska assessed the deceased stepfather's contributions to the living expenses of his stepdaughter for babysitting, clothes, food, medical care, housing, and utilities in the following manner.

[T]he child was unquestionably deprived of a source of support by reason of her stepfather's death.

The fact that support was also furnished the child by her natural father is immaterial. A child can be dependent upon more than one person. The statute speaks only of a child who is 'dependent' upon the deceased; it does not specify sole dependency as a condition of an award of compensation.[23]

The fact that state law imposes a support obligation upon the noncustodial parent, but not on the stepparent, is irrelevant to the determination of actual dependency in these cases.[24]

A further refinement in the definition of dependency is the distinction

20. *Id.* at 978; *see also* Robinson v. Eaves, 210 N.W. 578 (Iowa 1926) (applying broad definition of actual dependency in order to benefit stepchildren).

21. *Housley*, 475 P.2d at 979.

22. Employers Liab. Assurance Corp. v. Dull, 416 P.2d 821 (Alaska 1966).

23. *Id.* at 823.

24. *See, e.g.*, Fish v. Industrial Comm'n, 472 P.2d 97, 102 (Ariz. Ct. App. 1970) ("The entitlement of the children to death benefits arises out of the fact of support [by the stepfather] and not out of a legal duty.").

drawn in numerous state laws between partial and total dependency, with a preference assigned to claimants who were totally dependent on the deceased worker. Totally dependent survivors may be eligible for benefits to the exclusion of claimants who were only partially dependent on the deceased worker; alternatively, they may simply receive a larger share of the compensation award. Stepfamily members have enjoyed the benefit of both types of preference.

For example, the Arizona statute applied in *Diesel Drivers v. Industrial Commission*[25] reserved the highest benefit levels for totally dependent claimants. Thus, surviving spouses and children, who were conclusively presumed to be totally dependent on the deceased worker, were entitled to a maximum income award of two-thirds of the worker's average wage. In contrast, partially dependent claimants would receive only the fraction of this amount that represented the percentage of their support actually provided by the worker prior to death. The claimants in *Diesel Drivers* were the worker's four stepchildren and their mother. The mother clearly enjoyed the benefit of the conclusive presumption of total dependency for spouses, even though her earnings had, in fact, contributed to the family's support.

The issue in *Diesel Drivers* was whether the stepchildren, who had been supported by both of their natural parents and their stepfather, were entitled to receive benefits at the level set for totally dependent claimants. The Supreme Court of Arizona ruled that once the four stepchildren established actual, partial dependency on the deceased worker, then the conclusive presumption of total dependency benefiting "children" would be extended to them. Since the stepchildren in *Diesel Drivers* had received partial support from the deceased worker, they were eligible under this rule for the maximum level of benefits extended to totally dependent claimants.

The same liberal approach to classifying stepchildren as totally dependent survivors appears in the opinion of the North Carolina Court of Appeals in *Winstead v. Derreberry*.[26] Under the North Carolina statute, "wholly dependent" survivors received benefits to the exclusion of all other claimants; furthermore, the deceased worker's children, including the "stepchild . . . dependent upon the deceased," were conclusively presumed to be wholly dependent. The competing claimants in *Winstead* were the deceased worker's daughter, who clearly enjoyed the benefit of the presumption, and his two stepchildren, who had been receiving more than one-half of their support from the decedent and the remainder from their parents.

The *Winstead* court ruled that the stepchildren were entitled to receive benefits as "wholly dependent" survivors, along with the worker's daughter. According to the court, once the stepchildren established their "substantial dependence" on the decedent, they became entitled to the benefit of the

---

25. Diesel Drivers v. Industrial Comm'n, 593 P.2d 934 (Ariz. Ct. App. 1979).
26. Winstead v. Derreberry, 326 S.E.2d 66 (N.C. Ct. App. 1985).

conclusive statutory presumption in favor of "children."[27] Thus, like the stepchildren in *Diesel Drivers*, they enjoyed priority as wholly dependent claimants, even though they were not included in the automatic presumption of total dependency under the statute nor factually dependent upon the worker for all of their support.

In summary, stepfamily members, like other claimants, must establish their dependence upon the deceased worker in order to receive workers' compensation survivors' benefits. In some jurisdictions, designated stepfamily members, especially stepchildren, may benefit from a conclusive presumption of dependency. Even when legislation does not clearly extend this type of presumption to steprelatives, the courts have generally resolved questions of actual dependence in an extremely liberal manner. Due to this judicial attitude, as well as the broadly drawn statutory categories of eligible claimants described in the previous section, stepfamily relationships frequently receive recognition in the workers' compensation system.

---

27. The holding in *Winstead v. Derreberry* has been criticized for destroying the certainty and convenience of the conclusive presumption of dependency by requiring a factual determination regarding the "substantial dependence" of stepchildren. *See* Anne Ferrell Team, Note, Winstead v. Derreberry: *Stepchildren and the Presumption of Dependence Under the North Carolina Workers' Compensation Act*, 64 N.C. L. Rev. 1548 (1986).

CHAPTER 7

Custody and Visitation

I. Introduction

Child custody is a key aspect of the legal parent-child relationship. When both parents reside together with their minor children, they share the responsibility to care for their children and the authority to make many important decisions that affect the family. Parents make decisions, for example, about medical treatment, education, where the children will live, and with whom they will associate. Of course, as children mature, they are more likely to participate in this process.

When one parent is designated as the primary custodian, most often in a marriage dissolution proceeding, the noncustodial parent loses many aspects of his or her custodial authority. Thus, an order of visitation on behalf of the noncustodial parent typically entails the right to spend time with the children but no continuing decision-making authority. In contrast, a joint custody arrangement usually contemplates joint authority in the future, even though the parents live apart.

When an individual marries the parent who has the primary or joint custody of a minor child, a number of issues may arise regarding the custodial authority of the stepparent. First, during the period that the custodial parent, stepparent, and child reside together as a stepfamily, the stepparent is likely to share informally in many of the important decisions that affect the child's well-being. The issue explored in section II is whether the residential stepparent has any legal authority, like that of the custodial parent, that must be recognized by medical practitioners, educators, and other third parties. Currently, there are no clear answers to many of the practical questions that arise in this manner about authority within the stepfamily.

Additional issues involving the custodial rights of stepparents arise when the stepfamily is disrupted, either by divorce or by the death of the custodial parent. At these times of transition, stepparents frequently desire to protect their future relationships with stepchildren, by asserting legal rights of visitation or by seeking judicial appointment as the primary or joint custodian. These important issues of stepparent visitation and custody are explored in sections III and IV, respectively.

Visitation rights for stepparents have developed by analogy to the role traditionally assigned to the noncustodial parent following divorce. That is, when visitation is authorized, the stepparent becomes entitled to spend time with the stepchild in the future, even though the custodial parent may oppose this result. The status does not, however, involve any additional right to interfere with the custodian's authority vis-à-vis the child. As discussed in section III, the law is evolving to permit this type of visitation by stepparents in cases where continuation of the stepparent-child relationship would serve the child's best interests.

In contrast, the best interests of the child standard is not consistently applied to resolve contests between stepparents and parents when the issue is future custody of the child. Here, the legal system favors the placement of children with one or both parents, and third parties typically face a difficult burden in overcoming this parental preference. Furthermore, a clear line is drawn between biologic and adoptive parents, on the one hand, and all other adults; even the stepparent who played an in loco parentis role in the stepfamily for a substantial period of time is regarded as a "third party" for this purpose. Section IV discusses the legal standards that define the rights of stepparents, parents, and children in stepchild custody disputes.

II. Custodial Authority in the Stepfamily

A stepparent's custodial authority is defined, for the most part, in an informal fashion within the stepfamily. As a practical matter, the individual who marries a parent with the custody of minor children will likely become involved, to some degree, in the custodial parent-child relationship. For example, parents make many important decisions that affect the well-being of their children, including decisions about where the family will live, what kinds of food will be eaten, and what guests will be invited into the home. The stepparent, as an adult member of the household, will likely be involved in resolving many of these issues. Of course, custodial parents exercise control over their children in more direct ways as well. For example, parents make decisions about the religious training, education, medical care, and discipline of their children. As the children grow older, they are likely to have a voice in many of the decisions that affect them. In the stepfamily, the parties must also define the stepparent's role in the various aspects of childraising.[1]

Where the stepparent informally assumes shared responsibility for parenting children in the stepfamily, he or she may stand in loco parentis in the eyes of the common law. As discussed fully in other chapters, however, the in loco parentis status is not equivalent to the legal status of parenthood. As a result, other people who deal with stepchildren outside the home may be

---

1. *See generally* Myron Orleans et al., *Marriage Adjustment and Satisfaction of Stepfathers: Their Feelings and Perceptions of Decision Making and Stepchildren Relations*, 1989 FAM. REL. 371, 371 (concluding that a "stepfather's role in the family decision making process appears to be important for his marital adjustment").

reluctant to recognize the status of the stepparent, absent some clear legal authority for doing so. Thus, the issue of the stepparent's custodial authority becomes more complicated when third parties, such as medical practitioners or educators, enter the picture.[2]

In the medical field, the legal system requires that practitioners obtain the patient's informed consent to most medical procedures. Failure to do so may give rise to the patient's cause of action for damages under a variety of tort theories.[3] In this context, children are legally incapable of giving consent to their own medical treatment, based on an assumption about their lack of mature judgment and their inability to enter into binding contracts. In the case of a minor patient, therefore, informed consent must generally be obtained from the parent. The issue in the stepfamily is whether the residential stepparent, like the custodial parent, may consent to medical treatment for a minor stepchild.

Statutes in every state authorize the adult with formal legal custody, typically the parent, to consent to medical treatment for minor children.[4] An exceptional provision in the Missouri consent statute empowers parents to consent to medical treatment and expressly defines "parent" to include stepparents.[5] Furthermore, a few states authorize the person who is acting in the place of a parent to give consent.[6] Elsewhere, the authority of stepparents is less clear. For example, several statutes recognize in loco parentis authority, but only if the parent or legal guardian is not available.[7] Such

---

2. The discussion in the text assumes a situation where the custodial parent does not oppose the stepparent's attempt to assert custodial authority vis-à-vis third parties. If the parent and stepparent are in opposition, for example, where the stepparent supports medical treatment for the minor stepchild that is opposed by the parent, the third party would likely defer to the parent. As a legal matter, the parent's rights as legal custodian in this situation would be superior to any rights of the stepparent.

3. *See* FAY A. ROZOVSKY, CONSENT TO TREATMENT 6–12 (2d ed. 1990).

4. *See* JAMES D. MORRISSEY ET AL., CONSENT AND CONFIDENTIALITY IN THE HEALTH CARE OF CHILDREN AND ADOLESCENTS 149–261 (1986) (collecting statutes in every state that authorizes consent to medical care for minor patients). Many state legislatures have created exceptions to the general rule and allow minors to consent on their own behalf if they are "mature" or "emancipated," or if the medical treatment relates to drug dependency, birth control, or pregnancy. *See* ARNOLD J. ROSOFF, INFORMED CONSENT 211–31 (1981) (summarizing the state statutes that authorize consent by minors to their own medical treatment).

5. *See* Mo. ANN. STAT. § 431.061 (Vernon 1992).

6. *See* ARK. CODE ANN. § 20–9–602 (Michie 1991); GA. CODE ANN. § 31–9–2(a)(4) (1991) (authorizing "[a]ny person temporarily standing in loco parentis" to consent to child's medical treatment); MISS. CODE ANN. § 41–41–3 (Supp. 1992) (authorizing any person standing in loco parentis to consent to child's medical treatment); Mo. ANN. STAT. § 431.061 (Vernon 1992).

7. *See, e.g.,* ARIZ. REV. STAT. ANN. § 44–133 (1987) (authorizing consent from person standing in loco parentis in case of emergency when parent cannot be lo-

provisions may contemplate consent by stepparents in limited circumstances, but they clearly contain a preference for the parent.

Stepparents in most states have no statutory authority to give legally effective consent to medical treatment for their minor stepchildren. In the absence of clear legal guidelines, medical care providers have developed policies about the circumstances in which treatment will be provided to a minor patient based on the consent of a stepparent. Important factors generally include the immediacy of the child's medical need and the seriousness of the required procedure in each case.[8] For example, when the stepparent brings a child with a broken arm into the emergency room, the need for treatment is rather immediate, and the seriousness of the necessary procedure is not great. In this situation, the emergency room personnel may accept the stepparent's consent, even if they understand that the stepparent is not the legal guardian. In the alternative, an attempt may be made to contact the custodial parent, even though this involves a delay in providing treatment. In contrast, where the child requires major surgery and time is not of the essence, the doctors and hospital will likely insist on obtaining written consent from the adult who has clear legal authority. There are very few reported cases involving lawsuits by parents who have subsequently challenged the decisions made by medical practitioners to accept the consent of another adult.[9]

Of course, a general exception exists to the usual rules about informed consent in cases of medical emergency, where delay would create a serious threat to the patient's life or health. Here, the necessary treatment must go forward, even if no one is available to give consent, and authorization by the stepparent to emergency care for a minor patient may be preferable to no consent at all. Thus, in *Tabor v. Scobee*,[10] the liability of a surgeon for

cated); IDAHO CODE § 39–4303(b) (1993) ("If no parent . . . or legal guardian is readily available to do so, then consent may be given by . . . any other competent individual representing himself or herself to be responsible for the health care of [the child.]"); LA. REV. STAT. ANN. § 40:1299.53(A)(9) (West 1992) (authorizing consent from "[a]ny person temporarily standing in loco parentis" if no parent is "reasonably available"); NEV. REV. STAT. ANN. § 129.040 (Michie 1993) (same as Arizona); VA. CODE ANN. § 54.1–2969 (Michie 1991) (authorizing consent from person standing in loco parentis where minor "has been separated from the custody of his parent or guardian").

8. *See generally* MORRISSEY, *supra* note 4, at 23–27 (discussing situations in which health professionals may rely upon consent by nonparents to the treatment of minors).

9. *See, e.g.*, Taylor v. R.D. Morgan & Assocs., Ltd., 563 N.E.2d 1186 (Ill. App. Ct. 1990) (ruling that noncustodial parent was authorized to consent to medical treatment during period of visitation with the child when the custodial parent was unavailable); Danny R. Veilleux, Annotation, *Medical Practitioner's Liability for Treatment Given Child Without Parent's Consent*, 67 A.L.R.4th 511 (1989 & Supp. 1992) (collecting cases).

10. Tabor v. Scobee, 254 S.W.2d 474 (Ky. Ct. App. 1952).

battery depended upon the existence of an emergency to justify his removal of a twenty-year-old patient's fallopian tubes without prior consent. In *Tabor*, the surgeon decided to perform this additional procedure during a routine appendectomy; proper consent had been obtained in advance to remove only the appendix. The minor patient was accompanied by her stepmother, who remained in the hospital throughout the entire operation. On this record, the court ruled that the surgeon would be liable for battery, unless the evidence revealed that he had no opportunity to consult with the stepmother and obtain her consent to the extended surgery. According to the court, "the law rightfully requires the consent of the patient or one in loco parentis whenever it is possible to obtain her consent in time."[11] Notably, there was no discussion in the opinion about a preference for consent from the patient's parent or legal guardian in these circumstances.

Just as medical practitioners rely upon the judgment of parents regarding the medical care of minor children, so too educators must defer to parents on many important matters that involve a child's education.[12] For example, parents make decisions about the child's enrollment in a particular school or program, the release of student records, and the adults to whom school personnel may release the child. As in the medical field, the authority of the stepparent here is ill-defined by the legal system and frequently depends upon the policies and procedures adopted and implemented by schools and teachers.[13]

In 1974, Congress enacted the Family Education Rights and Privacy Act,[14] which established a national standard to govern the issue of access to student records. Congress intended to accomplish two related purposes by regulating the conduct of school personnel.

> The purpose of the Act is two-fold—to assure parents of students, and students themselves if they are over the age of 18 . . . , access to their educational records and to protect such individuals' rights to privacy by limiting the transferability of their records without their consent.[15]

---

11. *Id.* at 476.

12. *See* 1 JAMES A. RAPP, EDUCATION LAW 3–181 n.24 (1992) (collecting cases in which "a state or educational institution was required to defer to the educational wishes of parents").

13. *See generally* Donald S. Punger, *The Nontraditional Family: Legal Problems for Schools*, 15 SCH. L. BULL. 1 (1984) (describing various school policies that affect nontraditional families, including stepfamilies).

14. Family Education Rights and Privacy Act, 20 U.S.C. § 1232g (1988).

15. Nancy K. Schmidt Splain, Comment, *Access to Student Records in Wisconsin: A Comparative Analysis of the Family Educational Rights and Privacy Act of 1974 and Wisconsin Statute Section 118.125*, 1976 WIS. L. REV. 975, 987 (1976) (citing legislative history of the federal law).

Thus, the Act confers two sets of rights upon the parents of minor children: the right of access to the child's records and the right to determine who else may have access.

As to both purposes, the supplemental regulations of the Department of Education appear to confer rights upon many residential stepparents. Specifically, the regulations define the word "parent" to include, in addition to the custodial parent or other legal guardian, "an individual acting as a parent in the absence of a parent or guardian."[16] Although this language is not completely unambiguous, the regulations apparently confer the rights of a parent upon any adult, including a stepparent, who acts in loco parentis.[17]

The status of the stepparent is less clearly defined as to many other custodial issues arising in the field of education, which are regulated by state law. State legislatures have specified a wide range of parental rights and duties in the education field, including responsibility for the child's general school attendance and authority to excuse the child from subjects deemed objectionable by the parent.[18] For the most part, such state laws do not expressly recognize adults other than the parent, guardian, or other legal custodian of the child. In the absence of any legislative mandate, educational institutions are not likely to recognize a more expansive list of responsible adults.

In the stepfamily where the spouses are acting in a cooperative fashion to raise the children, school administrators may permit the stepparent to act in the place of the custodial parent. Thus, for example, one legal advisor to

---

16. Family Educational Rights and Privacy, 34 C.F.R. § 99.3 (1991); *see also* 23 U.S.C. § 1232g(b)(1)(H) (1988 & Supp. 1990) and 34 C.F.R. § 99.31(a)(8) (1992) (referring to the dependency provision of the federal income tax code, which includes stepparents, to identify those adults who have the right of access to student records under the Family Educational Rights and Privacy Act).

17. *See* Punger, *supra* note 13, at 3 (construing the Education Department's definition of parent to include a stepparent who stands in loco parentis to the child). The possible ambiguity in the regulation arises from the limitation of authority for nonparents to situations where the parent is "absent." There is no similar ambiguity about the authority of stepparents under another federal act, which controls access to the educational records of students with disabilities. The regulations of the Department of Education's Office of Special Education and Rehabilitative Services, which supplement the Education of Individuals with Disabilities Act, 20 U.S.C. §§ 1400–1485 (1988 & Supp. 1990), expressly define "parent" to include "persons acting in the place of a parent, such as a . . . stepparent with whom a child lives . . . ." 34 C.F.R. § 300.10 comment at 14 (1992).

18. For example, Title 15 of the Arizona Revised Statutes, which fills two volumes, deals with the subject of education. At least twenty separate provisions in this Title refer to the rights and duties of parents in educating their minor children. For example, a recently enacted provision establishes a program of instruction regarding AIDS in grades kindergarten through twelve, and authorizes "parents . . . to withdraw their child from instruction." ARIZ. REV. STAT. ANN. § 15–716 (Supp. 1992).

educators recommends a policy whereby schools would release children to a person other than the legal custodian, including a stepparent, upon the custodian's express instruction.[19] Furthermore, educators may choose to follow a course that is administratively convenient; if the stepparent is the person who has assumed primary responsibility for the child's day-to-day care, then the school may simply accept the stepparent's authority in many situations. Still, the continuing ambiguity regarding their legal status fore-closes a more clear-cut role for stepparents in this important aspect of childrearing.

In summary, stepfamily members have wide discretion to define the custodial role of the stepparent within the family. However, third parties who deal with children outside their homes, such as educators and doctors, may refuse to recognize the stepparent's authority. The relevant laws in these fields rarely require a different result.

III. Visitation Rights

The issues of stepparent authority vis-à-vis third parties, discussed in the previous section, typically arise at a time when the stepparent, custodial parent, and stepchild reside together in the intact stepfamily. In contrast, the issues of visitation and primary custody, discussed in the remaining sections of this chapter, usually arise after the marriage between the step-parent and the custodial parent has come to an end. Furthermore, these issues typically involve conflicts between the stepparent and one or both biologic parents.

Stepparents have sought visitation rights in two distinct situations after residential relationships with their stepchildren have come to an end. First, a stepparent may seek visitation rights in the divorce proceeding that termi-nates his or her marriage to the custodial parent, who will continue to be the primary custodian of the stepchild in the future. Second, the stepparent may raise the issue when the custodial parent dies, if the stepchild moves into the home of the other parent or another relative. In these situations, the termination of the stepparent's marriage to the custodial parent places the stepparent-child relationship in jeopardy. The recognition of visitation rights between stepparent and child is a means of protecting the relation-ship, in a reconstituted form, in the future.

The law of visitation first developed as a means of preserving the rela-tionships of children with both of their biologic parents when the parents do not live together. In this context, a very strong presumption exists that both parents are entitled to ongoing contact with their children. Therefore, when one parent assumes primary custody, the other retains visitation rights,

---

19. *See* Ronald L. Stenger, *The School Counselor and the Law: New Develop-ments*, 15 J.L. & EDUC. 105, 111 (1986).

unless this arrangement would be harmful to the children. Until recently, lawmakers tended to resist the extension of similar rights to other adults, including stepparents.

The traditional legislative and judicial approach to this topic was based on respect for the autonomy of parents; the rules protected the exclusive right of parents to determine who would have contact with their minor children. Lawmakers also expressed the view that any recognition of visitation rights for nonparents would make family life too complicated. In recent years, however, legislatures and courts have been called upon to balance these traditional concerns against the competing interests of children and other adults, including stepparents, in preserving established relationships with each other.[20] This balancing process has resulted in increased legal protection for stepparent-child relationships.[21]

A major development in the law of visitation for nonparents occurred during the 1970s and 1980s, a time of rising divorce rates, when child custody and visitation issues affected many families. During this period, every state legislature responded to public demand for the recognition of grandparent visitation rights.[22] Although stepparents have not received this type of recognition nationwide, current statutes in approximately one-third of the states do authorize stepparent visitation. Half of these statutes expressly refer to stepparents; the rest contain general language relating to nonparent visitation that is broad enough to include stepparents in certain cases.

The first category of statutes is exemplified by the following Virginia provision, which expressly authorizes judges to establish visitation rights between stepparents and stepchildren in marriage dissolution proceedings.

> In any case involving the custody or visitation of a child, the court may award custody or visitation to any party with a legitimate interest therein, including but not limited to grandparents, *stepparents, former stepparents*, blood relatives and family members . . . .[23]

---

20. *See, e.g.*, Katharine T. Bartlett, *Rethinking Parenthood As An Exclusive Status: The Need For Legal Alternatives When the Premise of the Nuclear Family Has Failed*, 70 Va. L. Rev. 879 (1984); Nancy D. Polikoff, *This Child Does Have Two Mothers: Redefining Parenthood to Meet the Needs of Children in Lesbian-Mother and Other Nontraditional Families*, 78 Geo. L.J. 459 (1990).

21. *See* Annotation, *Visitation Rights of Persons Other Than Natural Parents or Grandparents*, 1 A.L.R.4th 1270, §§ 5, 6 (1980 & Supp. 1992).

22. *See generally* Elaine D. Ingulli, *Grandparent Visitation Rights: Social Policies and Legal Rights*, 87 W. Va. L. Rev. 295 (1984–85) (discussing grandparent visitation statutes). The conflict between the rights of grandparents under these visitation statutes and the rights of the stepparent who adopts a stepchild is discussed in chapter 9.

23. Va. Code Ann. § 20–107.2 (Michie Supp. 1993) (emphasis added); *see also* Cal. Civ. Code § 4351.5(c) (West Supp. 1993); Kan. Stat. Ann. § 60–1616 (Supp.

In contrast, the Washington statute governing visitation rights at the time of marriage dissolution simply provides that "[t]he court may order visitation rights for *a person other than a parent* when visitation may serve the best interests of the child."[24] The courts have applied this type of open-ended provision, as well as the more specific stepparent statutes, in order to protect stepparent-child relationships.[25]

In most states, however, there is no statute that authorizes visitation rights either specifically for stepparents or generally for "any person." In the absence of such legislation, judges have taken inconsistent positions on the question of their own authority to establish stepparent visitation rights. On the one hand, the Arizona Court of Appeals has expressed the view that courts derive their authority over the welfare of children from underlying common law principles and are not dependent upon legislative involvement. In *Bryan v. Bryan*,[26] the court entertained the request of the stepfather for visitation rights in a marriage dissolution proceeding, despite the fact that the relevant Arizona statute mentioned visitation only for parents, with the following comment about judicial authority.

> We believe, however, that the statute is intended to bestow special protection upon the visitation rights of parents, not to grant the court authority to award visitation rights. That authority was recognized as an incident of the expressly granted authority to determine matters of custody long before the . . . adoption of the present statute.[27]

On the merits, the *Bryan* court affirmed the stepparent visitation order based on the trial court's determination that visitation would serve the interests of the stepchild.

The opposing view, that the courts have no independent authority to order stepparent visitation, was expressed by the Court of Appeals of Virginia in the case of *Kogon v. Ulerick.*

1992); La. Civ. Code Ann. art. 132 (West 1993) (relative by blood or affinity); N.H. Rev. Stat. Ann. § 458:17 (1992); Ohio Rev. Code Ann. § 3109.05.1(B)(1) (Baldwin 1992) (relative by affinity); Or. Rev. Stat. § 109.119 (1990); Tenn. Code Ann. § 36–6–302 (1991); Wis. Stat. Ann. § 767.245 (West 1993).

24. Wash. Rev. Code Ann. § 26.09.240 (West Supp. 1993) (emphasis added); *see also* Alaska Stat. § 25.24.150 (1991); Conn. Gen. Stat. Ann. § 46b–59 (West 1986); Haw. Rev. Stat. § 571–46(7) (1985); Me. Rev. Stat. Ann. tit. 19, § 214 (West Supp. 1992); Minn. Stat. Ann. § 518.175 (West 1990 & Supp. 1993).

25. *See, e.g.*, Hickenbottom v. Hickenbottom, 477 N.W.2d 8 (Neb. 1991); Hutton v. Hutton, 486 N.E.2d 129 (Ohio Ct. App. 1984).

26. Bryan v. Bryan, 645 P.2d 1267 (Ariz. Ct. App. 1982).

27. *Id.* at 1271; *see also* Evans v. Evans, 488 A.2d 157 (Md. 1985); Simpson v. Simpson, 586 S.W.2d 33 (Ky. 1979); Gribble v. Gribble, 583 P.2d 64 (Utah 1978).

> The common law right of visitation extends only to parents. Absent an express statutory grant of jurisdiction, the courts may not order visitation with a child by a non-parent over the objection of the custodial parent.[28]

Based on this analysis, the *Kogon* court reversed a custodial father's contempt conviction, which was premised on his failure to comply with the trial court's stepparent visitation order. The analysis and the result in *Kogon*, which left the stepfather with no opportunity to present the merits of his visitation request, reflect the traditional deference of the legal system to custodial parents in this situation.

There is a second jurisdictional hurdle that stepparents must overcome before they are entitled to a hearing on their visitation claims, especially in divorce cases. Divorce courts have jurisdiction only over issues that are related to the subject matter of the divorce, and those issues are typically defined by statute to include the status of the marriage, economic matters, and issues that affect the children. In a number of states, the statutes defining subject matter jurisdiction in the divorce courts refer to "children of the marriage" or the "children of both parties." This language lends itself to a narrow interpretation that excludes stepchildren.

The decision of the California Court of Appeals in *Perry v. Superior Court of Kern County*[29] illustrates the barrier created by this type of statutory limitation. There, the stepfather had resided for seven years with his stepson, from the time the child was nine months old. In the marriage dissolution proceeding between the stepfather and the custodial mother, the trial court ordered visitation for the stepfather with the following explanation.

> [T]he [stepfather] has filled the role of father in every respect most of the child's life. The fact that there is no "blood relationship" seems inconsequential, logically speaking, when viewing the ultimate issue which concerns the best interest of the child.[30]

On appeal, the *Perry* court reversed this decision on the ground that the marriage dissolution statute, which referred to "children of the marriage,"

---

28. Kogon v. Ulerick, 405 S.E.2d 441, 442 (Va. Ct. App. 1991). In fact, the Virginia legislature had authorized stepparent visitation orders prior to the decision in this case. The Virginia Court of Appeals ruled, however, that the relevant statute did not apply to Mr. Kogon because he was a "former stepparent," no longer a stepparent, following the divorce from his stepson's mother. *Id.* at 443. The Virginia legislature subsequently added the category of "former stepparents" to the statutes authorizing stepparent visitation orders. *See* VA. CODE ANN. §§ 16.1–241(A), 20–107.2 (Michie Supp. 1993).

29. Perry v. Superior Court of Kern County, 166 Cal. Rptr. 583 (Ct. App. 1980).
30. *Id.* at 584 (quoting the trial court).

did not establish jurisdiction over the stepchild. The court expressed deep dissatisfaction with this legislative restriction on its ability to protect the interests of the parties and their children.

> We do not find the result in this case particularly palatable. However, in view of the language in the relevant code sections, we feel compelled to hold the trial court had no jurisdiction to make any order concerning visitation in the proceeding before it. We are aware that in this modern society there are probably a considerable number of stepparents and stepchildren in situations substantially similar to that before us. The Legislature has the power to address this thorny problem of visitation by stepparents.[31]

The California legislature responded to this invitation from the *Perry* court by amending the statute to unambiguously confer jurisdiction over stepchildren in marriage dissolution proceedings. The current California Code contains the following provision.

> The . . . court has jurisdiction . . . to award reasonable visitation rights to a person who is a party to the marriage that is the subject of the proceeding with respect to a minor child of the other party to the marriage, if visitation by that person is determined to be in the best interests of the minor child. . . . Any visitation right granted to a stepparent . . . shall not conflict with any visitation or custodial right of a natural or adoptive parent who is not a party to the proceeding.[32]

The development of stepparent visitation law followed an easier course in the state of Alaska. There, the state divorce statute, like the provision construed by the California Court of Appeals in *Perry*, establishes jurisdiction over any "child of the marriage."[33] In *Carter v. Brodrick*,[34] the Alaska Supreme Court construed this language broadly to include stepchildren whose stepparent established an in loco parentis status in the stepfamily. Accordingly, the courts in Alaska are able to address the interests of stepchildren, even in the absence of a specific statute conferring this authority.

Once the jurisdictional hurdles are overcome, either by express legislation authorizing stepparent visitation orders or through liberal judicial construction of more general statutory provisions, the remaining legal issue is

---

31. *Id.* at 586. The opinion in *Perry* referred to several types of legal proceedings in California, other than marriage dissolution proceedings, in which the stepparent's visitation claim might properly be raised. *See id.* at 585.

32. CAL. CIV. CODE § 4351.5(b), (j) (West Supp. 1993).

33. *See* ALASKA STAT. § 25.24.150 (1991).

34. Carter v. Brodrick, 644 P.2d 850 (Alaska 1982).

the proper standard for resolving visitation disputes. Not surprisingly, the standard most often applied is the best interests of the child; the continuing relationship between child and stepparent will be protected, contrary to the wishes of the parent, only if this result will predictably enhance the child's future welfare.[35] Stepparents who receive a hearing on the issue of the child's best interests frequently prevail under this standard.[36]

The key factor that supports stepparent visitation claims is the widely accepted view that continuity in established family relationships serves the best interests of children. Thus, where the stepparent has resided with the stepchild and custodial parent for a period of time and meaningful bonds have been formed, continuation of the stepparent-child relationship may be important for the child's future well-being. The Oklahoma Court of Appeals clearly expressed this viewpoint in *Looper v. McManus*, a case involving the future relationship of an eight-year-old boy with his stepmother.

> Visitation . . . is aimed at fulfilling what many conceive to be a vital, or at least a wholesome contribution to the child's emotional well-being by permitting partial continuation of an earlier established close relationship.
>
> Usually such an affiliation is with a natural parent. But it need not be.[37]

The stepmother in *Looper* resided with her stepson during a four-year marriage to the boy's father, which ended in divorce, and for an additional year thereafter when she served as the child's primary custodian. During

---

35. Occasionally, judges have employed a standard other than the best interests of the child to resolve stepparent visitation disputes. *See, e.g.*, Klipstein v. Zalewski, 553 A.2d 1384 (N.J. Super. Ct. 1988) (applying the equitable estoppel standard developed by the New Jersey courts in stepparent support cases).

36. *See* Michael J. Lewinski, Note, *Visitation Beyond the Traditional Limitations*, 60 IND. L.J. 191, 206–10 (1984). Stepparents were granted visitation rights under the best interests of the child standard in the following cases: Bryan v. Bryan, 645 P.2d 1267 (Ariz. Ct. App. 1982); *In re* Banning, 541 N.E.2d 283 (Ind. Ct. App. 1989); Collins v. Gilbreath, 403 N.E.2d 921 (Ind. Ct. App. 1980); Evans v. Evans, 488 A.2d 157 (Md. 1985); Hickenbottom v. Hickenbottom, 477 N.W.2d 8 (Neb. 1991); Hutton v. Hutton, 486 N.E.2d 129 (Ohio Ct. App. 1984); Looper v. McManus, 581 P.2d 487 (Okla. Ct. App. 1978); Honaker v. Burnside, 388 S.E.2d 322 (W. Va. 1989). Conversely, the courts held that the child's best interests would be served by denying stepparent visitation in the following cases: Shoemaker v. Shoemaker, 563 So. 2d 1032 (Ala. Civ. App. 1990); Halpern v. Halpern, 184 Cal. Rptr. 740 (Ct. App. 1982); *In re* Raymond H., 501 N.Y.S.2d 726 (App. Div. 1986). The following cases were remanded to the trial court to resolve the issue of stepparent visitation under the best interests of the child standard: Carter v. Brodrick, 644 P.2d 850 (Alaska 1982); Simpson v. Simpson, 586 S.W.2d 33 (Ky. 1979); Spells v. Spells, 378 A.2d 879 (Pa. Super. Ct. 1977); Gribble v. Gribble, 583 P.2d 64 (Utah 1978).

37. Looper v. McManus, 581 P.2d 487, 488 (Okla. Ct. App. 1978).

this entire period, according to the court, the natural mother "ventured forth in search of excitement and romance"[38] and did not serve a parental role in her son's life. The mother's subsequent request for custody was granted according to the prevailing rule, discussed in the next section, which strongly favors parents as primary custodians. In spite of the mother's objections, however, the *Looper* court also ordered continuing visitation by the child's stepmother and paternal grandparents. In reaching this result, the court emphasized the value of continuity in the boy's relationships with these three adults, as well as the children of his father and stepmother, who remained in the stepmother's custody.

The protection of established relationships in this manner involves significant interference with the autonomy of custodial parents.[39] In the eyes of many judges, however, this parental interest becomes secondary when the child's meaningful relationship with a "parent figure" is at stake. For example, the Supreme Court of Nebraska disposed of a custodial mother's objections to future visitation between her daughter and her former husband, the girl's stepfather, with the following observation.

> [T]he wife is more interested in punishing the husband by denying him access to her daughter than she is in doing what serves the girl's best interests. The girl is not a piece of property; she is a living, breathing, and, as is any child, fragile person who is seemingly already distraught by the destruction of what she has known as her family. There is no need to further damage her by removing the emotional support of one who has cared for her during the marriage.[40]

Thus, the court was willing to recognize an additional family member in spite of the resulting diminution of the custodial mother's authority.

The recent cases that allow stepparent visitation nevertheless remain sensitive to concerns about parental autonomy. For example, the Alaska Supreme Court in *Carter v. Brodrick* emphasized that "we do not intend to open the door to a myriad of unrelated third persons who happen to feel affection for a child."[41] Thus, the threat to parental authority was a limited

---

38. *Id.* at 489.

39. In *The Myth of State Intervention In the Family*, 18 U. Mich. J.L. Ref. 835, 850–53 (1984–85), Professor Frances E. Olsen challenges the common assumption that this type of interference with parental rights involves "intervention" by the state.

40. Hickenbottom v. Hickenbottom, 477 N.W.2d 8, 17 (Neb. 1991). *But see* Shoemaker v. Shoemaker, 563 So. 2d 1032, 1034 (Ala. Civ. App. 1990) ("To force a former stepparent's . . . visitation upon a natural parent or the former stepchild, over either's objection, would appear to be a detriment to the best interests of the child . . . .").

41. Carter v. Brodrick, 644 P.2d 850, 855 n.5 (Alaska 1982).

one, because the visitation rights recognized in *Carter* were based on the stepparent's clearly defined in loco parentis status.

Of course, determinations about a child's best interests involve the exercise of judicial discretion in individual cases. This premise is illustrated by the divergent analysis and results in two cases involving infant children who resided in their stepfamilies for relatively brief periods of time. In the first case, *Halpern v. Halpern*,[42] a California trial judge denied stepparent visitation; in the second case, *Bryan v. Bryan*,[43] an Arizona court reached the opposite result. Both decisions were affirmed on appeal under the best interests of the child standard.

The stepchild in the *Halpern* case, Laurie Halpern, was born six months after her mother's marriage to Paul Halpern, who assisted as the Lamaze coach at his stepdaughter's birth. Thereafter, the stepfather worked at home and "took care of Laurie during the daytime, while [his wife] worked to support the family." The little girl "called Paul 'daddy' from the first time she could talk."[44] The Halperns separated when Laurie was eleven months old; thereafter, the mother assumed her primary custody. Based on this record, the trial court ruled that the stepdaughter's best interests would be served by denying the stepfather's request for future visitation rights.

First, the trial court did not assign much importance to the stepfather-child relationship, in light of Laurie Halpern's young age and the short duration of the stepfamily.

> I have to find the best interests of the child require there be no visitation because [the stepfather] is a nonparent. He absolutely has no relationship to the child bloodwise or otherwise . . . .
> . . . This child was well under two years of age, so very frankly it is just patently almost ridiculous to make the assumption . . . that the child knows there is a father. . . . [T]o try to arrive at any other conclusion based upon some psychiatric testimony, frankly, I just do not accept.[45]

Furthermore, the trial court believed that the requested visitation by the stepfather would be too disruptive for the parties in the future.

> I can't accept I should burden all of the parties in this matter, including Mr. Halpern, with conflicts, struggles and disruptions for

---

42. Halpern v. Halpern, 184 Cal. Rptr. 740 (Ct. App. 1982). The court in *Halpern* ignored the jurisdictional barrier, established in the earlier California case of *Perry v. Superior Court*, because neither party had raised the issue in their pleadings. The *Perry* case is discussed in the text accompanying notes 26–30.

43. Bryan v. Bryan, 645 P.2d 1267 (Ariz. Ct. App. 1982).

44. *Halpern*, 184 Cal. Rptr. at 742.

45. *Id.* at 743, 747 (quoting the trial court opinion).

years to come because of Mr. Halpern's present emotional state in connection with the child.[46]

On appeal, the California Court of Appeals affirmed the denial of visitation as a reasonable exercise of discretion by the trial court under the best interests of the child standard.

In contrast, the Arizona courts took a very different view of the step-parent's relatively brief role as a parent figure in *Bryan v. Bryan*. There, the stepfather had resided with his infant stepdaughter for approximately one year, from the time she was two months old. When his marriage to the custodial mother broke down, she moved out of the family home with her daughter. In the subsequent marriage dissolution proceeding, the trial court determined that the best interests of the child would be served by an order of visitation rights for the stepfather, in spite of the young age of the stepchild, the short duration of the marriage, and the mother's objections. On appeal, the Arizona Court of Appeals affirmed this determination.

> [T]he [stepfather] had been the child's only "father figure" during this period which, although short by some standards, was most of the child's life. From this evidence we believe the court could easily have concluded that . . . the child's best interest would be served by providing for some continuance of that relationship.[47]

The divergent results in the *Halpern* and *Bryan* cases clearly illustrate the different weight assigned by judges in specific cases to the factors that enter into the best interests of the child analysis.

In summary, the primary hurdles to the recognition of stepparent visitation rights have been jurisdictional ones. Once stepparents get into the courtroom, they tend to be successful in proving that the stepchild's best interests would be served by an ongoing relationship, especially in cases where meaningful family ties of substantial duration have been established in the stepfamily.

IV. Stepparent Custody

When the stepfamily is disrupted by divorce or the death of the custodial parent, the stepparent may seek to become the primary custodian of the stepchild. The stepparent faces difficult burdens, both procedural and substantive, if the custody request is contested by the natural parent. Indeed, the standards employed in custody disputes between parents and nonparents are much stricter than the best interests of the child standard,

---

46. *Id.* at 743 (quoting the trial court opinion).
47. *Bryan*, 645 P.2d at 1274.

discussed in the previous section, which is typically used to resolve contested requests for third-party visitation. The stricter legal standards offer increased protection to the parent in this situation, because the threatened interference with parental rights is so much greater.[48]

A variety of judicial forums are available in most states for resolving custody issues when the child's family has been disrupted in some way. For example, guardianship and habeas corpus procedures, as well as the civil child protection system, establish judicial authority to consider the legal custody of children.[49] Sometimes, however, the most convenient forum for raising custody issues is denied to stepparents because the divorce courts in a number of states have refused to assume jurisdiction over stepchildren.[50] This is the same limitation that has prevented stepparents in these same states from requesting visitation rights in divorce proceedings.[51]

The inability of the divorce courts to consider the future custody of

---

48. The interference with parental rights is even greater when the issue is termination of the parent-child relationship, and the strictest standards are applied in this setting. Chapter 9 describes the standards employed to determine whether the parent-child relationship can be terminated, without the parent's consent, as a prerequisite to stepparent adoption.

49. *See* HOMER H. CLARK, JR., THE LAW OF DOMESTIC RELATIONS IN THE UNITED STATES 456, 791–97 (2d ed. 1988) (discussing various bases for jurisdiction in child custody matters); Brigitte M. Bodenheimer, *The Multiplicity of Child Custody Proceedings—Problems of California Law*, 23 STAN. L. REV. 703 (1971). There are limits on the ability of stepparents to seek custody of their stepchildren in guardianship or civil protection proceedings. *Compare In re* J.W.F., 799 P.2d 710 (Utah 1990) (affirming stepfather's right to seek custody in a proceeding where the state sought to terminate natural parents' rights) *with* Jacobs v. Balew, 765 S.W.2d 532 (Tex. 1989) (denying stepfather's right to initiate a conservatorship proceeding where no issue was raised regarding the custodial mother's fitness).

50. *See, e.g.*, Indiana *ex rel.* McCarroll v. Marion County Superior Court, 515 N.E.2d 1124 (Ind. 1987) (ruling that the issue of a stepchild's safety could not be raised by the stepfather in a marriage dissolution proceeding); Winters v. Cooper, 827 S.W.2d 233 (Mo. Ct. App. 1991) (denying jurisdiction in a case where the dissolution court had determined that the custodial mother was unfit); *In re* Marriage of Miller, 825 P.2d 189 (Mont. 1992) (holding that the dissolution court had no authority to award custody of a stepchild to the stepfather, even though a child protection agency had determined that the mother's continuing custody would endanger the child).

51. Indeed, marriage dissolution courts have sometimes defined their jurisdiction even more narrowly when the issue is stepchild custody rather than stepchild visitation. *See* Olvera v. Superior Court, 815 P.2d 925 (Ariz. Ct. App. 1991) (refusing to extend the rule of Bryan v. Bryan, 645 P.2d 1267 (Ariz. Ct. App. 1982), which authorized stepchild visitation orders, to the issue of stepchild custody); Goetz v. Lewis, 250 Cal. Rptr. 30 (Ct. App. 1988) (ruling that a California statute, which expressly conferred authority on marriage dissolution courts to make stepchild visitation orders, did not authorize stepchild custody orders). *But see In re* Hinman, 8 Cal. Rptr. 2d 245 (Ct. App. 1992) (holding that consent of both parties conferred authority on marriage dissolution court to enter stepchild custody order).

stepchildren can have harsh consequences for stepfamily members, as illustrated by the case of *Palmer v. Palmer.*[52] There, the original divorce decree incorporated the agreement of the mother and stepfather to share joint custody of their three children and the stepson, who had resided with them from the time of his birth. Some time later, the divorce court amended the custody order by placing primary custody of all four children with the former husband, with restricted visitation rights for the mother, based on a finding of the mother's unfitness. On appeal, the Washington Supreme Court ruled that the divorce statute, which conferred jurisdiction over the "children of the marriage," did not include stepchildren.[53] As a result, the three siblings remained with their father, pursuant to the trial court's order, while the stepson was returned to the custody of his unfit mother. The *Palmer* court expressed its reservations about this outcome by observing that "[w]e do not decide whether or not proper proceedings should be brought to determine . . . the propriety of [the mother] as his custodian."[54]

In contrast to the outcome in *Palmer*, the Kansas Supreme Court long ago recognized that the welfare of stepchildren is a proper subject in divorce proceedings. In *State v. Taylor*,[55] the Kansas Supreme Court affirmed the criminal conviction of a father for kidnapping his son from the stepmother, to whom custody had been formally awarded in an earlier divorce proceeding. The *Taylor* court affirmed the authority of the divorce court to make such a stepparent custody award with the following explanation.

> In dissolving the marital relation and the breaking up of the home, the court necessarily took notice of the fact that there was an infant child in the home for whom provision must be made. . . . As a result of the marriage the child had been brought into the home, and . . . [the wife] assumed its care and stood in loco parentis towards it. We think the expression in the statute "minor children of the marriage," fairly interpreted, included the infant in question, and that the court had the responsibility and duty to make provision for its custody, care, and education when the marriage relation was dissolved.[56]

Thus, the Kansas Supreme Court in *State v. Taylor* broadly construed the statutory phrase "children of the marriage" to include stepchildren when in loco parentis ties were established in the stepfamily. In recent

---

52. Palmer v. Palmer, 258 P.2d 475 (Wash. 1953).

53. Subsequent to the decision in *Palmer*, the Washington legislature enacted the UNIFORM MARRIAGE AND DIVORCE ACT, 9A U.L.A. 147 (1973), which has been construed by the Washington Court of Appeals to include stepchildren in a marriage dissolution proceeding. *See In re* Marriage of Allen, 626 P.2d 16 (Wash. Ct. App. 1981).

54. *Palmer*, 258 P.2d at 477.

55. State v. Taylor, 264 P. 1069 (Kan. 1928).

56. *Id.* at 1070.

years, a few state legislatures have enacted statutes that eliminate the need for such broad construction of statutory language in order to protect the welfare of stepchildren in the divorce courts.[57] For example, the marriage dissolution statute in Oregon specifically provides that "a stepparent with a child-parent relationship . . . who is a party in a dissolution proceeding may petition the court . . . for custody or visitation . . . [and] may also file for post decree modification of a decree relating to child custody."[58]

Once the stepparent finds a forum for raising the issue of stepchild custody, he or she still faces a difficult contest with the natural parent. The applicable legal standards contain a preference for parental custody, which is designed to protect the interests of parents in their family relationships. The bias against third-party custody also involves an assumption that the interests of most children are best served by protecting the rights of their parents. In some cases, however, if the best interests of children are evaluated independently, a conflict arises between the rights of parents and the welfare of their children. Modern courts, confronted with this type of conflict in stepparent custody cases, have balanced the competing interests in a number of different ways.[59]

At one extreme, the strongest presumption in favor of the parent is rebuttable only if the stepparent can prove that the parent is unfit to care for the child, based on evidence of bad character or past behavior toward the child. This test does not consider the merits of the stepparent as custodian until the parent has been eliminated from the contest. At the opposite end of the analytical spectrum, the preference for the biologic parent may be completely eliminated; in this framework, the best interests of the child becomes the exclusive consideration. Finally, between the two extremes fall legal standards that require a nonparent to establish special and compelling reasons for interfering with the parent-child relationship.

The standard of parental unfitness, which is most protective of the biologic parent-child relationship, is the traditional standard employed for resolving custody disputes between parents and nonparents, including stepparents. The fitness standard has been codified in a number of state

---

57. See CONN. GEN. STAT. ANN. § 46b–57 (West 1986) (establishing jurisdiction in the superior court over "any minor child of either or both parties"); OR. REV. STAT. § 109.119(2) (1990).

58. OR. REV. STAT. § 109.119(2) (1990). The statute defines, in some detail, the elements of the "parent-child relationship" that must be established by the stepparent who requests custody. See id. § 109.119(4).

59. See Janet Leach Richards, *The Natural Parent Preference Versus Third Parties: Expanding the Definition of Parent*, 16 NOVA L. REV. 733 (1992) (describing the various standards employed to determine when the preference for parental custody can be set aside); Wendy Evans Lehmann, Annotation, *Award of Custody of Child Where Contest is Between Natural Parent and Stepparent*, 10 A.L.R.4th 767 (1981 & Supp. 1992) (collecting cases).

statutes.[60] For example, the following provision addresses the circumstances under which custody may be awarded to a nonparent in marriage dissolution proceedings in Kansas.

> If during the proceedings the court determines that there is probable cause to believe that the child is a child in need of care as defined by [the child protection laws] *or that neither parent is fit to have custody*, the court may award temporary custody of the child to another person or agency.[61]

In other words, the standard for awarding custody to stepparents, who are always regarded as "another person" for this purpose, is the same as the very high standard used to determine when the state should assume custody under the child protection laws.

In the absence of explicit statutory guidance, many courts have adopted this same standard of parental unfitness in stepchild custody cases.[62] For example, in *Stamps v. Rawlins*,[63] the Supreme Court of Arkansas reversed a divorce court's award of joint legal custody to a mother and stepfather, because this result was inconsistent with the mother's parental rights. The stepchild in *Stamps* was just three months old when his mother and stepfather married. When the marriage ended five years later, the trial judge found that the stepfather "was the only father that [the boy] had ever had and . . . treated [him] as his own child."[64] In reversing the award of joint custody to the stepfather, the state supreme court ruled that this evidence regarding the stepfather-child relationship was irrelevant under the legal standard of parental unfitness.

> [O]ur caselaw specifically establishes a preference for natural parents in custody matters, and provides that the preference must prevail unless it is established that the natural parent is unfit. . . .
> Here, the chancellor specifically found that the appellant mother

---

60. *See, e.g.*, KAN. STAT. ANN. § 60–1610(a)(4)(D) (Supp. 1992); ME. REV. STAT. ANN. tit. 19, § 752 (Supp. 1992); MISS. CODE ANN. §§ 93–5–24(1)(e), 93–13–1 (1972 & Supp. 1992); Mo. ANN. STAT. § 452.375(4)(a) (Vernon Supp. 1993); WIS. STAT. ANN. § 767.24(3) (West 1993).

61. KAN. STAT. ANN. § 60–1610(a)(4)(D) (Supp. 1992) (emphasis added).

62. *See* Berryhill v. Berryhill, 410 So. 2d 416 (Ala. 1982); Webb v. Webb, 546 So. 2d 1062 (Fla. Dist. Ct. App. 1989); Howell v. Gossett, 214 S.E.2d 882 (Ga. 1975); Selanders v. Anderson, 291 P.2d 425 (Kan. 1955) (awarding custody to mother, even though stepmother had been legal guardian for seven years following father's death); *In re* Hohmann's Petition, 95 N.W.2d 643 (Minn. 1959); Milam v. Milam, 376 So. 2d 1336 (Miss. 1979); Stuhr v. Stuhr, 481 N.W.2d 212 (Neb. 1992).

63. Stamps v. Rawlins, 761 S.W.2d 933 (Ark. 1988).

64. *Id.* at 935.

was a fit and proper person for custody. . . . Therefore, custody of
[the stepchild] should have been left in [the mother] . . . .[65]

Thus, in the absence of a prior determination of the mother's unfitness,
there was no opportunity to consider the merits of the stepfather's claim to
future custody or the child's interests in relation to his stepfather.

The same standard of parental unfitness has been applied when stepchild custody cases arise following the death of the custodial parent. In this
situation, the stepparent must establish the unfitness of the surviving parent, who now seeks sole custody of the child. The difficulty for the stepparent in carrying this burden is illustrated in the case of *Howell v. Gossett*,[66] which was decided by the Georgia Supreme Court. The father in
Howell initiated a habeas corpus proceeding to recover the custody of his
daughter from her stepfather following the mother's death in an automobile
accident. The trial court denied the father's request, based on evidence that
he had not provided support nor attempted to have any contact with his
daughter for the seven-year period prior to the lawsuit. The Georgia Supreme Court reversed, stating that the record contained "no evidence of
conduct . . . that would render the [father] unfit to have custody of his
daughter."[67] In the absence of such bad conduct, involving something
worse than the father's neglect for many years, he was automatically entitled to remove his daughter from the home she had shared with her mother
and stepfather.

When the issue of stepchild custody arises, as in *Howell*, following the
death of the custodial parent, the child's interests in stability and the continuity of family relationships are placed in serious jeopardy. First, the death
of the custodial parent involves the traumatic end of what was probably the
most important relationship in the child's life. Second, where family ties
have been formed with the residential stepparent, the abrupt removal of the
child from the family home and the stepparent's care constitute an additional threat to the child's sense of continuity in a family. Under the traditional standard, however, these matters become relevant only if the noncustodial parent is an unfit person.

The West Virginia court in *Honaker v. Burnside*[68] attempted to address

---

65. *Id.*

66. Howell v. Gossett, 214 S.E.2d 882 (Ga. 1975).

67. *Id.* at 884. One year after its decision in *Howell*, the Georgia Supreme Court
applied the same standard of parental unfitness in another stepchild custody case. In
White v. Bryan, 223 S.E.2d 710 (Ga. 1976), the court affirmed an award of custody to
the stepfather based on a finding that the natural father was unfit. In addition to the
father's past lack of involvement with his child, there was evidence that he abused
alcohol, and that his "lifestyle . . . [was] not conducive to a healthy environment for a
young girl." *Id.* at 711.

68. Honaker v. Burnside, 388 S.E.2d 322 (W. Va. 1989) (affirming an order of
the trial court that set out a schedule for gradually shifting custody of the child from
the stepfather to the father).

this concern about continuity for the child by establishing a transition period during which custody would be gradually shifted from the stepfather to the father. The *Honaker* court ruled that the noncustodial father was entitled to the custody of his six-year-old daughter following her mother's death because the evidence failed to establish his past unfitness. The court realized, however, that the removal of the girl from the home she had shared with her mother, stepfather, and half brother would likely add to the trauma she had already experienced. The transition period was an attempt by the court to help the child to adjust to this additional change. At the same time, future visitation rights were established between the child and her stepfather.

The interests of stepchildren in the continuity of stepfamily relationships have been addressed in a different fashion by judges who have broadened the definition of parental unfitness.[69] For example, in a case that was factually similar to *Howell v. Gossett*, the Arizona Supreme Court ruled that a lengthy period of indifference by the noncustodial father made him unfit for future custody. In *Clifford v. Woodford*,[70] the stepfather was awarded custody of his two stepdaughters upon his wife's death, following a period of ten years when they resided together as a stepfamily, based on evidence of the father's absence during this same period of time. The dissenting opinion strongly disagreed with this determination of parental unfitness, stating that the trial court's findings about the father's good character and morals and fine home were the only factors relevant to the issue of his fitness.[71] The disagreement highlights the amount of discretion exercised by judges in applying the parental unfitness standard.

In other states, legislatures and courts have expressly rejected parental unfitness as the sole ground for awarding custody to stepparents. For example, the Delaware Code authorizes the appointment of a guardian, other than the natural parent, "where the parents are unsuitable or where the child's interests would be adversely affected by remaining under the natural guardianship of his or her parents or parent."[72] The burden imposed on the stepparent here is less than the traditional requirement of proving parental unfitness.

The significance of the more lenient standard is illustrated by the

---

69. *See, e.g.*, Clifford v. Woodford, 320 P.2d 452 (Ariz. 1957); Clark v. Jelinek, 414 P.2d 892 (Idaho 1966) (abandonment); Patrick v. Byerley, 325 S.E.2d 99 (Va. 1985) (abandonment).

70. Clifford v. Woodford, 320 P.2d 452 (Ariz. 1957).

71. *Id.* at 461 (dissenting opinion).

72. DEL. CODE ANN. tit. 13, § 701(b) (1981); *see also* CAL. CIV. CODE § 4600(b),(c) (West Supp. 1993) (authorizing nonparent custody based on a "finding that an award of custody to a parent would be detrimental to the child and the award to a nonparent is required to serve the best interests of the child"); OKLA. STAT. ANN. tit. 10, § 21.1 (West Supp. 1993) (authorizing the appointment of a nonparent guardian following death of the custodial parent "if it would be detrimental to . . . the child for the noncustodial parent to have custody").

result in *Bailes v. Sours*,[73] where the Virginia Supreme Court affirmed the award of custody to a stepmother, following her husband's death, based on the "extraordinary circumstances" of the case. The special circumstances in *Bailes* included the following: the twelve-year-old boy had resided with his stepmother for ten years; the natural mother had maintained minimal contact with him during this period; he had been traumatized by the death of his father; he expressed strong opposition to leaving the home that he shared with his stepmother and half brother; and the trial court believed that such a transition would indeed be detrimental to his welfare. These are the same factors that the Georgia Supreme Court was unable to consider in *Howell v. Gossett* under the parental unfitness standard; in *Bailes* they resulted in an award of custody to the stepmother.

In applying a legal standard that reduced the level of protection for the rights of natural parents, the Virginia Supreme Court did not lose sight of the special interests of parents. Thus, the court observed that "[t]he presumption in favor of a parent over a non-parent is a strong one, not easily overcome, and the result we reach here must not be construed to weaken it."[74] Nevertheless, the mother's request for custody of her son following his father's death was denied in *Bailes*, based on proof relating to conditions in the stepfamily as well as the mother's past relationship with her son.[75]

The same adjusted legal standards, which impose a lesser burden on the stepparent than the traditional parental unfitness norm, may apply when the issue of stepchild custody arises in divorce proceedings between the custodial parent and stepparent.[76] In this situation, the stepparent is required to prove that special reasons exist to prefer him or her over the custodial parent, following a period of time when the parties resided together as a stepfamily. For example, in *In re Marriage of Allen*,[77] the Court

---

73. Bailes v. Sours, 340 S.E.2d 824 (Va. 1986).

74. *Id.* at 827.

75. As in *Bailes v. Sours*, stepparents obtained custody of stepchildren following the death of the custodial parent, without proving the noncustodial parent's unfitness, in the following cases: Cebrzynski v. Cebrzynski, 379 N.E.2d 713 (Ill. App. Ct. 1978) (compelling reasons); Tyrrell v. Tyrrell, 415 N.Y.S.2d 723 (App. Div. 1979) (extraordinary circumstances).

76. The courts applied this type of standard for resolving stepparent-parent custody disputes in marriage dissolution proceedings in the following cases: Palermo v. Palermo, 397 A.2d 349 (N.J. Super. Ct. App. Div. 1978); Worden v. Worden, 434 N.W.2d 341 (N.D. 1989); Commonwealth *ex rel.* Husack v. Husack, 417 A.2d 233 (Pa. Super. Ct. 1979) (convincing reasons); Neely v. Neely, 698 S.W.2d 758 (Tex. Ct. App. 1985) (detrimental effect of parent custody); Paquette v. Paquette, 499 A.2d 23 (Vt. 1985) (extraordinary circumstances); *In re* Marriage of Allen, 626 P.2d 16 (Wash. Ct. App. 1981) (extraordinary circumstances).

77. *In re* Marriage of Allen, 626 P.2d 16 (Wash. Ct. App. 1981), *discussed in* Sandra R. Blair, Note, *Jurisdiction, Standing and Decisional Standards in Parent-Nonparent Custody Disputes*, 58 WASH. L. REV. 111 (1982).

of Appeals of Washington affirmed the divorce court's award of primary custody to a stepmother over the objection of the custodial father.

The opinion in *Allen* first discussed the precise test employed to resolve custody disputes involving a nonparent. The court expressly rejected the best interests of the child standard as providing inadequate protection for the interests of the biologic family. On the other hand, the court dismissed the father's argument that the traditional standard of parental unfitness should be applied in his favor. Instead, the *Allen* court "look[ed] to a middle ground," which it defined as "extraordinary circumstances, where placing the child with an otherwise fit parent would be detrimental to the child."[78]

In *Allen*, the court found that extraordinary circumstances existed to justify the award of custody to the stepmother. The stepchild, Joshua Allen, was three years old when his custodial father and stepmother married. During the marriage, the stepmother and her three children from a prior marriage learned sign language in order to communicate with Joshua, who was deaf. The stepmother became actively involved in Joshua's education and social development. At the time of the divorce, four years later, the court concluded that "Joshua's future development would be detrimentally affected by placement with his father" for two reasons. First, the father, who did not know sign language, would be unable to maintain the level of interaction and communication that Joshua had been experiencing in his home. Second, the disruption of the child's family relationships with his stepmother and her three children would be harmful to him.[79] On the basis of this record, the *Allen* court concluded that the award of custody to the stepmother was proper and consistent with the "[g]reat deference . . . accorded to parental rights . . . and the goal of protecting the family entity."[80]

Thus, the appellate opinions in *Allen* and *Bailes*, and recent legislation enacted in Delaware and other states, have established legal standards that are less protective of parental rights in custody contests between parents and stepparents. Unlike the strict parental unfitness test, the adjusted standards permit the courts to consider specific evidence, unrelated to the parent, that sheds light on the child's circumstances. Still, a burden remains on the stepparent to establish proper reasons for removing a child from parental custody.

The most liberal alternative to the standard of parental unfitness is the best interests of the child standard, which appears to dispense with any preference for the parent in favor of an exclusive focus on the child. This familiar test, which is routinely applied to resolve custody disputes between two biologic parents, appears in a handful of third-party custody statutes[81]

---

78. *Allen*, 626 P.2d at 23.

79. *Id*. at 22–23.

80. *Id*. at 22.

81. *See* CONN. GEN. STAT. ANN. § 46b–57 (West 1986) (establishing best interests of the child standard for third-party custody and visitation cases); HAW. REV.

and has been invoked in recent years in a number of custody disputes between parents and stepparents.[82]

For example, in *Stanley D. v. Deborah D.*,[83] the Supreme Court of New Hampshire affirmed an award of joint legal custody to a mother and stepfather and sole physical custody to the stepfather, based on the best interests of the child. The high court first determined that the divorce court had jurisdiction over stepchildren, observing that "the . . . court was faced not only with the ending of a marriage, but also with the dissolution of a family."[84] Regarding the appropriate standard for resolving the issue of stepchild custody, the court referred to a New Hampshire statute that required the divorce courts generally to "make such decree as shall be most conducive to the child's benefit."[85] The court rejected the suggestion that the stricter standards designed to protect parental rights, which "requir[ed] proof of the natural parent's unfitness or other extraordinary circumstances,"[86] would be more appropriate in this situation. Finally, the court ruled that the award of physical and joint legal custody to the stepfather, who had "formed a psychological parent-child relationship with [his stepdaughter],"[87] would promote the best interests of the child.

Application of the best interests of the child standard apparently created a level playing field between the stepfather and biologic mother in *Stanley D.*[88] The standard is not always applied in this straightforward fashion in stepparent custody cases. State legislatures and courts may effectively inject a parental preference into the best interests of the child standard, by assuming that the interests of children are associated with parental custody. For example, the stepfather lost his claim to custody in *Henrikson v. Gable*, under a Michigan statute creating a "presumption that the best interests of the child are served by awarding custody to the parent . . .

STAT. § 571–46(2) (1985) (establishing best interests of the child standard for third-party custody cases); N.H. REV. STAT. ANN. § 458:17 (1992) (establishing best interests of the child standard for stepparent and grandparent custody cases).

82. Courts applied the best interests of the child standard to resolve stepparent custody issues in the following cases: Root v. Allen, 377 P.2d 117 (Colo. 1962) (awarding custody to stepfather following death of his wife); Stockwell v. Stockwell, 775 P.2d 611 (Idaho 1989); Atkinson v. Atkinson, 408 N.W.2d 516 (Mich. Ct. App. 1987) (adopting "equitable parent doctrine" whereby stepparent was treated like parent in custody contest); Stanley D. v. Deborah D., 467 A.2d 249 (N.H. 1983).

83. Stanley D. v. Deborah D., 467 A.2d 249 (N.H. 1983).

84. *Id.* at 250.

85. *Id.*

86. *Id.* at 251.

87. *Id.* at 250.

88. Recent scholarly proposals would confer the parental preference upon other adults who assume the role of a de facto parent. *See* Polikoff, *supra* note 20, at 472–73; Richards, *supra* note 59, at 760–66. This approach would place the stepparent who played an active parenting role in the stepfamily on an equal footing with the biologic parent in stepchild custody disputes.

unless the contrary is established by clear and convincing evidence."[89] This approach shifts an extra burden back to the stepparent to demonstrate why the child's welfare requires something other than an award of parental custody. Still, on the continuum of legal standards employed to resolve stepchild custody disputes, the best interests of the child standard provides the best opportunity for the stepparent to prevail against a natural parent.

In summary, stepparents who seek the custody of their stepchildren frequently face difficult hurdles in overcoming a well-established preference in the legal system for biologic parent-child relationships. A notable trend in the law acknowledges that real conflicts sometimes exist between this preference and the best interests of children. Thus, stepchildren may have a strong interest in continuing a residential relationship with their stepparent and stepsiblings following a divorce or the custodial parent's death. In these situations, courts and legislatures must undertake the difficult task of addressing and balancing the competing interests of parents, children, and stepparents. As discussed in this section, no consistent legal standard has been established to resolve stepparent custody claims.

---

89. Henrikson v. Gable, 412 N.W.2d 702, 703 (Mich. Ct. App. 1987); *see also In re* Doe, 784 P.2d 873, 879 (Haw. Ct. App. 1989) (ruling that statute authorizing custody award to nonparent on basis of the child's best interests, currently codified in HAW. REV. STAT. § 571–46(2) (1985), remains subject to a "priority in favor of the child's parents").

CHAPTER 8   **The Stepchild's Surname**

I. Introduction

One important aspect of the custodial authority of parents is the right to select their children's names. The authority of parents extends to the initial selection of children's names and any subsequent change of family names.[1] The legal issue considered in this chapter is whether a stepchild's name can be changed, over the father's objection, when the custodial mother has remarried and adopted her new husband's last name.

It has been customary in the United States that children born to married parents are given their father's last name at birth. Of course, the children of unmarried parents, a category that accounts for one in every five children born today,[2] frequently use their mother's surname. Moreover, the custom of a single "family name" has been rejected in other families as more women choose not to change their names upon marriage. Still, the custom of giving paternal surnames to children continues in many families. Furthermore, the relevant legal doctrines in this field are firmly premised on the assumption that children bear their father's surnames. As a result, the discussion in this chapter assumes that the noncustodial parent who resists a proposed name change is always the father.[3]

Although the process of changing a stepchild's name has certain practical consequences, the significance for family members is frequently a symbolic one. For the child, a choice between the father's name and the stepfamily name calls into question the child's loyalties and identity. For the noncustodial father, the child's abandonment of his surname may represent

---

1. *See* HOMER H. CLARK, JR., THE LAW OF DOMESTIC RELATIONS IN THE UNITED STATES 314–15 (2d ed. 1988).

2. *See* 1990 STATISTICAL ABSTRACT OF THE UNITED STATES, BUREAU OF THE CENSUS, UNITED STATES DEP'T OF COMMERCE, No. 90, BIRTH TO UNMARRIED WOMEN, BY RACE OF CHILD AND AGE OF MOTHER: 1970 TO 1987, at 67.

3. This is the only chapter in which generalizations are made about the gender of parents and stepparents. This approach is taken because the custom of assigning paternal surnames and the protective concern for the father's name have completely shaped the legal analysis in this area. Absent the gender-based preference, legal disputes about the stepchild's surname would likely be resolved by recognizing the authority of the primary custodian to make decisions about the child's name. *See infra* text accompanying note 30.

149

the symbolic termination of their relationship. For the mother and her husband, a common surname may represent stability and unity in the stepfamily they have created. As revealed in the following discussion, the rules of law regulating contested name changes for stepchildren have tended to assign priority to the interests of the father.

II. Procedural Issues

Litigation involving names may arise in several distinct procedural contexts.[4] First, divorce courts generally have the authority to issue orders affecting family names. Moreover, statutes in many states empower other courts to order a name change on behalf of individuals who petition for this relief.[5] Stepfamily members frequently petition for a formal name change under this latter type of statutory procedure, after the child has used the stepfamily name informally for a period of time. Conversely, the father may initiate a lawsuit seeking to enjoin the child from using the stepfather's surname.

The statutes governing name changes for children establish an impor-

---

4. *See generally* Kristine C. Karnezis, Annotation, *Rights and Remedies of Parents Inter Se With Respect to the Names of Their Children*, 92 A.L.R.3d 1091 §§ 9–11 (1979 & Supp. 1992) (describing "particular proceedings involving change of child's name").

5. *See* ALA. CODE § 12–13–1 (1986); ALASKA STAT. § 09.55.010 (Supp. 1992); ARIZ. REV. STAT. ANN. § 12–601 (1992); ARK. CODE ANN. § 9–2–101 (Michie 1991); CAL. CIV. PROC. CODE §§ 1275–1279.5 (West 1982 & Supp. 1993); COLO. REV. STAT. §§ 13–15–101, –102 (1987); CONN. GEN. STAT. ANN. § 52–11 (West 1991); DEL. CODE ANN. tit. 10, §§ 5901–5905 (1975 & Supp. 1990); D.C. CODE ANN. §§ 16–2501 to –2503 (1989); FLA. STAT. ANN. § 68.07 (West 1985 & Supp. 1993); GA. CODE ANN. §§ 19–12–1 to –4 (1991); HAW. REV. STAT. §§ 574–5, –6 (1985 & Supp. 1988); IDAHO CODE §§ 7–801 to –804 (1990); ILL. ANN. STAT. ch. 110, para. 21–101 (Smith–Hurd Supp. 1992); IND. CODE ANN. §§ 34–4–6–1 to –5 (Burns 1986 & Supp. 1992); IOWA CODE ANN. §§ 674.1 to .14 (West 1987 & Supp. 1993); KAN. STAT. ANN. §§ 60–1401, –1402 (1983 & Supp. 1992); KY. REV. STAT. ANN. §§ 401.010 to .040 (Baldwin 1990); LA. REV. STAT. ANN. § 13:4751 (West 1991 & Supp. 1993); ME. REV. STAT. ANN. tit. 19, § 781 (West Supp. 1992); MD. ANN. CODE art. 16, § 123 (1990); MASS. GEN. LAWS ANN. ch. 210, §§ 12 to 14 (West 1987); MICH. COMP. LAWS ANN. §§ 711.1, .2 (West 1993); MINN. STAT. ANN. § 259.10 (West Supp. 1992); MISS. CODE ANN. § 93–17–1 (Supp. 1992); MO. ANN. STAT. §§ 527.270 to .290 (Vernon 1953); MONT. CODE ANN. § 27–31–101 (1991); NEB. REV. STAT. §§ 61–102, –103 (1990); NEV. REV. STAT. ANN. §§ 41.270 to .290 (Michie 1986 & Supp. 1991); N.H. REV. STAT. ANN. § 547:3 (Supp. 1992); N.J. STAT. ANN. §§ 2A:52–1 to –4 (West 1987); N.M. STAT. ANN. § 40–8–1 (Michie 1989); N.Y. CIV. RIGHTS LAW §§ 60 to 64 (McKinney 1992); N.C. GEN. STAT. §§ 101–1 to –8 (1985 & Supp. 1992); N.D. CENT. CODE § 32–28–02 (Supp. 1991); OHIO REV. CODE ANN. § 2717.01 (Baldwin 1990); OKLA. STAT. ANN. tit. 12, §§ 1631–1637 (West 1993); OR.

tant role for parents in this legal process.[6] Typically, the petition to change a minor's name must be initiated by a parent or guardian, although the consent of a mature minor may be required.[7] A few states require the express consent of both parents,[8] although most permit one parent to proceed with notice to the other. The second parent, then, is entitled to object to the proposed name change in a hearing before the court.[9] The standards employed by the courts in these hearings to resolve contested name change petitions are explored fully in section III.

Prior to the enactment of state statutes on this subject, the common law regulated the process of changing names. The basic common law rule allowed any individual, including a minor child, to change his or her name simply by using the new name consistently over a period of time. In most jurisdictions, the enactment of statutes authorizing formal name changes by court order has not supplanted this common law procedure.[10] As a result, the interplay between the informal common law process and the formal statutory provisions for changing a stepchild's name has produced a rather complicated procedural framework in this field.

As a threshold matter, the informal name change option has certain practical limitations. Third parties, such as schools or government agencies, may insist on using the name that appears on a child's birth certificate

---

REV. STAT. § 33.410 (1988); 54 PA. CONS. STAT. ANN. §§ 701–705 (Supp. 1993); R.I. GEN. LAWS § 8–9–9 (1985); S.C. CODE ANN. §§ 15–49–10 to –50 (Law. Co-op. 1977 & Supp. 1992); S.D. CODIFIED LAWS ANN. §§ 21–37–1 to –10 (1987); TENN. CODE ANN. §§ 29–8–101 to –105 (1980); TEX. FAM. CODE ANN. §§ 32.01 to .05 (West 1986); UTAH CODE ANN. §§ 42–1–1 to –3 (1988); VT. STAT. ANN. tit. 15, §§ 811–816 (1989); VA. CODE ANN. § 8.01–217 (Michie Supp. 1993); WASH. REV. CODE ANN. § 4.24.130 (West Supp. 1993); W. VA. CODE §§ 48–5–1 to –6 (1992); WIS. STAT. ANN. §§ 786.36, .37 (West Supp. 1992); WYO. STAT. §§ 1–25–101 to –104 (1988).

6. A number of state statutes refer to name changes for minors and designate the parents as the child's representatives for this purpose. In other name change statutes, no express reference is made to children, but courts generally permit petitions on their behalf.

7. For example, the statutes in Delaware, Iowa, Michigan, Texas, and Vermont expressly require the consent of an older child in a name change proceeding.

8. For example, the statutes in Georgia, Iowa, Louisiana, Michigan, and North Carolina expressly require the consent of both parents, although they generally allow for a waiver of consent in certain circumstances involving parental misconduct.

9. *See, e.g.*, Hamman v. Jefferson County Court, 753 P.2d 743 (Colo. 1988) (reversing stepchild name change on ground that father had not received notice of proceeding). *But see In re* Fletcher, 486 A.2d 627 (Vt. 1984).

10. *See, e.g.*, CAL. CIV. PROC. CODE § 1279.5(a) (West 1982) ("Nothing in this title shall be construed to abrogate the common law right of any person to change one's name."). *But see* OKLA. STAT. ANN. tit. 12, § 1637 (West 1993) ("After the effective date of this act, no natural person . . . may change his or her name except as provided [in the name change statute] other than by marriage or decree of divorce or by adoption.").

in the absence of a court order authorizing a different name.[11] In this situation, a formal proceeding becomes a practical necessity if the stepchild, who has changed his or her name at home, is to be called the same name elsewhere. The incomplete effect of a stepchild's informal name change was described by one court in the following manner.

> [Her] medical, dental and school records state her surname to be [the stepfather's name]. However, the school administration is aware of her legal name and legal documents such as her passport, social security card, and bank account show the surname [of her father]. [Her] friends refer to her [by her stepfather's name].[12]

The father may preempt a stepchild's ability to formally or informally adopt a new name, by suing to enjoin the child's use of the stepfamily name. In *Brown v. Carroll*, an appellate court in Texas granted the father's request for "a permanent injunction ordering [the mother] to refrain from using any other surname for the children other than their legal surname, namely [their father's surname], and that she instruct the children that they use their legal surname."[13] Other courts have exercised their injunctive power in this situation more narrowly. The Supreme Court of Illinois, for example, affirmed a court order "enjoining [the custodial mother] and [her son] from changing [his] name in any legal proceeding or using any other name in official records or membership applications or records," but the high court refused to extend the injunction "to informal situations within the family . . . [such as] the name a child asks others to call him on the playground."[14] Even with this limitation, the father's lawsuit successfully preempted the child's future use of the stepfamily name for many important purposes.

In summary, the rights of the parties regarding the change of a step-child's surname are defined both by common law doctrines and by state statutes. Controversies over the child's name may be resolved in the divorce court or through a formal statutory name change proceeding or in an action brought by the father to enjoin usage of the stepfather's name. The substan-

---

11. *See* Donald S. Punger, *The Nontraditional Family: Legal Problems for Schools*, 15 SCH. L. BULL. 1, 2–3 (1984) (expressing opinion that school records must reflect the name that appears on the child's birth certificate unless both parents consent to the stepfamily name or a name change order has been issued by the court).

12. Rappleye v. Rappleye, 454 N.W.2d 231, 231–32 (Mich. Ct. App. 1990) (denying father's request to enjoin informal usage of stepfather's surname).

13. Brown v. Carroll, 683 S.W.2d 61, 63 (Tex. Ct. App. 1984).

14. *In re* Marriage of Presson, 465 N.E.2d 85, 90 (Ill. 1984); *cf.* Statham v. Domyan, 506 N.E.2d 613, 613 (Ill. App. Ct. 1987) (granting father's request for injunction against formal name change but permitting stepchild's "general use of [stepfather's] name and its use in official records").

tive standards employed by the courts to resolve the issue are examined in the next section.

III. The Standards Employed in Name Change Cases

Historically, the laws regulating name changes established a strong presumption that children would retain their paternal surnames in spite of changing family circumstances. The presumption existed primarily to protect the interests of the father in preserving his own name and in easily identifying his children.[15] The Oklahoma Supreme Court summarized the traditional, deferential attitude of the courts toward fathers in its 1980 opinion in *In re Tubbs*.

> The paternal interest has been alluded to by various terms—a natural right, a fundamental right, a primary or time-honored right, a common-law right, a protectible interest and even a legal right. . . . The paternal surname is said to have a tendency to identify the relationship between a father and his children whether it is bestowed as a matter of law or centuries-old custom.[16]

The priority of the father's interest, and the legal presumption protecting it, are still embodied in many modern name change statutes.

First, the statutes in several states require the consent of both parents, thus conferring an effective veto power upon the noncustodial father who opposes the proposed change of his child's surname. The father may lose this power to withhold consent, however, if he fails in some way to be a nurturing and supportive parent. The Georgia statute, for example, takes this approach to protecting the rights of parents.

> If the petition seeks to change the name of a minor child, the written consent of [the minor's] parent or parents if they are living and

15. *Cf. In re* Richie, 564 A.2d 239 (Pa. Super. Ct. 1989) (refusing to recognize any special interest of the father when the mother petitioned to change her daughter's name from the mother's surname, which the child had used since birth, to the stepfather's name).

16. *In re* Tubbs, 620 P.2d 384, 386–87 (Okla. 1980) (upholding father's right to personal notice of name change proceeding). Some courts have elevated the father's interest in his child's name to a constitutionally protected interest, especially when the issue before the court is the father's right to notice of the name change proceeding. *See, e.g.*, Carroll v. Johnson, 565 S.W.2d 10 (Ark. 1978); Eschrich v. Williamson, 475 S.W.2d 380 (Tex. Civ. App. 1972). *But see* Hamman v. Jefferson County Court, 753 P.2d 743, 752 (Colo. 1988) (Lohr, J., concurring in part and dissenting in part) (stating that parent's interest in child's name, "while certainly important to the parent, is not of constitutionally protected magnitude").

have not abandoned the child . . . shall be filed with the petition, except that the written consent of a parent shall not be required if the parent has not contributed to the support of the child for a continuous period of five years or more immediately preceding the filing of the petition.[17]

Absent abandonment or the extended period of nonsupport, this Georgia law apparently enables a noncustodial father to prevent his child's formal use of a new surname in the stepfamily setting.

The statutes in many other states authorize a name change, without the father's consent, if the result would serve the child's interests.[18] For example, the Indiana law provides that, "[i]n deciding on a petition to change the name of a minor child, the court shall be guided by the best interest of the child rule."[19] The best interests of the child standard, which is consistently invoked in many types of legal proceedings affecting children, assigns priority to the child's welfare over the private interests of the parents or other parties. Reference to the best interests of the child rule, however, has not eliminated the protective concern of lawmakers for the noncustodial father in this context. Thus, the same Indiana statute that invokes the best interests of children adds the following limitation.

> However, there is a *presumption in favor of a parent* of a minor child who: (1) [h]as been making support payments and fulfilling other duties in accordance with a decree issued [by the divorce court]; and (2) [o]bjects to the proposed name change of the child.[20]

This type of statutory presumption in favor of the father's surname creates a significant burden for stepfamily members who desire to change the stepchild's name.

In Virginia, the name change statute contains no presumption in favor of the father, but the state supreme court has nevertheless imposed the same type of burden on the proponent of change. The Virginia statute refers to the interests of the child, not the parent, in the following provision.

---

17. GA. CODE ANN. § 19–12–1(c) (1991); *see also* IOWA CODE ANN. § 674.6 (West 1987) (consent required unless abandonment or nonsupport is established); LA. REV. STAT. ANN. § 13:4751 (West 1991) (nonsupport for one year); MICH. COMP. LAWS ANN. § 711.1 (West 1993) (nonsupport and failure to maintain contact for two years); N.C. GEN. STAT. § 101–2 (1985) (abandonment).

18. *See In re* Grimes, 609 A.2d 158, 161 n.5 (Pa. 1992) (collecting cases in which courts adopted best interests of the child standard to resolve name change contests).

19. IND. CODE ANN. § 34–4–6–4(d) (Burns 1986).

20. *Id.* (emphasis added).

In case of a minor who has both parents living, the parent who does not join in the application shall be served with reasonable notice of the application and, should such parent object to the change of name, a hearing shall be held to determine whether the change of name is in *the best interest of the minor.*[21]

Nevertheless, in *Flowers v. Cain*, the Virginia Supreme Court held that a stepchild's surname could be changed under this statute, over the father's objection, only if the mother was able to demonstrate "substantial reasons . . . for the change."[22]

According to the *Flowers* court, "substantial reasons" would include the father's misconduct or abandonment of the child, which are the traditional grounds for waiving consent. The Virginia Supreme Court stated further that the wishes of a mature stepchild, or proof of substantial detriment to the child, might also justify a name change. Absent proof by the mother of one of these "substantial reasons" for change, however, the father's wishes regarding his child's name would prevail under the statutory "best interest of the minor" standard.

The impact of this continuing deference to the father is highlighted by the analysis and result in the *Flowers* case. There, the mother testified that "it meant something to the children to have their names changed because they thought so much of their stepfather."[23] The court disposed of this evidence by observing that the children were too young to make a mature decision for themselves; there was no further consideration of the children's bond with their stepfather. Furthermore, the mother had requested the name change in order to avoid confusion and embarrassment resulting from the children's use of a different last name at a time when the family was moving to a new community. In the view of the court, "this sort of confusion and embarrassment is no greater than would be experienced by any child who finds himself in a situation where his parents have divorced and his mother has remarried."[24] The mother's concern about the children's adjustment in their new community, therefore, did not establish a "substantial reason" for overriding the father's wishes in this matter.

The Virginia Supreme Court in *Flowers* was much more impressed by the evidence presented by the father. According to the court, "the evidence was overwhelming that the father had not abandoned the natural ties with his children [and] that he had not engaged in misconduct." Furthermore, the father "professed his continued love and devotion to the two children,

---

21. Va. Code Ann. § 8.01–217 (Michie Supp. 1993) (emphasis added).

22. Flowers v. Cain, 237 S.E.2d 111, 113 (Va. 1977), *cited with approval,* Beyah v. Shelton, 344 S.E.2d 909, 911 (Va. 1986).

23. *Flowers,* 237 S.E.2d at 114–15.

24. *Id.*

. . . he pronounced his embarrassment and anger caused by the proposal to change the children's names," and he had regularly supported the children and "exercised his scheduled visitation privileges sporadically."[25] Based on this record, the court concluded that the best interests of the children would be served by maintaining their father's last name.

Legal scholars and a growing number of judges have criticized the legal standards that continue to defer to the father's wishes in this manner under the auspices of the best interests of the child.[26] Indeed, a complete assessment of the child's interests involves the balancing of numerous additional factors. Besides the continuing consideration of the child's relationship with the father, other relevant factors may include the child's relationship with the mother who has assumed a new last name, the child's relationship with the stepfather and adjustment in the stepfamily, the name by which the child is actually known and the likely effect on the child of changing it, and the child's own wishes.

Notably, the child's best interests call into play factors relating to the custodial mother, which have been excluded from the traditional analysis in name change cases such as *Flowers v. Cain*. The New Jersey Superior Court, in *In re Rossell*,[27] illustrated this premise by paraphrasing the language of an earlier opinion of the court, which had emphasized the importance of surnames in the father-child relationship. The opinion in *Rossell* simply substituted "mother" wherever "father" had been used in the prior opinion, with the following result.

---

25. *Id.*

26. *See In re* Schiffman, 620 P.2d 579 (Cal. 1980); *In re* Rossell, 481 A.2d 602 (N.J. Super. Ct. 1984); Priscilla R. MacDougall, *The Right of Women to Name Their Children*, 3 Law & Ineq. J. 91, 131–51 (1985); Richard H. Thornton, *The Controversy Over Children's Surnames: Familial Autonomy, Equal Protection and the Child's Best Interests*, 1979 Utah L. Rev. 303, 316–34; Donald M. Shawler, Note, *Surname Selection for the Child of Divorced Parents: Honor Thy Father vs. the Child's Best Interests*, 1985 S. Ill. U. L.J. 335; Note, *Like Father, Like Child: The Rights of Parents in Their Children's Surnames*, 70 Va. L. Rev. 1303 (1984).

27. *In re* Rossell, 481 A.2d 602 (N.J. Super. Ct. 1984). The mother in *Rossell* sought to change her child's name from the father's surname to her own premarital surname. As more women retain their own names throughout marriage or reassume them following divorce, this type of lawsuit involving the child's surname has become quite common. *See* Note, *Like Father, Like Child, supra* note 26, at 1303; Karnezis, *supra* note 4, §§ 5, 9, 10, 11(b) (collecting cases). An additional twist on naming has occurred in cases where the mother, following divorce, seeks to change the child's name from the father's surname to a hyphenated combination of the father's name and the mother's premarital name or a combination of the father's name and the stepfather's name. *See, e.g., In re* Marriage of Schaefer, 515 N.E.2d 710 (Ill. App. Ct. 1987) (disallowing hyphenated combination of father's and stepfather's names when father objected); *In re* Andrews, 454 N.W.2d 488 (Neb. 1990) (authorizing "hyphenated combination reflecting both maternal and paternal surnames" over father's objection).

A child whose name is not changed may feel rejected by the
mother's . . . assumption of the surname of a new husband. Mother
may be considered "deserving of rejection or contempt" for the failure to share her new name with her child. The same failure may be
construed to be "an attempt by his mother to deceive him as to his
true identity," namely [as] the child of his mother.[28]

Of course, this type of attention to the stepchild's relationship with the
custodial mother does not appear in most judicial opinions. According to
the *Rossell* court, the historical failure to consider the mother's role and
interests in name change cases was sexist.

Names, as this case clearly illustrates, are intimately involved with
the status of women. Rules of law for changing names cannot be
premised upon unacceptable theories of inequality. The right of a
mother to have her child bear her name must be recognized as
equal to that of the father.[29]

Furthermore, from the child's perspective, rules based on gender have prevented the full consideration of all factors relevant to the best interests of the
child.

An additional factor affecting the best interests of stepchildren, which
has been ignored in the traditional analysis of contested name change
cases, involves the decision-making authority of the custodial mother. The
family privacy doctrine generally assumes that the interests of children are
best served when the decision-making authority of custodial parents is
reinforced by the state. Thus, when one parent is designated as the primary
custodian following divorce, this status entails the authority to make future
decisions about the child's education, medical care, and other important
issues without interference from the other parent or the state. This model of
custody is designed to promote the interests of the child by establishing a
clear voice of authority in the home and avoiding future legal entanglements
between the parents. Clearly, the existence of the name change proceeding,
wherein the noncustodial father can object to the mother's wishes regarding the child's surname, is a historical exception to this general principle.
Still, a broad definition of the stepchild's best interests would include consideration of this factor, relating to the reinforcement of the custodial
mother's authority, in name change cases.[30]

---

28. *Rossell*, 481 A.2d at 605 (paraphrasing *In re Lone*, 338 A.2d 883, 887 (N.J.
Super. Ct. 1975)).

29. *Id*. Professor Homer Clark has suggested that the presumption in favor of
the father's surname violates the Equal Protection Clause. *See* CLARK, *supra* note 1,
at 548.

30. Both judges and scholars have taken the position that the custodial parent's
decision about the child's surname is entitled to greater weight than a mere factor in

The Illinois name change statute incorporates all of these factors under the best interests of the child standard. In addition to the child's relationship with each parent, the statute also delineates the wishes of the child, the parents, and any person acting as a parent; the relationship of the child with a custodial stepparent and with siblings and stepsiblings; the child's adjustment to his or her home, school, and community; and "all [other] relevant factors."[31] Of course, it is axiomatic that the best interests of the child standard always provides judges with a great deal of discretion in weighing and balancing these factors in particular cases. This axiom is illustrated by a comparison of two recent cases decided by the Illinois Court of Appeals under this broadly written name change statute.

In *In re Craig*,[32] the Appellate Court of Illinois authorized a stepchild's name change over the noncustodial father's objection. The court characterized the case as a "difficult" one,[33] because the father had continued to support and love his daughter as a dedicated noncustodial parent. On the other hand, a number of competing factors supported the stepfamily's petition to change the child's name. These factors included the wishes of the twelve-year-old child, her affection for the stepfather with whom she had resided for seven years, her relationship with two stepsiblings who bore the stepfather's name, her desire to be known at school by the same name as her mother, stepfather, and stepsiblings, and her distress when outsiders became confused about names in her family. On balance, these considerations prevailed under the statutory best interests of the child standard, in spite of the strong relationship between the stepdaughter and her father.

In contrast, the Illinois appellate court took a very different approach to the issue of name changes for stepchildren, under the same statute, in another case decided during the same year as *Craig*. In *In re Schaefer*,[34] a mother petitioned to formally change her children's last name from their father's surname to a hyphenated combination of the father's and stepfather's surnames, which the children had been using informally for a period of several years. Although the record contained evidence about many of the statutory factors relating to the children's preferences and their ad-

---

the best interests of the child analysis. *See, e.g.*, *In re* Schiffman, 620 P.2d 579, 584 (Cal. 1980) (concurring opinion) (advocating a presumption that the custodial parent's decision about the child's surname is in the child's best interests); Kathryn R. Urbonya, Note, *No Judicial Dyslexia: The Custodial Parent Presumption Distinguishes the Paternal from the Parental Right to Name a Child*, 58 N.D. L. REV. 793 (1982).

31. ILL. ANN. STAT. ch. 110, para. 21–101 (Smith-Hurd Supp. 1992). In order to prevail under this statute, the proponent of a name change must satisfy the evidentiary standard of "clear and convincing" evidence.

32. *In re* Craig, 518 N.E.2d 728 (Ill. App. Ct. 1987).

33. *Id.* at 730.

34. *In re* Schaefer, 515 N.E.2d 710 (Ill. App. Ct. 1987).

justment in the stepfamily, the matters discussed in the *Schaefer* opinion
focused exclusively on the father.

> [The father] as the noncustodial parent is at a disadvantage in main-
> taining a strong relationship with his children. Maintenance of the
> Schaefer name goes far toward demonstrating his continuing inter-
> ests in and identity with the children . . . . It is undisputed that [the
> father] is willingly meeting his financial obligations toward his chil-
> dren. The record does not reflect any misconduct or neglect of the
> children by [the father]. Moreover, the children express love for both
> of their natural parents.[35]

Perhaps the interests of the children in *Schaefer* were indeed best served by
the court's refusal to hyphenate their last name. However, the court's analysis of this issue appears to be very incomplete in light of its failure to
address the numerous factors in the Illinois name change statute that are
unrelated to the father.

The detailed listing of factors relating to the child's best interests in the
Illinois name change statute represents a trend in the law away from the
traditional preference in favor of paternal surnames. Even as courts and
legislatures progress toward a neutral best interests of the child standard,
however, continuing deference to the father's wishes can still be discerned
in many cases. The same tension between the noncustodial parent-child
relationship and other factors that affect the child's welfare is reflected in
the laws regulating stepparent adoption, discussed in the next chapter.

---

35. *Id.* at 713.

CHAPTER 9

Stepparent Adoption

I. Introduction

A large proportion of the adoptions that take place in the United States involve the adoption of a stepchild by his or her stepparent.[1] Typically, a stepparent adoption occurs after the stepparent, custodial parent, and step-child have resided together for a period of time as a stepfamily. Through such an adoption, the stepfamily is transformed from the uncertain legal entity described in this book into a legal family. The process of adoption creates the full parent-child status between the adopting stepparent and the stepchild, with the same rights and responsibilities as biologic families in every legal context, including custody, surnames, child support, insurance and benefits, property and inheritance, incest, criminal law, and tort law. The motivation of the stepfamily members who initiate an adoption proceeding may involve some of these specific rights and duties or a more general desire to formalize the de facto family they have created.

The legal process of adoption is regulated by state statutes. Historically, the courts in England and the United States rejected the notion that a legal family status could be created between anyone other than biologic parents and their children. In the nineteenth century, state legislatures intervened by enacting formal adoption statutes that authorized designated courts to enter orders of adoption. The state statutes, which tend to be strictly construed by the courts, continue to govern the adoption process.[2]

While a great deal of variety exists among the various state adoption laws, there are common procedural and substantive elements.[3] Typically,

---

1. *See* 1991 STATISTICAL ABSTRACT OF THE UNITED STATES, BUREAU OF THE CENSUS, U.S. DEP'T OF COMMERCE, NATIONAL DATA BOOK 376 (stating that approximately one-half of adoptions are by relatives, defined to include stepparents); Patricia A. Wolf & Emily Mast, *Counseling Issues in Adoption by Stepparents*, 32 Soc. WORK 69, 69 (1987) (citing data from a study of adoption in Lancaster County, Pennsylvania, which revealed that "[s]tep-parent adoptions outnumber nonrelative adoptions . . . and have not experienced the same decrease during the past ten years").

2. For a general discussion of the historical development of the law of adoption, see JOAN H. HOLLINGER, ADOPTION LAW AND PRACTICE §§ 1.02–.04 (1990).

3. For a general discussion of the basic aspects of modern adoption law, see HOMER H. CLARK, JR., THE LAW OF DOMESTIC RELATIONS IN THE UNITED STATES 850–76 (2d ed. 1988).

an adoption proceeding is initiated by the individual seeking to adopt a child, by filing a petition. Given the significance of this action, natural parents and others with a custodial interest in the child are entitled to notice and an opportunity to be heard. Children of a certain age must be treated as interested parties for this purpose; indeed, an older child may be permitted to veto the proposed adoption. The universal standard employed in adoption cases is the best interests of the child; an adoptive parent-child relationship will be created only if this important transition would predictably enhance the future welfare of the child. A final order of adoption generally entails the child's removal from the biologic family and incorporation into the adoptive family for all legal purposes.

Children become available for adoption only after the legal relationships with their biologic parents have been severed. Parent-child relationships may be terminated for this purpose either in the adoption proceeding or in a prior judicial proceeding. Termination may be consensual, as when the noncustodial parent consents to a proposed stepparent adoption, or nonconsensual. Any involuntary waiver of parental rights immediately raises serious concerns relating to family autonomy and the constitutional rights of parents. In order to protect a parent's interest in maintaining his or her relationship with the child, traditional legal standards have required strong proof of parental unfitness in adoption cases. A tension sometimes arises in this situation between the parent's interest in maintaining ties with the child and the child's interest in being freed for adoption. In recent years, the standards governing the waiver of parental consent have begun to acknowledge this conflict and to take account of the interests of the child as well as the parent.

The classic model of adoption involves the removal of an infant from the natural family and placement with "strangers" unrelated to the child. This model assumes that all ties between the child and his or her natural family members will be severed. Stepparent adoption does not fit easily into this model primarily because the adoptive parent is married to the custodial parent, whose legal and custodial relationship with the child will continue unaltered following the adoption. This special feature of stepparent adoption, involving change in the child's life that is less complete than the typical adoption by strangers, has influenced the development of the law in several ways.

First, certain procedural requirements, such as home evaluations and waiting periods, have been eased when the adoptive household consists of the custodial parent, stepparent, and child.[4] To a more limited extent, the substantive standards for dispensing with the consent of the noncustodial parent have also been adjusted in ways that facilitate stepparent adoption. Finally, the special circumstances of adopted stepchildren have led to the

---

4. *See, e.g.*, ALA. CODE § 26–10A–27 (1992) ("Any person may adopt his or her spouse's child according to the provisions [regulating adoptions], except that . . . [n]o investigation . . . shall occur unless otherwise directed by the court, and . . . [n]o

thorough reconsideration of adoption as an all-or-nothing proposition for both the biologic parent and the adoptive stepparent. One alternative model, for example, would permit continuing visitation rights for the non-custodial parent following a stepparent adoption. This chapter examines the special legal issues that arise when stepparents seek to adopt their stepchildren.

II. Waiver of Consent Based on Unfitness

The adoption of a child can proceed only after legal relationships between the child and his or her biologic parents have been severed. Parents may consent to a termination of their rights and obligations, thereby freeing their child for adoption. In the absence of such a voluntary release, however, the biologic parents are presumptively entitled to have the continuing custody and control of their child and to prevent the child's adoption.

The adoption petition of a stepparent will generally be supported by his or her spouse, whose custodial and legal relationship with the child would remain unaffected by the proposed adoption. Before an adoptive relationship can be created between stepparent and child, however, the child's relationship with the noncustodial parent must be legally terminated. Significantly, a parent's legal rights are not lost for this purpose by virtue of the fact that he or she is not the primary custodian of the child. The rights of the noncustodial parent are entitled to protection, whether or not the parents were ever married to each other[5] and whether or not a prior court order has addressed the rights and duties of the noncustodial parent.[6] Thus, when a decision is made in the stepfamily that adoption would be desirable, the

---

report of fees and charges . . . shall be made unless ordered by the court.") Furthermore, procedural rules that are designed to preserve confidentiality in the adoption process have no relevance to stepparent adoptions, where the natural and adoptive parent are known to each other.

5. The rights of unmarried fathers in this context have been addressed on several occasions by the United States Supreme Court. As a matter of constitutional law, the father who serves an active parenting role is entitled to the same protection as married parents. *See* CLARK, *supra* note 3, at 855–62 (discussing "constitutional position of the father of an illegitimate child"); Robert S. Rausch, Note, *Unwed Fathers and the Adoption Process*, 22 WM. & MARY L. REV. 85 (1980).

6. The adoption statutes in a number of states appear to waive the requirement of consent from the parent who lost primary custody in an earlier divorce proceeding. Modern courts have refused to read these statutes literally, holding that noncustodial parents retain the right to veto a proposed adoption unless other grounds for terminating their rights can be established. For example, the Minnesota Supreme Court held that the consent of a divorced, noncustodial mother was required, even though the state statute provided that "consent shall not be required of a parent who has abandoned the child, or of a parent who has lost custody of the child through a divorce decree." *See In re* Parks, 127 N.W.2d 548, 550, 553 (Minn. 1964). Indeed, a

noncustodial parent's objection may present an insurmountable hurdle in achieving this goal. In the absence of the noncustodial parent's consent, an adoption petition initiated by the custodial parent and stepparent can proceed only if statutory grounds exist for involuntarily severing the noncustodial parent-child relationship.

Statutes in every jurisdiction set forth standards for involuntarily terminating the parent-child relationship.[7] The traditional statutory standards have protected the interests and autonomy of parents by requiring proof that their past conduct justifies this decisive legal action. For example, the following Illinois statute establishes the standard of "unfitness" to determine when adoption is permitted without the consent of both parents.

[C]onsents shall be required in all cases, unless [the parent] shall be found by the court, *by clear and convincing evidence . . . to be an unfit person . . . .*

[T]he grounds of such unfitness [are] any one or more of the following:

  (a) abandonment of the child;
  (b) failure to maintain a reasonable degree of interest, concern or responsibility as to the child's welfare;
  (c) desertion of the child for more than 3 months . . . ;
  (d) substantial neglect of the child if continuous or repeated;
  (e) extreme or repeated cruelty to the child;
  (f) two or more findings of physical abuse . . . ;
  (g) failure to protect the child from conditions within his environment injurious to the child's welfare;
  (h) other neglect of, or misconduct toward the child . . . ;
  (i) depravity;
  (j) open and notorious adultery or fornication;
  (k) habitual drunkenness or addiction to drugs . . . ;
  (l) failure to demonstrate a reasonable degree of interest, concern or responsibility as to the welfare of a new born child during the first 30 days after its birth;
  (m) failure by a parent to make reasonable efforts to correct the conditions which were the basis for the removal of the child [by the state] . . . ;
  (n) evidence of intent to forego his or her parental rights . . . .[8]

---

literal construction of this type of statute would likely violate the constitutionally protected interests of noncustodial parents. *See generally* E. LeFevre, Annotation, *Consent of Natural Parents as Essential to Adoption Where Parents Are Divorced,* 47 A.L.R.2d 824, §§ 4, 5 (1956 & Later Case Serv. 1991) (collecting cases).

7. *See* Larry K. Laskiewicz, Comment, *A Survey of State Law Authorizing Stepparent Adoptions Without the Noncustodial Parent's Consent,* 15 AKRON L. REV. 567 (1982).

8. ILL. ANN. STAT. ch. 40, paras. 1501, 1510 (Smith-Hurd Supp. 1992) (emphasis added).

Notably, most of these statutory bases for establishing unfitness are directly related to the parent's past treatment of the child. Other grounds in the Illinois statute, such as "open and notorious adultery or fornication," emphasize past behavior that reveals the parent's general character.

Even after this type of parental unfitness has been established, the adoption court must still determine whether a proposed adoption would serve the child's interests. In a stepparent adoption proceeding, the court may determine that maintenance of the child's legal relationship with an unfit noncustodial parent is more important than the formalization of relationships within the stepfamily.[9] In reaching this very result, one court observed that the denial of a stepfather's adoption petition would "give [the] 12-year-old son the better part of two worlds,"[10] in spite of the court's prior determination that the father was unfit.

The conduct by noncustodial parents most frequently relied upon to establish their unfitness in stepparent adoption proceedings involves their failure to maintain contact with the child, to support the child, or to otherwise carry out the responsibilities of parenthood over a period of time. For example, in *In re Adoption of Syck*,[11] the custodial father and stepmother attempted to establish grounds for terminating the rights of the noncustodial mother by relying upon Section (b) of the Illinois adoption law, set out previously, which provides that parental "unfitness" includes the "failure to maintain a reasonable degree of interest, concern or responsibility as to the child's welfare."

The marriage between the biologic parents, Lorrie and Mark Syck, was dissolved in 1984, when their son Paul was almost two years old. The parties agreed then that Mark would serve as primary custodian and that Lorrie would be entitled to spend designated times with her son. Lorrie exercised this right for several months, until she moved from Illinois to Pennsylvania, where she assumed responsibility for her ailing father. During the next four years she neither saw nor spoke with her son, who resided with his father and grandparents until 1985 and thereafter in the stepfamily created by Mark's marriage to Lisa Syck. During this four-year period, Lorrie sent numerous cards and letters to Paul, called Mark and his parents many times, but provided no financial support for her son. When Lorrie

---

9. *See In re* J.A.A., 618 P.2d 742 (Colo. Ct. App. 1980) (denying adoption by stepfather who was "fit and proper person to adopt the child" in spite of three-year abandonment by natural father, because "it would be in the best interest of the child to maintain and develop a relationship with his natural father"); Knapp v. Cotten, 577 So. 2d 241 (La. Ct. App. 1991); *In re* Hinton, 390 So. 2d 972 (La. Ct. App. 1980); Adoption of Latiolais, 376 So. 2d 555 (La. Ct. App. 1979), *aff'd*, 384 So. 2d 377 (La. 1980); Domingue v. Thibodeaux, 200 So. 2d 784 (La. Ct. App. 1967); *In re* Adoption of R.M.B., 645 S.W.2d 29 (Mo. Ct. App. 1982); *In re* Adoption of S.T.V., 733 P.2d 841 (Mont. 1987).

10. *In re* Adoption of R.M.B., 645 S.W.2d 29, 30 (Mo. Ct. App. 1982).

11. *In re* Adoption of Syck, 562 N.E.2d 174 (Ill. 1990).

subsequently refused to cooperate in Lisa's and Mark's plan for Paul's adoption, they requested the termination of her parental rights.

Based on this record, the lower courts determined that Lorrie Syck had "fail[ed] to maintain a reasonable degree of interest, concern or responsibility" and terminated her parental rights. On appeal, the state high court reversed, ruling that Lorrie's level of involvement with her son, notably her efforts to communicate with him, demonstrated the "degree of interest as to the child's welfare required by the adoption statute." Clearly, the relevant statutory standard conferred wide judicial discretion in assessing the quantity and quality of contact by the mother with her child during the relevant four-year period.

Many courts, like the Illinois Supreme Court in *Adoption of Syck*, tend to construe the statutory waiver of consent standards strictly against the proponent of adoption, as a device for protecting the rights of parents.[12] The Court of Appeals of Kansas stated this position clearly in *In re Adoption of B.J.H., Jr.*, when it denied the petition of a stepfather to adopt his stepchild.

> In order to grant a decree of adoption in opposition to the wishes and against the consent of the natural parent, the conditions presented by statute which make consent unnecessary must be clearly proved and the statute construed in support of the right of the natural parent. . . . [T]he inclination of the court is in favor of maintaining the natural relation.[13]

An important feature of this judicial preference for natural parents involves measuring the quantity and quality of the parent-child relationship from the parent's perspective. In *Adoption of Syck*, for example, where the mother's contacts with her son over a four-year period were limited to cards and letters, the Illinois trial court terminated her rights after observing that "cards and letters to a child of this age would in essence have the practical effect of no contact at all in a maternal sense."[14] The state supreme court, on the other hand, emphasized several factors that justified the mother's failure to communicate with her son, including her youth, poverty and lack of employable skills, her father's illness, and the role played by her former husband and his parents in obstructing the long-distance relationship between mother and son. In other words, her failure to maintain meaningful

---

12. There is a constitutional dimension to the rights of the parent in this context. The United States Supreme Court has ruled that the grounds for terminating parental rights must, as a constitutional matter, be established by a minimum standard of clear and convincing evidence, which exceeds the evidentiary standard typically employed in civil trials. *See* Santosky v. Kramer, 455 U.S. 745 (1982) (invalidating "fair preponderance of the evidence" standard under New York statute governing state-initiated termination proceedings).

13. *In re* Adoption of B.J.H., Jr., 757 P.2d 1268, 1272 (Kan. 1988).

14. *Adoption of Syck*, 562 N.E.2d at 182.

contact with the child was excused due to the mother's special circumstances.

The impact of viewing the evidence of unfitness from the parent's point of view is similarly illustrated in the case of *Adoption of B.J.H., Jr.* There, the Kansas trial court had terminated the rights of a noncustodial father on the statutory ground that he had "failed or refused to assume the duties of a parent for two consecutive years." The Court of Appeals of Kansas reversed this decision and criticized the trial court for judging the father's behavior in terms of its minimal impact on the child.

> The trial court . . . distinguished between visitation, contacts, communications, or contributions and "attempts" at accomplishing the same, and held that, although Father initiated a number of good faith attempts to exercise visitation, they were never followed through in a manner of real meaning or benefit to the child . . . .
>
> The wording of the [trial court's] opinion places undue consideration on the "effect upon the child" and improperly weighs and tests the evidence "from the standpoint of the child."[15]

By emphasizing the father's level of activity, rather than its impact on the child, the court concluded that he was fit and entitled to veto the proposed stepparent adoption.

As in the *Syck* and *B.J.H., Jr.* cases, stepparent adoption petitions frequently fail, even though the noncustodial parent's past involvement was sporadic and of questionable significance to the child. In numerous cases, the failure to spend time with the child has been forgiven if occasional contacts were made, if unsuccessful efforts were made to communicate with the child, if other significant events in the parent's life distracted him or her, or if nonaccess resulted from emotional tension between the parents. Likewise, nonsupport has been excused based on the parent's poverty, the parent's intention to protest the denial of visitation rights by withholding support, the partial or occasional compliance with support obligations, or the promise of future support.[16]

Yet this high level of deference to the noncustodial parent is not the universal rule in the stepparent adoption cases that turn on the issue of parental fitness. For example, the Alaska Supreme Court held in 1986 that something more than casual or occasional involvement with the child was

---

15. *Adoption of B.J.H., Jr.*, 757 P.2d at 1272–73.

16. For a general discussion of the manner in which the courts have applied these statutory standards for involuntarily terminating parental rights, see CLARK, *supra* note 3, at 895–905; *see also* C.C. Marvel, Annotation, *What Constitutes Abandonment or Desertion of Child By Its Parent or Parents Within Purview of Adoption Laws*, 35 A.L.R.2d 662, § 11 (1954 & Later Case Serv. 1989) (collecting cases).

required before the parent was permitted to veto a proposed adoption. The relevant statute dispensed with consent "if the parent for a period of at least one year has failed significantly without justifiable cause . . . to communicate meaningfully with the child, or . . . to provide for the care and support of the child as required by law or judicial decree."[17] In *In re J.J.J.*, the court expressly lowered the level of protection for parents under this statute.

> In this court's prior decisions . . . we have declined to dispense with a noncustodial parent's right to withhold consent to a stepparent adoption as long as the noncustodial parent has made a few perfunctory communications or an occasional gesture of support. . . .
> We take this opportunity to clarify that, in order for a noncustodial parent to block a stepparent adoption, he or she must have maintained *meaningful* contact with a child, and must have provided regular payments of child support, unless prevented from doing so by circumstances beyond the noncustodial parent's control.[18]

In *J.J.J.*, the court reviewed the conduct of a noncustodial father during the two-year period between the parents' marital separation and the filing of the stepfather's adoption petition. During this time, almost all of the father's support contributions had been made in response to collection efforts by a state child support agency. Furthermore, a period of more than one year had elapsed during which no communication with the child occurred, although the father subsequently attempted to renew contact with his son. Based on this record, the Alaska Supreme Court concluded that the noncustodial father in *J.J.J.* had lost the right to withhold consent to his son's adoption.

A similar view, that past "perfunctory gestures" on the part of the noncustodial parent should not bar a child's adoption, has been expressed by the Kansas legislature. The state adoption statute, which includes the "fail[ure] . . . to assume the duties of a parent for two consecutive years" as a ground for waiving consent to adoption, also provides that "the court may disregard incidental visitations, contacts, communications or contributions" in applying this standard.[19] In *In re Adoption of B.C.S.*,[20] the Kansas Supreme Court upheld a stepparent adoption under the terms of this statute, over the objection of a noncustodial father who had maintained incidental contact with the children.

The results in cases like *Adoption of B.C.S.*, *In re J.J.J.*, *Adoption of Syck*, and *Adoption of B.J.H., Jr.* reveal a lack of consistency in the laws that define "unfitness" as a ground for waiving parental consent to a proposed stepparent adoption. A great deal of variation exists both in the statement of

---

17. *In re* J.J.J., 718 P.2d 948, 953–54 (Alaska 1986).
18. *Id.* at 952–53.
19. KAN. STAT. ANN. § 59–2136(d) (Supp. 1992).
20. *In re* Adoption of B.C.S., 777 P.2d 776, 781 (Kan. 1989).

legal standards and their application to particular cases. After reviewing the statutes and numerous reported decisions in this field, Professor Homer Clark aptly observed that "the usual principles of stare decisis have less impact here than in cases where the conflicts are less emotional and the interests involved less complex."[21]

The consistent feature involved in the statutory standards discussed in this section, however, is their exclusive focus on the conduct of the parent. Under the parental unfitness standard, however defined, the courts are unable to consider other factors that may influence a child's welfare, such as the child's adjustment in the stepfamily. As discussed in the next section, the best interests of the child standard has emerged as an alternative basis for determining when a stepparent adoption should proceed without parental consent. In contrast to the parental unfitness standard, the best interests standard permits the consideration of additional factors that are unrelated to the noncustodial parent.

III. Waiver of Consent Based on the Best Interests of the Child

Once a child has been freed for adoption, the best interests of the child standard is uniformly applied to determine whether a proposed adoptive placement will receive state approval. As described in the previous section, however, the best interests of the child standard has not been the traditional norm for making the threshold determination about the child's availability for adoption; rather, the parental unfitness standard has been employed for this purpose. In recent years, the delay involved in addressing the child's interests under this two-step process has become the subject of criticism and reevaluation. As a result, a number of state courts and legislatures have replaced the traditional rules for regulating the rights of parents in this context with a best interests of the child standard. Where the laws have been revised in this fashion, the noncustodial parent is not authorized to withhold consent to a stepparent adoption if the result would be inconsistent with the future welfare of the child. This trend in the law of stepparent adoption is examined in the following discussion.

The two stepparent adoption cases discussed at length in the preceding section illustrate the traditional approach. According to the Illinois Supreme Court in *In re Adoption of Syck*, "there is a two step process of first ruling on parental unfitness and then, if called for, ruling on whether adoption is in [the] child's best interests."[22] The Kansas Supreme Court in

---

21. CLARK, *supra* note 3, at 894.

22. *In re* Adoption of Syck, 562 N.E.2d 174, 183–84 (Ill. 1990) (ruling that the trial court improperly factored the child's interest in being adopted into its assessment of the noncustodial parent's right to veto a proposed stepparent adoption).

B.J.H., Jr. applied the same standard and reversed the trial court, for considering the child's interests in the hearing to determine the rights of the noncustodial father.

> [T]he wording of the trial court's opinion . . . indicates the "best interests" of the child was given undue consideration. There is *no question but that the trial court's decision is socially desirable*, but unless the legislature establishes different tests in adoption cases we must continue the presently mandated strict construction in favor of maintaining the rights of a natural parent.[23]

Thus, the appellate court in *B.J.H., Jr.* expressed the view that consideration of the child's interests would be "socially desirable," while it reversed the trial court precisely for taking this approach.

In recent years, other jurisdictions have followed the approach described by the Kansas court as socially desirable by including the interests of the child as a ground for waiving the noncustodial parent's consent in stepparent adoption cases. For example, the Uniform Adoption Act, which has been enacted in several states,[24] authorizes such a waiver when the parent has abandoned or neglected the child, "or . . . in the case of a parent not having custody of a minor, his consent is being unreasonably withheld *contrary to the best interest of the minor*."[25] The commentary accompanying this provision describes a contested stepparent adoption case to illustrate the application of the best interests of the child standard.

> The final ground . . . concerns unreasonable withholding of consent to adoption. It can be used in a case where a stepparent and the [custodial parent] are in custody of the child but the [noncustodial parent] refuses to give consent and withholding of consent is found by the court to be contrary to the best interests of the child.[26]

The adoption statute in Arizona employs a slightly different formula for invoking the child's interests. The statute identifies those parents from whom consent to adoption is not required, including those who are incompetent or whose rights have been involuntarily terminated based on grounds of abandonment, neglect, mental illness, or imprisonment for a felony, and then adds the following caveat: "The court may waive the re-

---

23. *In re* Adoption of B.J.H., Jr., 757 P.2d 1268, 1274 (Kan. 1988) (emphasis added).

24. UNIF. ADOPTION ACT, 9 U.L.A. 1 (Supp. 1992) (listing five states that have enacted this provision).

25. *Id.*, § 19(c), at 72 (1988) (emphasis added).

26. *Id.*, § 19 comment, at 73. *But see* Kottsick v. Carlson, 241 N.W.2d 842 (N.D. 1976) (holding that the noncustodial father's consent to stepparent adoption could be waived under the Uniform Adoption Act only upon a determination of his unfitness).

quirement of the consent of any person required to give consent when . . . the court determines that *the interests of the child will be promoted thereby.*"[27]

Whatever the particular statutory formula, the best interests of the child standard requires judicial consideration of all aspects of a proposed stepparent adoption as they affect the child. In many cases, formalization of the child's relationship with the residential stepparent would be beneficial by introducing a sense of permanency and the positive legal aspects of the parent-child status in the stepfamily. On the other hand, the potential detriment resulting from the loss of all legal connection with the noncustodial parent, incident to a stepparent adoption, is a competing factor to be weighed in the best interests of the child analysis.

On balance, if the benefits of a stepparent adoption outweigh the costs of losing the noncustodial parent, then the best interests of the child would be served by moving ahead with the adoption. If the noncustodial parent objects, then a clear conflict is created between the interest of the noncustodial parent in maintaining his or her legal status and the welfare of the child. Of course, the traditional standards relating to parental fitness protect the parent in this situation by permitting the adoption only if the noncustodial parent has failed to perform his or her duties. Modern statutes, including the Uniform Adoption Act, which introduce the interests of the child into the waiver of consent determination, have shifted the legal balance away from the parent. The judicial opinions in stepparent adoption cases, however, reveal a wide range in the willingness of judges to actually base their decisions about involuntary termination of parental rights upon an analysis of the child's interests.

For example, in *In re H.J.P.*,[28] the Washington Supreme Court was unwilling to attach any significance whatsoever to the "best interest of the child" language in the following statute, which was enacted by the state legislature in 1985 to regulate the termination of parental rights specifically in stepparent adoption cases.

> [T]he parent-child relationship of a parent may be terminated upon a showing by clear, cogent, and convincing evidence that *it is in the best interest of the child to terminate the relationship* and that the parent has failed to perform parental duties under circumstances showing a substantial lack of regard for his or her parental obligations and is *withholding consent to adoption contrary to the best interest of the child.*[29]

---

27. Ariz. Rev. Stat. Ann. § 8–106(C) (1989 & Supp. 1992) (emphasis added); *see also* Ariz. Rev. Stat. Ann. § 8–533(B) (1989) (listing grounds for involuntary termination of parental rights).

28. *In re* H.J.P., 789 P.2d 96 (Wash. 1990).

29. *Id.* at 100 (emphasis added) (quoting Wash. Rev. Code § 26.33.120(1) (1985)).

Prior to 1985, the statutory standard for waiving consent of the noncustodial parent in stepparent adoptions had been "desertion" or "abandonment" of the child, which the state courts had characterized as evidence of parental "unfitness."

The noncustodial father in *H.J.P.* challenged the constitutionality of the revised statute on the ground that any consideration of the child's interests, under the standard for terminating parental rights, would violate the constitutional rights of parents. Specifically, the father argued that the Due Process Clause required nothing short of the traditional standard of a parent's unfitness before his or her consent to the child's adoption could be waived. The United States Supreme Court has never answered the question of whether a parent's rights can be lawfully terminated on the basis of the child's best interests. Lower courts that have addressed the issue have reached conflicting results.[30] The Washington Supreme Court avoided this constitutional issue in *H.J.P.* by construing the revised stepparent adoption statute to require proof of parental unfitness in the form of "failure to perform parental duties."

Under this narrow construction of the Washington statute, the language regarding the best interests of the child is simply not relevant in determining whether the noncustodial parent is entitled to veto a stepparent adoption. Instead, "[t]he court must resolve the jurisdictional [fitness] issue before it can address the best interests of the child."[31] In this manner, the Washington Supreme Court reverted to the two-step analysis employed under the traditional statutes, wherein the interests of the child come into play only after a threshold determination has been made that "the biological parent, by behavior, has forfeited all rights in the child."[32] Thus, the decision in *H.J.P.* effectively negated the legislative effort to introduce the interests of the child as a factor in making waiver of parental consent decisions in stepparent adoption cases.

A similar reluctance to embrace legislative reform appears in the opinion of the Virginia Supreme Court in *Malpass v. Morgan*,[33] where the court narrowly construed the following provision in the state adoption statute.

---

30. Professor Clark has summarized the uncertain state of the law regarding this constitutional issue as follows.

> The statutes of a few states authorize termination of parental rights . . . when the best interests of the child demand those forms of relief . . . . [S]ome courts have held that this is insufficient to meet the constitutional standard of precision or to comply with substantive due process requirements. Other courts have held such statutes valid. A closely related line of cases is concerned with whether "unfitness" must be proved before parental rights may be terminated. Here also the cases are in disagreement.

CLARK, *supra* note 3, at 891.

31. *H.J.P.*, 789 P.2d at 102.

32. *Id.* at 101.

33. Malpass v. Morgan, 192 S.E.2d 794 (Va. 1972), *discussed in* Note, Malpass

If after hearing evidence the court finds that the valid consent of any person . . . whose consent is . . . required is *withheld contrary to the best interests of the child,* . . . the court may grant the [adoption] petition without such consent.[34]

In *Malpass*, the Virginia Supreme Court held that this legislative standard was not satisfied by the trial court's determination that a proposed stepparent adoption would "promote the best interests" of the stepchild.

[W]e think something more is required to support a finding that consent is withheld contrary to the best interests of a child. . . .
Where, as here, there is no question of the fitness of the nonconsenting parent . . . it must be shown that *continuance of the relationship between the [child and the nonconsenting parent] would be detrimental to the child's welfare.*[35]

Predictably, this narrow construction of the best interests of the child standard under the Virginia adoption statute was premised on the rights of the biologic parent.

We have established the rule in Virginia that in custody and adoption cases the welfare of the child is of paramount concern and takes precedence over the rights of parents. . . . There is, however, a condition to the rule . . . that the rights of parents may not be lightly severed but are to be respected if at all consonant with the best interests of the child.[36]

Although the Virginia court did not go as far as the Washington Supreme Court in *H.J.P.* and establish a requirement of parental unfitness, the analysis in *Malpass* nevertheless narrowed the focus of the best interests of the child inquiry to the biologic parent-child relationship. As a result, any consideration of the potential benefits for the child in the adoptive household of the custodial parent and stepparent becomes possible only *after* an initial determination that the noncustodial parent-child relationship is "detrimental to the child's welfare."

The impact of this limitation is underscored by the result in *Malpass*,

v. Morgan: *Determining When a Parent's Consent to Adoption is Withheld Contrary to the Best Interests of the Child*, 60 Va. L. Rev. 718 (1974).

34. The quoted statute is currently codified in Va. Code Ann. § 63.1–225(E) (Michie Supp. 1993) (emphasis added).

35. *Malpass*, 192 S.E.2d at 798–99 (emphasis added).

36. *Id.* at 799 (citations omitted); *cf.* Frye v. Spotte, 359 S.E.2d 315, 320 (Va. Ct. App. 1987) (affirming trial court order granting adoption petition of stepfather over objection of natural father, because facts satisfied the test of *Malpass v. Morgan* that continuation of father-child relationship would be detrimental to the children).

where the Virginia trial court had based its determination that adoption would "promote the best interests of the child" on three types of evidence. First, the trial judge made findings about the minimal level of the noncustodial father's involvement with his son during the six-year period between the parents' separation, when the child was one year old, and the time of the custodial stepfather's adoption petition. Second, the trial court considered evidence about the stepfamily, which was summarized in the following manner: "Suffice to say, the record shows that the child justifiably looks upon [the stepfather] as his father and that the lad is being reared in a warm and loving home."[37] Finally, the trial court assessed the impact of the father's recent return to Virginia and exercise of visitation rights, which had caused friction among the parties.

On appeal, the Virginia Supreme Court made no reference to the second category of evidence, which focused on the stepfather-child relationship. This information was irrelevant under the standard formulated in *Malpass*, which limited the best interests of the child analysis to the question of whether the father-child relationship was detrimental to the child. The Virginia Supreme Court reviewed the remaining evidence relating to the father, concluded that the father-child relationship was not detrimental to the child, and denied the stepfather's petition for adoption.

In contrast to the approaches of the Washington and Virginia Supreme Courts, the District of Columbia Court of Appeals has applied a straightforward test for determining the best interests of the child under the adoption statute in the District. Furthermore, the court has expressly held that the termination of parental rights on this basis in the stepparent adoption setting does not violate the constitutional rights of the noncustodial parent. In *In re J.O.L. II*,[38] the court enumerated the following factors to be considered by trial courts, under the statutory best interests of the child standard, in determining whether parental consent should be waived and stepparent adoption authorized.

(1) [Q]uestions of family stability,
(2) present and future effects of adoption or non-adoption on the child,
(3) interaction between the child and the contestants,
(4) who the child perceives as his or her psychological parent,
(5) the child's adjustment to his or her living situation, school, and community, and
(6) mental and physical health of all interested parties.[39]

This broad standard requires the courts to weigh and balance all of the factors that affect the child's interests.

---

37. *Malpass*, 192 S.E.2d at 796.
38. *In re* J.O.L. II, 409 A.2d 1073 (D.C. 1979), *vacated on other grounds*, 449 U.S. 989 (1980).
39. *Id*. at 1075.

For example, the trial court in *J.O.L.* considered information about both the noncustodial father and the stepfamily. Notably, the father had failed to communicate with his children for a period of five years, following a series of earlier efforts at visitation that had caused problems for the children. In the meantime, the stepfather had become their psychological father, and the children were well adjusted in the stepfamily home. After weighing all of the factors, the trial court determined that the interests of the children would best be served by the proposed adoption.

> When viewed from the children's point of view, the choice is between giving final security to the family unit of which these children are in every way an integral part or leaving them to wander upon a course of uncertainty in the hope that someday they will be able to accept the benefit from respondent's love. . . . Based on this record, a ruling favoring the adoption is warranted.[40]

Thus, a broad best interests of the child analysis opened the door to full consideration of the potential benefits that the stepchildren would likely derive from the proposed adoption.[41]

As the opinion in *J.O.L.* makes clear, a stepparent adoption frequently involves certain benefits and minimal risk in the adoptive home for the child who already resides with the custodial parent and petitioning stepparent. Based on these special factors, Professor Homer Clark has expressed the view that the standards for waiving the consent of noncustodial parents and authorizing adoption should be relaxed in stepparent cases.

> A distinction should be made in [contested adoption] cases between the child who has been taken from his natural parents by a state . . . agency . . . and a child who has been . . . living with one natural parent and a stepparent. . . . In the [stepfamily] the child has very likely been integrated into a new family on a permanent basis and the risk . . . of shifting about between foster homes does not exist. In

---

40. *Id.* at 1076 (quoting trial court opinion).

41. In a similar fashion, the following Massachusetts adoption statute makes clear that the best interests of the child standard involves consideration of both the noncustodial parent-child relationship and the existing custodial placement.

> Whenever a petition for adoption is filed by a person having the care or custody of a child, the [parent's] consent . . . shall not be required if . . . the court hearing the petition finds that the allowance of the petition is in the best interests of the child . . . . [T]he court shall consider the ability, capacity, fitness and readiness of the child's parents . . . to assume parental responsibility and shall also consider the ability, capacity, fitness and readiness of the petitioners . . . to assume such responsibilities.

MASS. GEN. LAWS ANN. ch. 210, § 3(a), (c) (West 1987); *see also* Adoption of a Minor,

those circumstances the courts should be much more ready to terminate parental rights than in the foster care cases notwithstanding some contact between the natural parent and the child.[42]

The adoption laws in a number of states reflect this view, incorporating a preference for stepparent adoption, compared with other types of adoption, into the standards regulating the waiver of parental consent.[43] Thus, the Colorado Supreme Court provided the following explanation for the special priority assigned to the interests of stepchildren under state adoption law.

[P]ublic policy favors stepparent adoption because the adoption helps solidify an already existing family unit consisting of one of the biological parents. . . . [T]he modern trend is to make stepparent adoption easier.[44]

The court further explained that stepparent adoption is "made easier" than other adoptions by placing greater emphasis on the best interests of the stepchild.

The conflict between the best interests of the child and the natural parent's right to parenthood, which can arise *in a stepparent adoption* . . . is resolved in Colorado law by placing *primary importance on the best interests of the child.*[45]

---

389 N.E.2d 90, 91 (Mass. 1979) (applying this statute in a stepparent adoption proceeding).

42. CLARK, *supra* note 3, at 900–01. An opposing view has been expressed from time to time by judges who believe that the condition of stepchildren in the stepfamily is so excellent that no change is required to assure their welfare. For example, in a case involving a child whose biologic parents had never been married to each other, an appellate court in New York expressed skepticism about the benefit to be derived from formalizing the stepfamily through stepparent adoption.

[I]t is hard to see what appreciable benefit would inure to the child should the adoption be approved at this time . . . . No order of adoption will ever erase [the fact that the child had been born to unmarried parents] from his mind. Nor is an adoption required in order to give a home to a homeless boy or because of an absent, unknown or hostile parent. Although we recognize that the child presently enjoys the trappings and benefits of a family unit created by the natural mother and her spouse, it is also equally true that an order of adoption cannot by itself contribute or add anything to the quality of this child's upbringing.

In re Gerald G.G., 403 N.Y.S.2d 57, 60 (App. Div. 1978).

43. *See* HOLLINGER, *supra* note 2, at § 2.10[3][c](discussing grounds for dispensing with consent of noncustodial parent in stepparent adoptions).

44. E.R.S. v. O.D.A., 779 P.2d 844, 849–50 (Colo. 1989).

45. *Id.* at 850 (emphasis added).

Predictably, the greater weight placed on the interests of the child, at the expense of the noncustodial parent, will facilitate the approval of stepparent adoption petitions.

In summary, the best interests of the child standard is employed as an alternative to the parental unfitness standard in a number of state laws, as the basis for determining when stepparent adoptions can proceed without the consent of the noncustodial parent. In comparison to the traditional criterion of parental unfitness, the best interests standard enhances the authority of the courts to proceed with an adoption over the parent's objection, by eliminating the exclusive focus on the biologic parent-child relationship. In the stepfamily setting, there may be benefits involved in preserving the noncustodial parent-child status; on the other hand, there may be benefits for the child involved in formalizing the stepfamily. The courts that apply the best interests of the child standard in stepparent adoption cases must balance these competing considerations.

An alternative approach to identifying the circumstances under which stepparent adoption should be available is discussed later, in section VI. The alternative involves a new definition of adoption, wherein the child would be permitted to retain legal ties to both biologic parents while establishing new legal ties with an adoptive parent. Within this framework, the biologic parent-child relationship need not be terminated in order to free the child for adoption; thus, the standards for waiving parental consent to adoption and terminating parent rights are less critical. Although this model of adoption has received considerable scholarly attention, lawmakers have not been very open to this type of reform. As a result, the courts must continue the difficult process of choosing between the stepparent and the noncustodial parent in contested stepparent adoption cases. As discussed in this section, there is an observable trend in the law toward relying on the best interests of the child standard for this purpose.

IV. The Legal Consequences of Adoption

The parent-child relationship involves many benefits, rights, and obligations in diverse areas of the law, including support, inheritance, workers' compensation, state and federal taxation, tort and criminal law, surnames, and custody. The discussion of the stepparent-child relationship in other chapters of this book reveals that many important aspects of the legal parent-child status have not been extended to stepfamily relationships. In contrast, an adoption formalizes the stepparent-child relationship and guarantees its recognition for virtually all legal purposes.

Essentially, the legal effect of an adoption order is the child's removal from the biologic family and complete integration into the adoptive family. This model of adoption attempts to establish the adoptive family as a legal and social unit identical to the traditional, biologic family. For example, the

Arizona adoption statute describes the adoptive parent-child relationship as follows.

> Upon entry of the decree of adoption, the relationship of parent and child and all the legal rights, privileges, duties, obligations and other legal consequences of the natural relationship of child and parent shall thereafter exist between the adopted person and the adoptive petitioner the same as though the child were born to the adoptive petitioner in lawful wedlock. The adopted child shall be entitled to inherit real and personal property from and through the adoptive petitioner and the adoptive petitioner shall be entitled to inherit real and personal property from and through the adopted child . . . .[46]

The same Arizona statute is equally clear in describing the termination of the biologic parent-child relationship.

> Upon entry of the decree of adoption, the relationship of parent and child between the adopted person and the persons who were his parents just prior to the decree of adoption shall be completely severed and all the legal rights, privileges, duties, obligations and other legal consequences of the relationship shall cease to exist, including the right of inheritance, except that where the adoption is by the spouse of the child's parent, the relationship of the child to such parent shall remain unchanged by the decree of adoption.[47]

The final proviso affirms that the termination of family ties is restricted in the stepparent adoption context to the child's relationship with the noncustodial parent; the custodial parent-child relationship remains unaffected by the adoption.

This model of adoption, whereby all legal rights and obligations between the child and the noncustodial parent must be severed prior to stepparent adoption, is not without its critics. Especially in cases where the stepchild has established positive ties with the noncustodial parent and, perhaps, with other relatives, the sudden denial of these relationships may appear to be harsh and destructive for the child as well as the relatives.

These harsh effects have been mitigated somewhat by two doctrines that extend continuing recognition to the biologic family after adoption. First, in a number of states, limited rights of inheritance between the child and members of the noncustodial parent's family may survive the child's adoption by a stepparent. Second, and more recently, noncustodial parents and grandparents have sought continued rights of visitation with children

---

46. Ariz. Rev. Stat. Ann. § 8–117 (1989).
47. Id.

following their adoption in the stepfamily. These continuing economic and associational rights in the biologic family following stepparent adoption are discussed in the next two sections.

V. Inheritance Rights in the Biologic Family Following Adoption

Mutual rights of inheritance between parent and child, along with the parental support duty, constitute the major economic aspects of the parent-child relationship.[48] Under a strict model of adoption, these financial rights and duties in the biologic family are unquestionably terminated by an adoption decree. Indeed, it is likely that the relinquishment of support responsibility is a motivating factor in the decisions of many noncustodial parents who consent to the adoption of their children by a stepparent. Conversely, custodial parents and stepparents realize that adoption entails loss of the noncustodial parent as a source of child support and the assumption of full financial responsibility by the stepparent.[49]

Unlike the shifting of child support responsibility, which is a legal certainty following a stepparent adoption, there is no uniformity among the various state laws regulating inheritance rights between a child and his or her biologic relatives following adoption. Of course, every property owner is entitled to execute a will that leaves property at death to selected beneficiaries; by executing a valid will, the biologic relatives can always devise property to an adopted child. In the event that the property owner dies without a will, the inheritance laws in most states completely sever all rights between an adopted child and his or her biologic family. In other states, however, limited rights of inheritance survive a stepparent adoption.[50]

An early rationale for maintaining inheritance rights in the biologic family following a child's adoption reflected the common law view that inheritance laws must assure the passage of property through bloodlines.[51]

---

48. Of course, the parent-child relationship entails many economic consequences in addition to support and inheritance rights, in fields such as tort law, public benefit programs, taxation, insurance, employee benefits, and workers' compensation. As a general rule, the adopted child is severed from the biologic family for all of these purposes and integrated as a member of the adoptive family. *See* HOLLINGER, *supra* note 2, at § 12.06.

49. *See id.* at § 12.02 (discussing impact of adoption on child support obligations).

50. *See id.* at § 12.03 (discussing postadoption inheritance rights in both the biologic family and the adoptive family).

51. *See* Jan E. Rein, *Relatives By Blood, Adoption and Association: Who Should Get What and Why*, 37 VAND. L. REV. 711, 713 (1984) ("The traditional preoccupation with blood ties is now on the wane.").

Of course, the statutes reflecting this view apply evenhandedly to all types of adoption, not just stepparent adoptions. Frequently, limitations are imposed on the inheritance rights that are maintained between the adopted child and his or her natural family, for example, by limiting the categories of relatives still entitled to inherit.[52]

Other state statutes preserve inheritance rights only in the case of a stepparent adoption. For example, the Uniform Probate Code, which has been enacted in several states, takes this approach in the provisions governing the intestate distribution of property.

> An adopted individual is the child of his or her adopting parent or parents and not of his or her natural parents, but adoption of a child by the spouse of either natural parent has no effect on . . . the relationship between the child and that natural parent or . . . the right of the child . . . to inherit from or through the other natural parent.[53]

This limited continuation of inheritance rights in the biologic family is intended to reflect normal testamentary desires following a stepparent adoption; the Uniform Probate Code drafters assumed that most family members would wish to benefit adopted children in these circumstances.[54]

A further refinement of the inheritance rights that survive stepparent adoption appears in several state statutes that only apply if the adoption occurs after the noncustodial parent has died. The statutes preserve inheritance rights between the adopted stepchild and the surviving relatives of the deceased parent. In all other cases, where the noncustodial parent's rights have been terminated either by consent or by court order, no inheri-

---

52. In the states that permit continuing inheritance between the child and his or her biologic relatives following adoption, the various limitations on inheritance include restrictions on the types of property that may be inherited and restrictions on the categories of relatives who enjoy the benefit of these special provisions. For example, inheritance may be permitted by the child from the biologic relatives following adoption, but not vice versa. *See* Cathy J. Jones, *Stepparent Adoption and Inheritance: A Suggested Revision of Uniform Probate Code Section 2–109*, 8 W. NEW ENG. L. REV. 53, 66–76 (1986) (summarizing state laws governing inheritance).

53. UNIF. PROBATE CODE § 2–114, 8 U.L.A. 82 (Supp. 1992); *see also* HOLLINGER, *supra* note 2, at 12–16 n.26 (listing states that have enacted the Uniform Probate Code inheritance provision). An earlier version of this provision had established continuing inheritance rights for both the child and the noncustodial parent following a stepparent adoption; the current provision, quoted in the text, deleted the inheritance rights of the noncustodial parent and his or her relatives. *See* UNIF. PROBATE CODE § 2–109 (1969) (repealed).

54. *See* Jones, *supra* note 52, at 63–64 (citing Uniform Probate Code Proceedings).

tance rights survive in the biologic family.[55] This legislative distinction apparently assumes that meaningful ties between the adopted stepchild and his or her biologic relatives are more likely to exist if the child was freed for adoption due to the parent's death.

The various statutes described in this section extend limited inheritance rights between the stepchild and the noncustodial parent, whose economic relationship with the child is otherwise terminated in a stepparent adoption proceeding. These laws constitute an exception to the classic adoption model, wherein all legal connections between the biologic family and the child come to an end. The next section describes another important aspect of the traditional adoption model, the termination of custody and visitation rights in the biologic family, and the exceptions that have been recognized when adoption takes place in the stepfamily.

VI. Visitation Following Adoption

In recent years, considerable controversy has surrounded an important noneconomic issue in the adoptive stepfamily, namely, the rights of grandparents and noncustodial parents to visit with children following their adoption. The traditional model of adoption recreates the same type of parental autonomy in the adoptive family that is enjoyed in the intact biologic family. This includes the exclusive authority of adoptive parents to determine what persons will have access to the children. As a result, biologic relatives relinquish all legal rights to child custody and visitation following adoption; their access to the adopted children continues only to the extent permitted by the adoptive parents.

As in the intact natural family, this type of autonomy in the adoptive family is intended to promote the best interests of the child by establishing a single line of family authority. Competing policy concerns come into play, however, when children have enjoyed meaningful relationships with biologic family members prior to their adoption. In this situation, the interests of the child and the biologic relatives may be seriously harmed by an abrupt termination of established relationships. In recent years, many state legisla-

---

55. *See* HOLLINGER, *supra* note 2, at 12–19 n.36 (collecting statutes that permit inheritance by the adopted stepchild from relatives of the deceased noncustodial parent) and n.37 (collecting statutes that preserve reciprocal rights of inheritance between the adopted stepchild and relatives of the deceased noncustodial parent). The Alaska adoption statute follows the pattern of maintaining inheritance rights between the child and the relatives of a deceased parent following the child's adoption by a stepparent; in other cases, the statute confers discretion upon the adoption court to determine whether inheritance rights between the child and the natural relatives should survive the stepchild's adoption. *See* ALASKA STAT. § 25.23.130(a)(1) (1991).

tures and courts have balanced these competing interests by creating and enforcing grandparent visitation rights following adoption in the stepfamily. However, no similar postadoption rights have been established for parents.

Under the common law principle of parental autonomy, grandparents traditionally had no rights of access to their grandchildren, absent parental permission. During the 1970s and 1980s, state statutes were enacted that authorized the courts to grant grandparent visitation, contrary to the wishes of the child's custodian, according to a best interests of the child standard.[56] Initially, these grandparent visitation statutes failed to state whether visitation orders were intended to survive a subsequent adoption of the grandchild. Such a result would, of course, create an exception to the basic rule set forth in the adoption statutes, that adoption automatically severs all legal ties with the child's biologic family.

Although a number of state courts addressed this apparent conflict between the grandparent visitation statutes and the adoption laws, no uniform rule emerged from their decisions.[57] On the one hand, for example, the Alabama Supreme Court took the position that "adoption, like birth, creates legal relationships under which adoptive parents gain certain rights which pre-empt any visitation rights by natural parents or grandparents."[58] The court emphasized the "societal importance in the establishment of a permanent and stable family unit" and refused to recognize visitation rights for biologic relatives following adoption.

Conversely, the Illinois Supreme Court ruled that the best interests of the child standard in the Illinois grandparent visitation statute took priority over the provisions of the adoption statute that expressly severed all ties in the biologic family. Accordingly, autonomy in the adoptive stepfamily was just one factor to be considered in determining the best interests of the child.

> Of course the child's best interest is not entirely severable from the interests of the parents in a reconstituted family, and certainly the parents' attitude toward grandparental visitation is an important factor for the court to consider . . . . Such factors as the length and quality of the relationship between grandparents and child, [and] the

---

56. For general discussion of the grandparent visitation legislation, see CLARK, *supra* note 3, at 828–33; Edward M. Burns, *Grandparent Visitation Rights: Is It Time for the Pendulum to Fall?*, 25 FAM. L.Q. 59 (1991); Elaine D. Ingulli, *Grandparent Visitation Rights: Social Policies and Legal Rights*, 87 W. VA. L. REV. 295 (1984–85).

57. *See* HOLLINGER, *supra* note 2, at 13–86 to 13–87 nn.25–29 (collecting cases).

58. *Ex parte* Bronstein, 434 So. 2d 780, 783–84 (Ala. 1983). The state legislature subsequently enacted a statute that changed the law regarding grandparent visitation in Alabama. *See* Palmer v. Bolton, 574 So. 2d 44 (Ala. 1990) (discussing the new visitation statute).

child's need for continuity . . . must also be considered. These factors will certainly outweigh the opposition of parents that is based on the mere inconvenience to them of such visits, or on their animosity toward the child's other natural parent.[59]

This view of the Illinois Supreme Court, recognizing grandparent visitation following a stepparent adoption, was subsequently incorporated into a 1985 amendment to the Illinois visitation statute. The amended law provides that the "adoption of the minor by the spouse of a legal parent after termination of the parental rights of the other parent does not preclude granting visitation privileges to a grandparent."[60] Indeed, a number of state legislatures in recent years have addressed the conflict between grandparent visitation statutes and adoption statutes in the same manner.[61]

However, this legislative trend is not without exceptions. The Delaware grandparent visitation statute, for example, provides that "when the natural or adoptive parents of the child are cohabiting as husband and wife, grandparent visitation shall not be granted over both parents' objection."[62] The lack of uniformity among state legislatures and courts on this issue highlights the tension between the important policies that underlie grandparent visitation rights, on the one hand, and the goal of creating autonomy in the adoptive family, on the other.

Threats to autonomy in the adoptive family have come from natural parents, as well as grandparents, seeking visitation rights with adopted stepchildren. Prior to an adoption, the law protects rights of access between the child and both biologic parents. Furthermore, as described in section II, the adoption of a minor stepchild can take place only after the rights of the noncustodial parent have been legally terminated. When termination occurs and adoption follows, however, the natural parent retains no legal right to spend time with the child. Under the traditional adoption model, future

---

59. Lingwall v. Hoener, 483 N.E.2d 512, 516–17 (Ill. 1985); *see also In re C.G.F.*, 483 N.W.2d 803 (Wis. 1992), *cert. denied*, 113 S. Ct. 408 (1992).

60. Act of Sept. 20, 1985, ch. 40, 1985 ILL. LAWS 84–66 (amended 1991). The current Illinois visitation statute provides that grandparent visitation orders are not permitted if the child is adopted by "an individual or individuals who are not related to the biological parents of the child." *See* ILL. ANN. STAT. ch. 40, para. 607(b)(2)(B) (Smith-Hurd Supp. 1992).

61. *See* HOLLINGER, *supra* note 2, Appendix 1–A (collecting state statutes that authorize grandparent visitation following stepparent adoption); *see generally* Peter A. Zablotsky, *To Grandmother's House We Go: Grandparent Visitation After Stepparent Adoption*, 32 WAYNE L. REV. 1, 2 (1985) (expressing the view that "the best interest of the child is the only relevant and useful standard in analyzing grandparent visitation rights after stepparent adoption and that this consideration mandates that grandparent visitation rights not be automatically terminated upon stepparent adoption").

62. DEL. CODE ANN. tit. 10, § 950(7) (Supp. 1990).

contact between the biologic parent and the adopted child depends upon the willingness of the adoptive parents to permit it.

Recent efforts by noncustodial parents to establish the legal right to spend time with their children following a stepparent adoption, similar to the recently established rights of grandparents, have been largely unsuccessful. Proponents of visitation rights for noncustodial parents have urged that the best interests of children would be served, in some cases, by continuing relationships with both biologic parents following a stepparent adoption. According to this analysis, visitation rights would avoid the disruption of meaningful parent-child relationships and would also encourage more noncustodial parents to voluntarily consent to stepparent adoptions. These arguments have failed to persuade most judges, who fear that visitation rights for parents in this setting would pose an unacceptable threat to autonomy in the adoptive family.[63]

The Kentucky Court of Appeals expressed this viewpoint in *Jouett v. Rhorer* in the following manner.

> If a child is subject to the parental control of two families—which are alien and often hostile to each other—the resulting injuries to the child's emotions and future well-being are a matter of deep concern to the public. It is for this reason so many courts have held that public policy demands that an adoption shall carry with it a complete breaking off of old ties.[64]

The trial court in *Jouett* had granted a stepfather's petition to adopt the stepson with whom he had resided for two years and simultaneously denied the stepfather's request to terminate all rights of the natural father. The Court of Appeals reversed and remanded the case, with directions that the trial court was not authorized to preserve any rights for the natural father in the event of adoption by the stepfather: "[I]t seems clear to us the Legislature intended that the adoption of a child necessarily brings to an end all connections, legal and personal, with any natural parent."[65] In other words, the adoption court was required to choose between a continuing relationship with the father or an adoptive relationship with the stepfather.

The Supreme Court of Alaska reached a similar result in *In re J.J.J.*,[66] where it ruled that the trial court was not empowered to maintain visitation rights for the biologic father, whose consent to a stepparent adoption had been involuntarily waived. Unlike the Kentucky court in *Jouett*, however,

---

63. *See* Danny R. Veilleux, Annotation, *Postadoption Visitation by Natural Parent*, 78 A.L.R.4th 218 (1990 & Supp. 1992) (collecting cases).

64. Jouett v. Rhorer, 339 S.W.2d 865, 868 (Ky. 1960).

65. *Id.*

66. *In re* J.J.J., 718 P.2d 948 (Alaska 1986).

the Alaska Supreme Court expressly questioned the wisdom of this legislative policy.

> [T]he very problem now before us is an increasingly common occurrence, given the increase in divorce and remarriage in our society. . . .
>
> Well-known commentators have proposed "incomplete adoption" as a middle approach that would better accommodate the interests of both the stepparent and the noncustodial natural parent by giving . . . rights to each. However, the Alaska legislature apparently has not yet considered this modern approach that would allow the courts a more reasonable choice in deciding stepfamily cases. . . . We are therefore left with the harsh choices inherent in deciding between adoption or no adoption at all.[67]

The state legislature subsequently acted on the suggestion of the Alaska Supreme Court in *J.J.J.*, that another option should be available in stepparent adoption cases. The current Alaska statute, which is not limited to stepparent adoptions, contains the following provision: "Nothing in this chapter prohibits an adoption that allows visitation between the adopted person and that person's natural parents or other relatives."[68] This statute is unique in creating a clear authority for the adoption courts to order continuing visitation by natural parents whose rights are otherwise terminated.

In a handful of cases decided in other jurisdictions, the courts have been willing to assume this authority in the absence of such a legislative mandate. For example, in *In re Adoption of Children by F*,[69] a New Jersey court provided for future visitation rights between stepchildren and their natural father in an order authorizing an adoption by the stepfather. According to the court, this outcome was first proposed by the father, who took the position that he would consent to the stepfather's adoption of his children only if visitation rights were preserved. According to the court, several factors supported a waiver of the statutes that normally severed all ties between adoptive children and their parents. These factors included the noncustodial father's conditional consent, the mother's role in keeping the children separated from their father in the past, the wishes of the children, and the court's belief that their interests would be served by a continuing relationship with their father. In *Adoption of Children by F*, the court characterized the residual visitation rights between the father and his children as belonging to the children. Thus, the court appointed a guardian ad litem "whom the children may contact to enforce this right, should their

---

67. *Id.* at 951–52 (citation omitted).
68. ALASKA STAT. § 25.23.130(c) (1991).
69. *In re* Adoption of Children by F, 406 A.2d 986 (N.J. Super. Ct. 1979).

natural mother or adoptive father attempt in the future to frustrate their attempt to maintain a relationship with their natural father."[70]

It was unclear in this case whether the adoption could have proceeded absent the court's willingness to recognize visitation rights for the father. Of course, the father made it clear that he would not consent to the adoption without the assurance of future visitation. The New Jersey court never stated, however, whether the father's right to withhold consent could have been involuntarily terminated based on his past behavior. If, in fact, there were no grounds for taking this step, then no adoption would have taken place absent the judicial grant of visitation rights.

By way of contrast, the recognition of enforceable visitation rights for the noncustodial father was clearly *not* a necessary condition for the adoption of the stepdaughter in *In re Adoption of N.*[71] There, the father had lost his right to withhold consent to his daughter's adoption based upon the statutory ground of abandonment. Nevertheless, the New York adoption court determined that the child's interests would best be served by maintaining ties with her father following a stepparent adoption.

Adoption of N was an unlikely case for creating an exception to the general rule that adoption terminates the child's legal ties with the noncustodial parent, because no actual ties existed between the stepdaughter and her father at the time of her adoption. Indeed, the record revealed no contact between the father and child for a period of two years, although the father did provide explanations for this past behavior. The child had come to recognize her stepfather as a psychological parent and "appear[ed] to have forgotten [the father]."[72] Nevertheless, the court ordered bimonthly visits with the father in the presence of the natural mother or adoptive stepfather. Furthermore, the adoption court retained jurisdiction to resolve future differences between the parties. In many more compelling cases involving children who know and care for their noncustodial parents, the general rule denying postadoption visitation rights has foreclosed such a result.

Apparently, the concept of enforceable rights for the noncustodial father following adoption was first introduced in *Adoption of N* by the parties themselves. Prior to the adoption proceeding, the custodial mother and stepfather had contacted the father, advising him that they would permit his future visitation if he would consent to an adoption. Although the father initially rejected this offer, and the court later determined that the father's consent was unnecessary, the court itself pursued the issue of visitation. The opinion in *Adoption of N* recites that "the court consulted with both attorneys . . . and suggested a resolution which might satisfy all adult parties and be for the best interest of the child as well."[73] At the time the court

---

70. *Id.* at 989.

71. *In re* Adoption of N., 355 N.Y.S.2d 956 (Sur. Ct. 1974).

72. *Id.* at 958.

73. *Id.* at 959.

entered its order, the parties had agreed to the visitation arrangement contained therein.

The type of private agreement, initially proposed by the mother and stepfather in *Adoption of N*, presents a scenario which is not unique to that case. Especially when the custodial parent knows that the other parent has the legal right to veto a stepparent adoption, such a compromise arrangement may be the only avenue to formalizing the stepfamily. The terms of a private agreement may be attractive to the noncustodial parent as well, if visitation is assured at the same time that the legal support obligation shifts completely to the adoptive stepfamily.

With very few exceptions, the courts have refused either to incorporate such private agreements into orders of adoption or to enforce their terms. Of course, informal agreements involving postadoption visitation may regulate the parties' relationships for as long as all parties are willing to comply with such understandings. However, in the event that the adoptive parents breach their promise to allow visitation by the natural parent, the courts rarely enforce the agreement. According to the predominant view, neither the parties nor the court can waive the legislative rules requiring termination of the noncustodial parent's rights following a stepparent adoption.

An exception to this general rule appears in the opinion of the Maryland appellate court in *Weinschel v. Strople*.[74] There, the mother and father executed a separation agreement at the time of their divorce providing that the children would reside with their father in the future. The agreement also stated that the mother's visitation rights would continue in the event that the father's new wife adopted the children. When the stepmother subsequently adopted the children, both the mother's written consent and the formal adoption order expressly incorporated the terms of the separation agreement regarding continuing visitation.

The issue of enforceability arose two years later, when the father and adoptive mother attempted to terminate the mother's visits due to a scheduling conflict. The Maryland court in *Weinschel* held that the provision of the separation agreement preserving the mother's rights would be enforceable, as long as continuing visitation promoted the welfare of the children. The opinion carefully distinguished earlier cases in which adoption courts had not been permitted to preserve postadoption visitation rights, by emphasizing the absence of any agreement between the parties there.

The court considered the existence of a contract to be crucial, because the provision of the adoption statute terminating parental rights could only be waived with the consent of the adoptive parents.

---

74. Weinschel v. Strople, 466 A.2d 1301 (Md. Ct. Spec. App. 1983); *see also* Michaud v. Wawruck, 551 A.2d 738, 741 (Conn. 1988) (holding that enforcement of visitation agreement between natural parent and adoptive foster parents was consistent with the policy of the state adoption statutes).

> We read [the adoption statute] as protective of the adoptive parents and their status with the adopted child. It insulates the adoptive parent and child from attack by a disruptive, displeased, dissatisfied or disappointed natural parent. . . . The [statute], however, is a shield not a sword. It does not purport to mandate that the adoptive parents and the natural parents may not under any circumstance agree to visitation privileges by the natural parents . . . .[75]

Thus, the agreement in *Weinschel* was held to be specifically enforceable, under contract law principles, to the extent consistent with the best interests of the children.[76]

Unlike the Maryland court in *Weinschel*, most courts consider an adoption consent that allows visitation rights for the consenting parent to be legally ineffective; absent an unconditional consent, no adoption can take place. Furthermore, the consenting parent who executes an unconditional consent, with an informal understanding about future visitation, retains no enforceable visitation rights.[77] Thus, under the current laws governing adoption, families desiring to create enforceable visitation rights for the noncustodial parent at the time of a stepparent adoption are generally unable to do so. In the eyes of the law, only two options are available: adoption coupled with the complete termination of parental rights or no adoption at all.[78]

---

75. *Id.* at 1306.

76. A unique provision in the current Maryland adoption statute authorizes postadoption visitation agreements, although it does not address the issue of subsequent enforceability: "After the adoption, if it is in the child's best interest, the adoptive parent and a nonconsenting natural parent may agree to visitation privileges between the child and the natural parent or siblings." MD. CODE ANN., FAM. LAW § 5–312(e) (1991). This statute was not in effect at the time of the *Weinschel* decision.

77. The noncustodial parent who consents to a stepparent adoption based on an informal understanding about future visitation may subsequently attempt to set aside the adoption by alleging that no proper consent was given. The statute of limitations may prevent this type of challenge to the adoption after a relatively brief period of time. *See* HOLLINGER, *supra* note 2, Appendix 1–A (collecting state statutes). Of course, such a lawsuit is not a means to achieving the goal of adoption in the stepfamily coupled with enforceable visitation. *Compare In re* Adoption of Singer, 326 A.2d 275, 278 (Pa. 1974) (setting aside adoption because "[a]lthough [father's] signature did appear on the unconditional consent form, it was nevertheless conditioned upon the retention of [his parental] rights") *and* McLaughlin v. Strickland, 309 S.E.2d 787, 790 (S.C. Ct. App. 1983) (same), *with In re* S.O., 795 P.2d 254, 256 (Colo. 1990) (holding father's consent to be valid as an unconditional consent in spite of evidence that "the parties understood that [he] would continue to visit [the child] after the adoption").

78. *See In re* Adoption of Jennifer, 538 N.Y.S.2d 915, 919 (Fam. Ct. 1989) ("Since [the] Court has determined that it lacks the legal authority to order visitation for Jennifer and her father, as part of [the] adoption, or to accept a surrender . . .

The all-or-nothing approach to stepparent adoption has been criticized by many scholars who favor alternative rules that would enable the adoption courts to preserve visitation rights for the noncustodial parent.[79] According to this view, a more flexible approach would promote the interests of stepchildren by encouraging more noncustodial parents to consent to stepparent adoption and by permitting adopted stepchildren to maintain ties with both biologic parents in appropriate cases. As discussed fully in this section, this viewpoint has not been widely incorporated into the laws regulating stepparent adoption in the United States.[80] In this legal context, priority has generally been assigned to the competing value of autonomy in the adoptive family.

The issue of parental visitation poses a significant threat to the classic adoption model, which envisions a complete break with the child's biologic family. To date, the recognized exceptions to this model are the inheritance laws, discussed in the previous section, and the grandparent visitation statutes that contemplate grandparent visitation following a stepparent adoption. The additional creation of ongoing rights for the noncustodial parent would have a much greater theoretical and practical impact on the traditional model of the family following adoption. To date, few lawmakers have been willing to implement this type of reform.

---

conditioned on visitation, the only way to assure [the] child legally enforceable contact with her father is to deny the petition.").

79. *See, e.g.*, Brigitte M. Bodenheimer, *New Trends and Requirements in Adoption Law and Proposals for Legislative Change*, 49 S. Cal. L. Rev. 10 (1975); Susan F. Koffman, Comment, *Stepparent Adoption: A Comparative Analysis of Laws and Policies in England and the United States*, 7 B.C. Int'l & Comp. L. Rev. 469, 509–15 (1984); Judy E. Nathan, Note, *Visitation After Adoption: In the Best Interests of the Child*, 59 N.Y.U. L. Rev. 633 (1984); Linda F. Smith, *Adoption—The Case for More Options*, 1986 Utah L. Rev. 495, 547–57; *cf.* Katherine T. Bartlett, *Rethinking Parenthood As an Exclusive Status: The Need for Legal Alternatives When the Premise of the Nuclear Family Has Failed*, 70 Va. L. Rev. 879 (1984) (proposing a more flexible approach to the concept of legal parenthood in various contexts).

80. An alternative model for introducing flexibility into the all-or-nothing rule of traditional adoption law would confer a legal status other than parenthood upon the stepparent, while preserving the legal noncustodial parent-child relationship. Professor Brigitte Bodenheimer recommended this approach to striking a balance between the interests of parents and stepparents in an early law review article on this subject entitled *New Trends and Requirements in Adoption Law and Proposals for Legislative Change, supra* note 79, at 44–47. *See also* Koffman, *supra* note 79, at 502–09 (discussing formal, nonadoptive status available to stepparents under English law).

CHAPTER 10

Neglect and Abuse of
Stepchildren

I. Introduction

Parents and other adults who serve as the custodians of minor children have
the responsibility and authority to care for, educate, and discipline their
children. Under the doctrine of family privacy, the state confers wide discretion on parents to determine the manner in which their children will be
raised. At the same time, the state is ready to intervene in the family to
protect children when the responsible adults fail to provide adequate care.
Such a failure may result from affirmative acts, such as physical or sexual
abuse, or from acts of omission. Parental inaction or neglect can cause
harm, for example, when the child does not receive necessary food or shelter; medical, educational, or other care; emotional support; supervision; or
protection against third parties. Public awareness about the need for intervention in neglectful or abusive families has produced a heightened level of
state activity in this field during the second half of the twentieth century.[1]

The avenues for state intervention in the abusive or neglectful family
include both civil law and criminal law procedures. The child protection
laws in every jurisdiction establish public agencies that identify troubled
families and work to protect the children, primarily through treatment and
rehabilitation. However, when such efforts to preserve the family as a func-
tioning unit fail, the ultimate form of protective intervention is the permanent removal of children from the home and the legal termination of family
relationships.[2]

In contrast, the primary goals of the criminal justice system are the
deterrence and punishment of behavior that is unacceptable according to
societal norms. Abusive adults may be prosecuted under general laws defining assault, battery, homicide, and other crimes. In addition, special statutes have been enacted in every state that define specific crimes against

---

1. *See* Douglas J. Besharov, *"Doing Something" About Child Abuse: The Need to
Narrow the Grounds for State Intervention*, 8 HARV. J.L. & PUB. POL'Y 539, 539–45
(1983) (discussing legal history in the area of child abuse and neglect).

2. The legal standards for terminating the rights of parents without their consent are discussed in chapter 9.

children. When a troubled family first comes to the attention of the state, decisions must be made about whether to intervene in the family and the proper form of intervention under the civil or criminal laws. In reality, a clear preference exists for resolving the large majority of neglect and abuse cases in the child protection system.[3]

Not surprisingly, the laws that regulate neglectful and abusive conduct in the family are not restricted to biologic parents or other adults with formal custody. Thus, stepparents who assume informal responsibility for their stepchildren are subject to many of the same civil law and criminal law sanctions, when they misuse the authority that comes with their status. This chapter discusses the significance of the stepparent-child relationship in the civil and criminal laws that address the issues of neglect and abuse of children in the family.[4]

II. Civil Neglect and Abuse Laws

Child neglect and abuse most often come to the attention of the state through reports by teachers, doctors, relatives, or other persons who have contact with children outside the home. Indeed, statutes in every jurisdiction impose a duty on designated persons to report suspected abuse or neglect to child protection agencies.[5] The agencies, in turn, are responsible for investigating such allegations. If the child is determined to be in jeopardy, then an agency decision must be made about the best course to follow in order to protect the child in the future.

The less intrusive forms of intervention involve social, educational, and psychological counseling and services for family members, designed to help them function better as a family unit. In some cases, a child must be temporarily removed from the home until dangerous conditions improve. Ultimately, such conditions may provide the basis for permanently removing a child from the home and severing legal family ties. Even when family participation is voluntary, each of these forms of state intervention under the child protection laws involves a serious curtailment of privacy and autonomy in the family.

As a general rule, the decisions made by child protection agencies

---

3. *See* Douglas J. Besharov, *Child Abuse: Arrest and Prosecution Decisionmaking*, 24 Am. Crim. L. Rev. 315 (1987).

4. The topic of sexual abuse of stepchildren is reserved for discussion in chapter 11. Social scientists have observed that the rates of both physical and sexual abuse in stepfamilies are high, compared with the rates in biologic families. *See* Jean Giles-Sims & David Finkelhor, *Child Abuse in Stepfamilies*, 33 Fam. Rel. 407 (1984) (discussing various theories that explain why abuse occurs in the stepfamily).

5. *See* Besharov, *supra* note 1, at 542–45 (discussing enactment of state mandatory reporting laws in response to federal legislation during the 1960s).

are not affected by the fact that the child resides in a stepfamily. Furthermore, the focus of many state neglect and abuse laws is on the family or household in which the child resides, without regard to the particular composition of the household. For example, in 1988 the Maryland legislature enacted a subtitle to the Family Law Code, entitled Child Abuse and Neglect, which established a legal framework for protecting children within the family. Notably, abuse is defined in the Code as physical harm caused "by any household or family member."[6]

First, the Maryland statute identifies certain individuals, including educators, police officers, human service workers, and health practitioners, who must report suspected abuse to either the child protection agency or to a law enforcement agency.[7] Upon receiving a report, the agency must assess "the safety of the child, wherever the child is, and of other children in the household." Under certain circumstances, the child may be "removed from [the] household" without the consent of family members. Upon the child's return, the child protection agency must "establish proper . . . monitoring of the household . . . for at least three months."[8] The clear focus in this system is on the welfare of the child in the home; in the case of a stepfamily, the stepparent would necessarily be involved in the state's assessment of, and intervention in, the stepchild's household.[9]

The ultimate goal of the civil child protection system is to assure the child's welfare within the family. Toward this end, the adults in an abusive family may be required to participate in a treatment plan for improving conditions within the home. Although voluntary compliance with such a plan is common, the agency may seek a court order to coerce compliance by uncooperative family members.

For example, the New Hampshire Child Protection Act lists the conditions that may be imposed upon the "parents, guardian, relative [defined to include stepparents] or other custodian" of a neglected or abused child. These conditions include individual or family therapy or medical treatment, attendance by the child at a day care center, home visitation by a homemaker or parent aide, and abstention from "acts of commission or omission that tend not to make the home a proper place for the child."[10] Under this statute, the stepparent, along with other family members, may find himself

---

6. MD. CODE ANN., FAM. LAW § 5–701(b) (1991).

7. *Id.* §§ 5–704, –705, –708.

8. *Id.* § 5–706(b)(3), –713(a).

9. The broad definition of family relationships under the child neglect and abuse laws may also provide procedural protection for nontraditional family members. *See In re* Herron, 212 N.W.2d 474 (Iowa 1973) (ruling that stepfather was entitled to personal notice of neglect proceeding under statute requiring notice to "individual standing in loco parentis").

10. N.H. REV. STAT. ANN. § 169–C:19(I)(a) (1990).

or herself subject to a number of coercive measures designed to assure the stepchild's welfare.[11]

Of course, the state's authority to intrude on family autonomy in this manner is limited to situations where the level of care provided for children falls below minimum standards. In defining the minimally adequate level of care, difficult questions arise regarding the scope of acceptable behavior within families. For example, the use of physical force by parents against their children may be privileged if it falls within the bounds of proper corporal punishment, but the state will intervene if those boundaries are exceeded. The doctrines that define the scope of the parental privilege to discipline children, and their application in the stepfamily, are the subject of the next section.

III. The Right to Discipline Stepchildren

The custodial responsibilities of parents entail the right and duty to discipline their children, and the state permits parents to use corporal punishment for this purpose. This privilege of parents is an exception to the general rule that the use of physical force by one individual against another is unlawful. Still, any use of force that exceeds the lawful exercise of parental authority remains subject to criminal prosecution and also provides a basis for state intervention under the child protection laws. This section analyzes the scope of the parental discipline doctrine and its application to stepparents, especially in the criminal law context.

In the context of the civil child protection system, described in the last section, the parental privilege to discipline children may be raised as a defense when the state seeks to intervene in the family on the ground that a child has been physically abused.[12] For example, this defense was suc-

---

11. Not all of the state civil neglect and abuse statutes are drafted as broadly as the Maryland and New Hampshire provisions discussed in the text. For example, the Montana Code authorizes the court to order treatment and services in neglect and abuse proceedings only as to the "youth, parents, guardians or persons having legal custody." MONT. CODE ANN. § 41–3–403 (1991). *See also In re* Jodi B., 278 Cal. Rptr. 242 (Ct. App. 1991) (ruling that stepfather was not a "parent" entitled to receive remedial services prior to permanent removal of his stepchild into state custody).

12. The domestic authority doctrine has been recognized in the civil child protection system under both statutes and case law. *See, e.g.,* GA. CODE ANN. § 49–5–180(5)(A) (1990) (authorizing physical forms of discipline as long as there is no physical injury to the child); Mo. ANN. STAT. § 210.110(1) (Vernon Supp. 1993) (establishing immunity for discipline including spanking administered in a reasonable fashion); Natural Mother v. Hinds County Welfare Dep't, 579 So. 2d 1269 (Miss. 1991). The doctrine may also provide a defense to private lawsuits by children to recover damages from their parents for assault and battery. *See* RESTATEMENT (SECOND) OF TORTS §§ 147–51 (1965).

cessfully asserted in *Natural Mother v. Hinds County Welfare Department*,[13] a case involving the alleged abuse of two boys, eight and nine years old, in the home of their custodial mother and stepfather. In *Hinds*, the child protection agency first received a report from the noncustodial father that he had observed bruises on his sons' buttocks. In the child abuse proceeding initiated by the agency, the trial court determined that the bruises were a result of the stepfather's spanking the boys with a leather belt following their repeated misconduct at home and at school. The court ruled that this behavior constituted child abuse and ordered the welfare department to supervise the children in their home for a period of six months. The Mississippi Supreme Court reversed this decision, holding that the stepfather's behavior fell within the scope of proper discipline within the family. Notably, the court considered the stepfather to be entitled to the same disciplinary privilege as a natural parent.

The privilege of reasonable parental discipline, or "domestic authority," has been asserted also as a defense to criminal prosecutions for child abuse, assault, homicide, and other crimes against children. The Georgia statute defining the doctrine of criminal justification spells out the significance of parental authority in this context as follows.

> The fact that a person's conduct is justified is a defense to prosecution for any crime based on that conduct. The defense of justification can be claimed . . . [w]hen the person's conduct is the reasonable discipline of a minor by his parent or a person in loco parentis.[14]

Notably, the statutory defense is not limited to parents or other adults with formal custody; the Georgia statute expressly includes adults who stand in loco parentis to the disciplined child. Criminal justification statutes in a majority of states similarly include adults who have informally assumed the custodial responsibility for minor children.[15]

In a number of states, the parental privilege to discipline children is a matter of common law rather than statute. Here, the courts have followed the same pattern of broadening the class of protected adults beyond the legal custodians of children. For example, the stepfather in *Nicholas v.*

---

13. Natural Mother v. Hinds County Welfare Dep't, 579 So. 2d 1269 (Miss. 1991).

14. Ga. Code Ann. § 16–3–20(3) (1992).

15. *See, e.g.*, Ariz. Rev. Stat. Ann. § 13–403(1) (1989); Ark. Code Ann. § 5–2–605(1) (Michie 1987); Tex. Penal Code Ann. § 9.61(a)(1) (West 1974) (expressly including stepparents along with parents and others acting in loco parentis); Wayne R. LaFave & Austin W. Scott, Criminal Law 452 (2d ed. 1986) (discussing statutes that extend the right to discipline children to nonparents). *But see* La. Rev. Stat. Ann. § 14:18(4) (West 1986) (establishing justification defense only for "parents, tutors or teacher").

State,[16] who was charged with assaulting his stepson, was permitted to raise the defense of justification based on the existence of an in loco parentis relationship. Under the Alabama common law, "one standing in loco parentis [was entitled to] render reasonable chastisement to a child to the same extent as the parent."[17]

In *Nicholas*, the stepfather proved that he "had taken the child . . . into his family upon marrying the child's mother, and had in every way treated him as a member of the family."[18] Based on this record, the court concluded that he stood in loco parentis and was, therefore, entitled to invoke the justification defense. Nevertheless, the stepfather was convicted of assault and sentenced to prison for three months, because the beating of his preschool age stepson with a rubber belt for one hour did not constitute reasonable discipline. According to the reviewing court in *Nicholas*, "[t]he brutish nature of [his] conduct bespeaks the appropriateness of the [stepfather's conviction]."[19]

As in *Nicholas*, stepparents who reside with their stepchildren usually qualify to take advantage of the parental discipline defense under the statutory and common law rules defining eligible adults.[20] The more difficult issue in most cases, and the decisive issue in *Nicholas*, is whether the behavior of a parent or stepparent falls within the scope of conduct permitted under the parental authority doctrine. The task of defining a legal standard that draws a clear and just line between authorized force and criminal conduct in the family is a complex one. This process, which involves the balancing of family privacy interests against society's protective concern for children, is complicated by the absence of any societal consensus about the propriety of using even minimal force against children.[21] The courts and legislatures have attempted to accommodate the wide range

16. Nicholas v. State, 28 So. 2d 422 (Ala. Ct. App. 1946); *see also* Keser v. State, 706 P.2d 263 (Wyo. 1985) (holding that stepfather was entitled to invoke common law defense of justification in prosecution for child abuse).

17. *Nicholas*, 28 So. 2d at 425. The Alabama legislature subsequently codified the common law rule of justification applied in the *Nicholas* case. *See* ALA. CODE § 13A–3–24(1) (1982).

18. *Nicholas*, 28 So. 2d at 425.

19. *Id.*

20. *See* H.D. Warren, Annotation, *Criminal Liability for Excessive or Improper Punishment Inflicted on Child by Parent, Teacher, or One In Loco Parentis*, 89 A.L.R.2d 396 §§ 12–15 (1963 & Later Case Serv. 1993) (collecting cases in which stepparents and others standing in loco parentis asserted the defense of justification to criminal prosecution). *But see* Moreno v. State, 26 S.W.2d 652, 654 (Tex. Crim. App. 1930) ("We do not think the record indicates that the accused [stepmother] occupied such relation to the injured party that justified or excused her for the acts deemed violative of the [assault] statute.").

21. *See* Besharov, *supra* note 3, at 340 (describing conflicting viewpoints on the issue of corporal punishment).

of considerations and viewpoints in this context by developing standards that permit the use of force, but only in a manner that is consistent with the welfare of children.

The laws in this area employ two distinct factors to distinguish between proper discipline and criminal behavior. The first factor relates to the parent's purpose in using force against a child; the parent must not be motivated by selfish interests that are unrelated to the child's welfare. The second factor focuses directly on the nature of the parent's conduct; conduct that is too severe or harmful to the child is always unlawful. The Model Penal Code, for example, provides that the use of force against a child is justifiable only under the following circumstances.

> [T]he force is used for the purpose of safeguarding or promoting the welfare of the minor, including the prevention or punishment of his misconduct; and . . . the force used is not designed to cause or known to create a substantial risk of causing death, serious bodily injury, disfigurement, extreme pain or mental distress or gross degradation . . . .[22]

Thus, under the Code, the absence of either element—proper purpose or moderate behavior—would defeat a claim that the use of force against a child was justified.[23]

The difficult issue that arises under the second prong of the justification standard is identifying the point at which force becomes excessive. Admittedly, many of the reported cases present pictures of abuse in the family that clearly fall outside the scope of justifiable conduct under any humane standard.[24] Nevertheless, there is a place where a line must be drawn between acceptable discipline and excessive force, and individuals may draw the line in different places on the continuum of forceful behavior.[25]

In *State v. Singleton*,[26] an appellate court in Washington rejected the claim of a stepfather, convicted of assault, that the standard of acceptable behavior should be defined in terms of his own personal experiences as a severely disciplined child. The trial court had instructed the jury that state

---

22. MODEL PENAL CODE PART I § 3.08(1)(a), (b) (Official Draft and Revised Comments 1985).

23. *See, e.g.*, Commonwealth v. Moore, 395 A.2d 1328 (Pa. Super. Ct. 1978) (rejecting stepfather's defense of justification to charges of aggravated assault and child endangerment under the Model Penal Code).

24. *See, e.g.*, Bearden v. State, 294 S.E.2d 667, 668 (Ga. Ct. App. 1982) (holding that trial court properly refused to deliver a jury instruction regarding the stepfather's right to discipline his stepchild, because the "injuries sustained by the victim . . . could not be determined to have been reasonable discipline").

25. *See* Besharov, *supra* note 3, at 341.

26. State v. Singleton, 705 P.2d 825 (Wash. Ct. App. 1985).

law authorized the use of force that was "reasonable and moderate" and rejected a proposed jury instruction that "reasonable discipline is to be measured by the jury standing in the defendant's shoes." In affirming the stepfather's conviction, the appellate court emphasized that reasonableness in this context has an objective meaning that does not take into account the personal experiences or subjective standards of the defendant.

The stepfather in *Singleton* had barricaded his wife, his ten-year-old stepson, his fifteen-year-old stepdaughter, and another child in the living room of the family home for a period of two hours. During this time, he "struck each of the children in turn, spanking them with a heavy-duty leather glove and, allegedly, with a piece of kindling wood." Furthermore, the stepchildren "were beaten repeatedly for refusing to choose who would be beaten next."[27] Based on this record, the jury concluded that the force employed by the stepfather was immoderate and unreasonable, according to the objective standard of lawful parental authority, even if the defendant believed that he was operating within the realm of proper discipline.[28]

A clearly defined standard of lawful conduct in this field provides guidance to family members and to others who must judge their behavior.[29] One approach to clarifying the standard of acceptable conduct involves reliance upon certain objective factors. For example, the *Singleton* court observed that "the age, size, sex and physical condition of both child and parent, the nature of the child's misconduct, the kind of marks or wounds inflicted on the child's body [and] the nature of the instrument used for punishment" were objective factors employed by other courts for this pur-

27. *Id.* at 826.

28. According to the drafters' commentary about the Model Penal Code endangerment provision, earlier legal standards tended to emphasize the subjective element of purpose in determining when the use of force against a child was unlawful. *See* MODEL PENAL CODE PART I § 3.08, comment at 140 (Official Draft and Revised Comments 1985). Even under this type of subjective standard, however, the second element of the Code standard, involving the nature of the parent's conduct, could become relevant in proving that the parent had an evil purpose. *See, e.g.,* Cates v. State, 748 S.W.2d 9, 11 (Tex. Ct. App. 1987), *vacated on other grounds,* 776 S.W.2d 170 (Tex. Crim. App. 1989) ("The jury could infer, from the severity of the injuries, from the fact that the child was kept locked in a closet after the beating, and from the instrumentalities used to accomplish the beating, that [the stepfather] acted . . . intentionally.").

29. Stepparents have challenged the criminal statutes in this field on the constitutional ground that they are void for vagueness for failing to spell out the behavior that is unlawful. The courts generally have not been receptive to these claims by stepparents. *See, e.g.,* State v. Fulton, 657 P.2d 1197 (N.M. Ct. App. 1983); Keser v. State, 706 P.2d 263, 268 (Wyo. 1985). *See generally* Milton Roberts, Annotation, *Validity and Construction of Penal Statutes Prohibiting Child Abuse,* 1 A.L.R.4th 38 §§ 3, 4 (1980 & Supp. 1992) (collecting cases involving constitutional challenge on vagueness grounds).

pose.[30] Of course, this approach still involves the exercise of discretion in determining the weight to be assigned to each factor in a particular case.

The Washington legislature has enacted a statute that eliminates much of the discretion inherent in the traditional standards that define excessive force. The statute contains the following list of specific acts, which are presumed to be unlawful.

[T]he physical discipline of a child is not unlawful when it is reasonable and moderate and is inflicted by a parent . . . for purposes of restraining or correcting the child. . . .

The following actions are presumed unreasonable when used to correct or restrain a child: (1) Throwing, kicking, burning, or cutting a child; (2) striking a child with a closed fist; (3) shaking a child under age three; (4) interfering with a child's breathing; (5) threatening a child with a deadly weapon; or (6) doing any other act that is likely to cause and which does cause bodily harm greater than transient pain or minor temporary marks. . . . This list is illustrative of unreasonable actions and is not intended to be exclusive.[31]

Individuals making judgments about their own conduct or that of another person can assess whether the behavior falls into one of these statutory categories or is similar, in terms of moderation and reasonableness, to the listed items. The analysis of criminal responsibility does not end with this determination; the statute provides an opportunity to rebut the presumption of unlawfulness, based on all of the facts of a particular case. Still, the Washington legislature has attempted to clarify the traditional standards in this area by identifying specific types of behavior in the family that presumptively fall outside the protection of the parental discipline doctrine.

In summary, stepparents who serve a supervisory role in the stepfamily usually have the same rights as parents in disciplining children. Although there is no consensus in our society about the basic question of corporal punishment, the family privacy doctrine requires the state to defer to family members on this issue. Still, the privilege to discipline children by using force is limited by a standard of reasonableness. Not surprisingly, the line between reasonable discipline and excessive force is not always easy to draw. The person who makes the judgment about acceptable conduct in the first instance is the parent or stepparent, as he or she decides how to behave toward a child. When questionable conduct in the family comes to the attention of the state, third parties may second-guess this judgment, either in the process of administering the civil child protection laws or in the criminal justice system.

---

30. *Singleton*, 705 P.2d at 827.
31. Wash. Rev. Code Ann. § 9A.16.100 (West 1988).

IV. Criminal Violence

The use of excessive force against children in the family may simultaneously violate more than one criminal law.[32] First, there are general laws in every state that define crimes, such as assault, battery, and homicide; these laws apply to parents or stepparents whose use of force is not justified by the privilege to discipline their children. In addition, state legislatures have enacted a variety of special laws defining violent crimes against children within the family, such as cruelty, endangerment, and child abuse. The issue discussed in this section is whether stepparents are subject to prosecution for these additional crimes of violence against children in the family. As a general rule, these offenses have been defined broadly enough to encompass the stepparent who serves an informal custodial role in the stepfamily.

The decision of the state to prosecute the abusive parent or stepparent for a crime specifically relating to children may have significant consequences for the defendant. First, a greater stigma frequently attaches to a conviction for child abuse than to a conviction for assault. Second, the penalties for using improper force against children in the family may be greater than the penalties for similar crimes committed against a stranger.[33] Finally, the laws creating testimonial privileges between spouses, which may prevent one spouse from testifying against the other in certain criminal proceedings, are sometimes suspended in child abuse cases.[34] Thus, a prosecution for criminal child abuse may be more onerous for the defendant than a prosecution for assault or homicide based on the same behavior.

The state statutes that define special crimes of child abuse must identify the categories of adults to whom they apply; nationwide, there is no uniform treatment of this issue. Some state statutes provide that "any person" may commit the offense of child abuse, although the majority are

---

32. *See, e.g.*, Anderson v. State, 487 A.2d 294 (Md. Ct. Spec. App. 1985) (describing relationship between statutory crime of child abuse and common law crime of assault and battery).

33. *See* People v. Noble, 635 P.2d 203 (Colo. 1981) (rejecting equal protection challenge based on greater penalty for crime of child abuse versus crime of reckless manslaughter). In contrast, the Model Penal Code defines just one crime specifically relating to the maltreatment of children, a misdemeanor called "endangering the welfare of a child." The drafters' commentary acknowledges that a misdemeanor conviction may provide inadequate redress for child abuse in some cases, stating that "the case of serious injury as a result of child abuse can be reached under the Model Code provisions on assault and other forms of physical injury . . . ." MODEL PENAL CODE PART II § 230.4, comment at 454 (Official Draft and Revised Comments 1980).

34. *See, e.g.*, State v. Suttles, 597 P.2d 786 (Or. 1979) (holding that the state statute waiving the testimonial privilege of spouses in cases of child abuse extended to criminal as well as civil proceedings).

limited to adults with a special relationship to the abused child. Whatever the statutory designation, stepparents who assume de facto custodial responsibility for their stepchildren are generally subject to prosecution when they exploit their status in the stepfamily.

The first category of abuse statutes, which do not expressly limit the individuals who may commit the offense,[35] is illustrated by the Georgia law applied in the case of *Morrow v. State*.[36] There, the defendant stepfather was convicted for beating his stepchild, under a statute providing that "[a]ny person commits cruelty to children when he maliciously causes a child under the age of 18 cruel or excessive physical or mental pain."[37] In spite of the unqualified statutory reference to "any person," the defendant appealed his conviction on the ground that this statute "does not apply to stepparents who do not have legal custody of the child."[38] The *Morrow* court rejected this narrow interpretation of the phrase "any person" and affirmed the stepfather's conviction.

Currently, the majority of state statutes defining child abuse limit criminal responsibility to persons with a special relationship to the abused child. Beyond the categories of parents and other adults with formal legal custody, the various statutory formulas include "any person [with] control and custody,"[39] a "household member,"[40] "a person [with the] care of a dependent,"[41] a "person who has . . . responsibility for supervision of a child,"[42] and a person standing in loco parentis to the child.[43] The purpose of such limitations is to establish a special liability when the adult standing in a position of power and trust toward a child abuses that status. As a general rule, these statutory terms have been construed broadly to include stepparents and others who assume an informal custodial role in the family.[44]

---

35. *See, e.g.*, Ariz. Rev. Stat. Ann. § 13–3623 (Supp. 1992); Ark. Code Ann. § 5–27–204 (Michie 1987); Colo. Rev. Stat. § 18–6–401 (1986 & Supp. 1992); La. Rev. Stat. Ann. § 14:93 (West 1986); Utah Code Ann. § 76–5–109 (Supp. 1993).
36. Morrow v. State, 271 S.E.2d 707 (Ga. Ct. App. 1980); *see also* Long v. State, 681 S.W.2d 840 (Tex. Ct. App. 1984).
37. *Id.* at 708. The Georgia cruelty to children statute is currently codified in Ga. Code Ann. § 16–5–70(b) (1992).
38. *Morrow*, 231 S.E.2d at 708.
39. Conn. Gen. Stat. Ann. § 53–20 (West 1985).
40. Haw. Rev. Stat. § 709–906(1) (1985).
41. Ind. Code Ann. § 35–46–1–4 (Burns 1985); N.C. Gen. Stat. §§ 14–318.2 & 318.4 (1986).
42. Md. Ann. Code art. 27, § 35A (1992); Mont. Code Ann. § 45–5–622 (1991).
43. Ohio Rev. Code Ann. § 2919.22(A) (Baldwin Supp. 1992).
44. *See* People v. Parris, 267 N.E.2d 30 (Ill. App. Ct. 1971); Shoup v. State, 570 N.E.2d 1298 (Ind. Ct. App. 1991) (holding that criminal neglect statute, limited to "person[s] having the care of a dependent," included stepparent who assumed responsibility for child's care and discipline); State v. Smith, 485 S.W.2d 461 (Mo. Ct.

For example, the defendant stepfather in *People v. Parris*[45] was convicted of cruelty to children under the following statute, which limited criminal responsibility to individuals who have the "legal control" of children.

> Any person who shall wilfully and unnecessarily expose to the inclemency of the weather, or shall in any other manner injure in health or limb, any child, apprentice, or other person *under his legal control*, shall be fined not exceeding $500, or imprisoned in the penitentiary for a term of not less than one year and not exceeding five years.[46]

The defendant appealed his conviction on the ground that, as a stepparent, he did not have "legal control" of his stepchildren. The appellate court in *Parris* rejected this argument and ruled that the stepfather's in loco parentis status in the stepfamily satisfied the statutory custody requirement.

> They all lived under the same roof, and ate at the same table from a common source of support. . . . [The stepfather] certainly exercised the parental right of discipline over his stepchildren. . . . [H]e was head of the household and stood in the position of in loco parentis . . . to his stepchildren. As such he had them in his "legal control" within the meaning of the statute.[47]

While affirming the conviction, the appellate court remanded the *Parris* case for resentencing, on the ground that the stepfather's sentence of imprisonment for one to five years was too severe. The stepfather had been convicted for beating his four young stepchildren after they disobeyed his instructions about how to behave on a particular occasion. The court observed that the incident appeared to be an isolated one, for which the stepfather was contrite, and that his imprisonment would cause the family to lose its breadwinner. Based on this record, the appellate court concluded that a fine and probation would be a more appropriate punishment.[48]

App. 1972) (holding that criminal neglect statute, limited to persons with "care and control of" children, would include stepfather if jury found that he stood in loco parentis to child); Lovisi v. Commonwealth, 188 S.E.2d 206 (Va. 1972) (holding that cruelty to children statute, limited to "any person employing or having the custody of any child," included stepparent who stood in loco parentis to child). *See generally* Annotation, *Who Has Custody or Control of Child Within Terms of Penal Statute Punishing Cruelty or Neglect by One Having Custody or Control*, 75 A.L.R.3d 933 (1977 & Supp. 1992) (collecting cases).

45. People v. Parris, 267 N.E.2d 30 (Ill. App. Ct. 1971).

46. *Id.* at 42 (emphasis added). The statute is currently codified in Ill. Ann. Stat. ch. 23, para. 2368 (Smith-Hurd 1988).

47. *Parris*, 267 N.E.2d at 42.

48. *Id.* at 43.

The Illinois law applied in *Parris* included the supervisory or custodial relationship between abuser and child as an element of the crime of cruelty to children. The defendant's supervisory or custodial status may have additional consequences under other criminal laws governing child abuse.[49] For example, the Wisconsin abuse statutes provide, in an open-ended manner, that "whoever . . . causes great bodily harm" to a child may commit child abuse. However, if the person convicted of abuse was a "person . . . responsible for the [child's] welfare," then the sentence imposed may be enhanced by as much as five years of imprisonment.[50] Here, the offense may be committed by any person, but it is more abhorrent when the defendant enjoyed a special relationship with the victim. Predictably, stepparents who stand in loco parentis in the stepfamily would be included in the designation of "person[s] responsible for the child's welfare" under this sentencing statute.

A final consequence, which depends upon the existence of a special supervisory relationship, relates to the type of conduct that is deemed to be abusive. In a number of state statutory schemes, the failure to act to protect a child may be a crime in certain circumstances. As a general rule, the existence of a special relationship between adult and child is a necessary element of this type of criminal liability. The doctrine of omission, and its application in the stepfamily, are discussed in the next section.

V. Criminal Neglect

The most common forms of criminal child abuse involve affirmative acts, such as assault, battery, or sexual abuse. Maltreatment of children in the family can also involve acts of omission by the adults who are responsible for their care and protection. The neglect of children in their homes, involving inadequate nourishment, shelter, medical care, education, emotional support, supervision, or protection from danger, is a common basis for state intervention within the civil child protection system. In contrast, criminal prosecutions based on neglect or the failure to act are rare, especially when the negligent adult is not the legal custodian of the children.

As described in this section, lawmakers have generally been more cautious about imposing criminal responsibility for acts of omission than for affirmative acts of child abuse. Still, parents and other adults with special custodial responsibility for dependent children have been held accountable for the basic aspects of their welfare. The custodial relationship gives rise to affirmative duties toward the child, the breach of which may constitute the crime of child abuse.

---

49. Other child abuse statues establish several degrees of liability, reserving the highest degree for abusive adults who have a special relationship with the victim. *See, e.g.,* ARK. CODE ANN. §§ 5–27–203 (Michie 1987).

50. WIS. STAT. ANN. § 948.03 (West Supp. 1992).

According to a recent survey, thirty-five states expressly include acts of omission in the definition of criminal child abuse.[51] Elsewhere, courts have sometimes construed abuse laws broadly to include the failure to act.[52] Where lawmakers have defined child abuse to include acts of omission as well as affirmative acts, the same category of responsible adults may be designated as to both types of behavior.[53] More often, the category of adults who may be prosecuted for their failure to act to protect a child is defined more narrowly.

For example, the Texas statute defining the offense of injury to a child applies to "any person," but the provision dealing with injury resulting from omission lists only those "persons with the care, custody or control" of the child.[54] Similarly, in Georgia, the offense of cruelty to children may be committed by "any person" who maliciously causes physical or mental pain; on the other hand, only a "parent, guardian, person supervising the child, or person having immediate charge or custody" may be responsible for "willfully depriv[ing] the child of necessary sustenance."[55] Notably, the Mississippi child abuse statute expressly includes stepparents in a provision defining a specific type of negligent behavior, namely, the condonation of abuse by another adult. Under the Mississippi provisions, "any parent, guardian, or other person" may be liable for affirmative acts of abuse, but only the "parent, guardian, custodian, stepparent, or person who lives in the household" may be criminally responsible for condoning abuse by another adult.[56] Finally, the Ohio statute regarding child endangerment provides that "no person" shall affirmatively abuse a child; whereas "no person who is the parent, guardian, custodian, person having custody or control or person in loco parentis shall create a substantial risk to the health or safety of a child, by violating a duty of care."[57] These statutes illustrate the premise

---

51. *See* Anne T. Johnson, *Criminal Liability for Parents Who Fail to Protect*, 5 LAW & INEQ. J. 359, 365–68 (1987).

52. *See, e.g.*, Pope v. State, 396 A.2d 1054 (Md. 1979); State v. Willoquette, 385 N.W.2d 143 (Wis. 1986). Beyond liability under specific child abuse statutes, the parent's failure to act to safeguard a child's welfare may constitute the more general crime of criminal negligence or negligent homicide. *See, e.g.*, Commonwealth v. Clark, 471 N.E.2d 349 (Mass. 1974); Johnson, *supra* note 51, at 370.

53. *See, e.g.*, IDAHO CODE § 18–1501 (1987) (establishing liability for "any person" who "causes or permits" a child to suffer); IOWA CODE ANN. § 726.6 (West Supp. 1993) (establishing liability for both affirmative acts and acts of omission committed by "the parent, guardian or person having custody or control over a child").

54. TEX. PENAL CODE ANN. § 22.04 (West Supp. 1993); *see also* UTAH CODE ANN. § 76–5–109(2) (Supp. 1993).

55. GA. CODE ANN. § 16–5–70 (1992).

56. MISS. CODE ANN. §§ 97–5–39, –40 (Supp. 1992).

57. OHIO REV. CODE ANN. § 2919.22 (Baldwin Supp. 1992); *see also* ARIZ. REV. STAT. ANN. §§ 13–3619, –3623 (1989 & Supp. 1992).

that criminal responsibility is frequently defined more narrowly for acts of omission. Nevertheless, many of the omission statutes are still broad enough to include stepparents who stand in loco parentis in the stepfamily.

The explanation for the restricted scope of responsibility for acts of omission, as contrasted with affirmative acts of child abuse, relates to a basic principle of criminal responsibility. As a general rule, the failure to act can lead to criminal liability only if an affirmative legal duty has been breached as a result of the omission.[58] This limitation reflects the philosophical view that laws requiring a person to perform specified acts are more intrusive on individual autonomy than are criminal restraints on affirmative activity.[59]

Thus, the existence of an affirmative duty to protect the child is an essential element of crimes involving the neglect of children. The Model Penal Code, which has been enacted in several states, expressly incorporates this principle into the offense of endangering the welfare of children, which is defined as "knowingly endanger[ing] the child's welfare by violating a duty of care, protection or support."[60] Clearly, parents and other adults with the formal custody of children owe affirmative duties, under both common law and state statutes, to act to safeguard their children's welfare. The neglect of these duties may give rise to criminal liability; for example, parents have been successfully prosecuted for failing to obtain necessary medical care for their children or for failing to prevent abuse by other adults.[61] Before criminal responsibility can be similarly imposed upon a stepparent, it must be established that the defendant owed a legal duty to protect the child, which was breached by the failure to act.[62]

The importance of an underlying legal duty to act is starkly illustrated

---

58. *See* LaFave & Scott, *supra* note 15, at 203–07; Model Penal Code Part I § 2.01(3) (Official Draft and Revised Comments 1985) ("Liability for the commission of an offense may not be based on an omission unaccompanied by action unless . . . the omission is expressly made sufficient by the law defining the offense; or . . . a duty to perform the omitted act is otherwise imposed by law.").

59. *See, e.g.*, Paul H. Robinson, *Criminal Liability for Omissions: A Brief Summary and Critique of the Law in the United States*, 29 N.Y.L. Sch. L. Rev. 101, 104 (1984).

60. Model Penal Code Part II § 230.4 (Official Draft and Revised Comments 1980).

61. *See, e.g.*, Roberts, *supra* note 29, §§ 12(b), 21 (collecting criminal cases involving acts of omission).

62. In Stehr v. State, 139 N.W. 676 (Neb. 1913), the Supreme Court of Nebraska affirmed the conviction of a stepfather for manslaughter, based on his failure to obtain medical care for his stepson, without discussing the issue of legal duties associated with his status as a stepparent. The child's mother, who was also with the child when he became ill and died, was not prosecuted for her inaction. The likely explanation for placing the burden to act on the stepfather in this case relates to the sexist view of marriage under the common law, whereby the husband was regarded as assuming many of his wife's legal responsibilities.

by the reversal of the defendant's conviction for child abuse in *Florio v. State.*[63] There, the defendant was the "live-in boyfriend" of the deceased child's mother and had assumed responsibility as "babysitter, disciplinarian and caretaker" of the child.[64] The state alleged that he had criminally injured the child "by failing to seek and provide proper medical care for [the child] and by failing to give [him] adequate nutrition . . . and by failing to move and reposition [him]."[65] The relevant Texas statute provided that "a person" commits the offense of injury to a child "if he . . . by act or omission" causes physical or mental injury to a child. Following a jury trial, the defendant was convicted of this offense and sentenced to sixty years in prison. On appeal, the *Florio* court reversed the conviction, because the defendant owed no independent statutory duty to protect the child. According to the court, under general principles of criminal responsibility in Texas, a person must have a *statutory* obligation to act before criminal liability can be imposed for the failure to act. The court found that no Texas statute imposed any responsibility for children upon individuals such as the defendant. Furthermore, the statement in the child abuse statute itself, that the failure of "a person" to act may constitute a crime, had not created the requisite underlying duty.

Following the decision in *Florio*, the Texas legislature amended the child abuse statute by imposing an express duty to act on the limited category of adults who assume the "care, custody, or control of a child." The legislature added the following provision.

> An omission . . . is conduct constituting an offense under this section if: (1) the actor has a legal or statutory duty to act; or (2) the actor has assumed care, custody, or control of a child . . . .[66]

Under this provision, a conviction would be possible on the facts of the *Florio* case, based on the defendant's failure to aid the child with whom he resided, if a court determined that he had indeed "assumed care, custody, or control of [the] child."

In other states, the affirmative duty to act can be derived from sources other than a state statute. For example, the following commentary to the Model Penal Code child endangerment provision, which has been enacted in several jurisdictions, refers to several types of nonstatutory obligations.

> [T]he duty itself need not be stated in the penal code but may arise from contractual obligation, from settled principles of tort or family law, or from other legal sources. . . . The objective is to confine crim-

---

63. Florio v. State, 784 S.W.2d 415 (Tex. Crim. App. 1990).
64. *Id.* at 417.
65. *Id.* at 416.
66. Tex. Penal Code Ann. § 22.04(b) (West Supp. 1992).

inal punishment for endangering the welfare of children to . . . acts violative of some settled obligation springing from the supervisory relationship of actor to child.[67]

Thus, in a case like *Florio*, the Model Penal Code would impose criminal liability if the defendant owed a duty toward the neglected child arising from their relationship to each other. The duty in this setting could be created either by a state statute or by common law.

The common law in loco parentis doctrine is a potential source of the prerequisite duty to act, in cases where stepparents jeopardize the welfare of children in their care through their acts of omission. The doctrine provides that the adult who voluntarily assumes a parental role stands in the place of a parent in the eyes of the law. Of course, as discussed at length throughout this book, the rights and duties of parenthood are assigned to stepparents and other adults in a very selective fashion, and the in loco parentis status is not the full legal equivalent of parenthood. The issue here is whether the affirmative duty to safeguard a child's welfare is one legal responsibility that should be recognized when a stepparent or other adult assumes informal custodial authority in the family.

The highest court in Maryland has affirmed the existence of such an affirmative duty on the part of adults who stand in loco parentis to minor children. In *Pope v. State*,[68] the court construed the state child abuse statute, which referred to "[a]ny parent, adoptive parent, or other person who has the permanent or temporary care or custody or responsibility for the supervision of a minor child."[69] According to the court, the statute applied to two categories of adults in addition to parents and formal custodians: those who stood in loco parentis to abused children, and those to whom parents had temporarily delegated custodial responsibility.

The conviction of the defendant in *Pope* was reversed because her relationship to the abused child, who died as a result of his mother's beating, did not fall into either of these statutory categories. Joyce Lillian Pope had opened her home to the mother and her three-month-old baby on a temporary basis on a Friday night. Thereafter, she helped to care for the child until the mother killed him, in the defendant's presence, on Sunday morning. The court conceded that the defendant's failure to intervene to stop the abusive conduct, as well as her failure to seek medical care in a timely fashion, were acts of omission that fell within the definition of "abuse" in the statute.[70] Nevertheless, Joyce Lillian Pope was not criminally

---

67. MODEL PENAL CODE PART II § 230.4, comment at 450–51 (Official Draft and Revised Comments 1980).

68. Pope v. State, 396 A.2d 1054 (Md. 1979).

69. *Id.* at 1060.

70. Although the Maryland child abuse statute did not expressly refer to acts of omission, the court had earlier construed the law to include omissions in State v. Fabritz, 348 A.2d 275 (Md. 1975).

responsible for her failure to act, because her role in caring for the child did not constitute the "temporary care or custody or responsibility for the supervision of" the deceased child.

Thus, the court's construction of the abuse statute relieved the defendant in *Pope* from criminal responsibility for her acts of omission. At the same time, the court clearly established responsibility for adults, including stepparents, who have assumed a more significant role in the child's life. In other words, a stepparent standing in loco parentis who failed to safeguard the welfare of the stepchild, in circumstances like those in the *Pope* case, would be criminally liable under the Maryland abuse statute.

There are very few reported cases involving the prosecution of stepparents and other nonparents for their failure to act to protect children in their care.[71] The reported opinions, including those in *Florio* and *Pope*, reveal a degree of judicial reluctance to convict adults who do not have formal legal custody for neglecting to care for children. This attitude reflects the more general conservatism, discussed earlier, about imposing criminal liability for inaction in the absence of a clear legal duty to act. Still, the Maryland Court of Appeals in *Pope* believed that stepparents who play an in loco parentis role in the stepfamily may be regarded as assuming the affirmative duty to protect their stepchildren. According to this analysis, the stepparent who shares actual responsibility with the custodial parent for the care of a stepchild must act to safeguard the child from harm. The failure to do so may result in criminal liability.

---

71. *See* Roberts, *supra* note 29, §§ 21–22 (collecting cases).

CHAPTER 11

Regulation of Sexual Activity

I. Introduction

The law decisively forbids sexual activity between close relatives, such as siblings or parents and children, in the biologic family.[1] This ban on sexual activity is intended to promote the well-being of the family and its members and the larger society as well. Typically, the legal regulation of sexual behavior in the family takes two forms. First, the state statutes governing marriage deny any recognition to attempted marriages between close relatives. Second, a variety of criminal laws punish attempted marriages, as well as sexual activity outside of marriage, between close relatives. This chapter discusses the extent to which steprelatives, especially stepparents and their stepchildren, are included in these civil and criminal regulations.

II. Historical Background

In earlier centuries, steprelatives were included in the civil and criminal laws that regulated incestuous relationships. First, in pre-Reformation England, the Catholic Church developed a set of marriage restrictions that applied both to persons related by blood and persons related by marriage.[2] For example, marriage between brothers and sisters was forbidden; marriage between stepbrothers and stepsisters was similarly forbidden because they stood in a close relationship of affinity created by the marriage between their parents. According to English legal historians Sir Frederick Pollock and Frederic Maitland, the rules regarding steprelatives and relatives-in-law reflected "the axiom that the sexual union makes man and woman one flesh. All my wife's . . . blood kinswomen are connected with me by way of affinity."[3]

Selected materials from Chapter 11 appear in an article by the author entitled *A Legal Definition of the Stepfamily: The Example of Incest Regulation*, which appears in Volume 7 of the BRIGHAM YOUNG UNIVERSITY JOURNAL OF PUBLIC LAW.

1. *See generally* GEORGE THORMAN, INCESTUOUS FAMILIES 10–15 (1983) (defining incest in the biologic family).

2. *See* HOMER H. CLARK, JR., THE LAW OF DOMESTIC RELATIONS IN THE UNITED STATES 21–24 (2d ed. 1988).

3. 2 FREDERICK POLLOCK & FREDERIC MAITLAND, THE HISTORY OF ENGLISH LAW 388 (2d ed. reissued 1968); *see also* SYBIL WOLFRAM, IN-LAWS & OUTLAWS:

Subsequently, during the reign of Henry VIII, statutes were enacted in England that significantly narrowed the scope of the ecclesiastical marriage restrictions by reducing the number of forbidden relationships.[4] However, these sixteenth-century statutes continued the evenhanded treatment of persons related by blood and persons, including steprelatives, who were related to each other by marriage.[5]

Derived from the laws of England, the early marriage laws in the United States included the prohibition on marriage between persons related by affinity. As a result, when steprelatives attempted to marry, their unions were regarded as void and of no legal effect. Disapproval was also expressed in laws that criminalized such relationships; attempted marriages or sexual activity outside of marriage between close steprelatives was subject to criminal prosecution.[6]

As time passed, the traditional restrictions on marriage and sexual activity between steprelatives were lifted in many states, as lawmakers reexamined the historical and religious assumptions on which they were premised. Currently, only a dozen states invalidate the marriage between a stepparent and his or her stepchild, contracted after the stepparent's prior marriage to the stepchild's natural parent has come to an end. Similarly, in many of the modern criminal statutes that regulate sexual activity in the family, stepfamilies are not regulated as strictly as biologic families.

The historical development in this field and the inconsistency among modern state laws invite inquiry into the reasons for retaining or rejecting the historical ban on sexual relationships between steprelatives. The following section describes the various justifications for the legal regulation of sexual conduct in the family and their applicability in the stepfamily context.

III. Policy Analysis

The legal analysis of stepfamily relationships has been influenced by the multiple theories propounded by sociologists and legal scholars to justify the general regulation of incestuous family relationships.[7] Ironically, the

---

KINSHIP AND MARRIAGE IN ENGLAND 16–20 (1987) (exploring the broad concept of relationship by affinity in the early English marriage laws).

4. *See* Concerning Precontracts of Marriages, and Touching Degrees of Consanguinity, 32 Hen. 8, ch. 38 (1540) (Eng.).

5. A complete discussion of the sixteenth-century English incest statutes appears in WOLFRAM, *supra* note 3, at 23–30.

6. *See* MODEL PENAL CODE PART II § 230.2, comment at 400–01 (Official Draft and Revised Comments 1980) ("In general, moreover, the law of incest enforced these civil limitations by criminal sanctions.").

7. *See generally* WOLFRAM, *supra* note 3, at 161–85 (discussing historical development of the various theories that explain incest regulation).

various theories point in divergent directions on the issue of stepfamily restrictions. For example, one traditional justification involves the biomedical concern that the offspring of close relatives will suffer abnormally high rates of recessive genetic abnormalities. This analysis, which is premised on the common genetic makeup of close biologic relatives, obviously has no application to persons, such as steprelatives, who are not related by blood.[8] In contrast, a second explanation draws upon religious history, viewing the current laws as an extension of earlier ecclesiastical doctrines.[9] Under this analysis, the clear religious tenets that outlawed sexual and marital relationships between steprelatives over the centuries continue to have modern vitality.

Another theory relies upon community norms as the source and rationale for laws regulating incestuous relationships.[10] For example, most people would predictably disapprove of the marital or sexual relationship established between a parent and his or her adult child; the ban on such relationships reflects this viewpoint. The pertinent inquiry relating to relationships of affinity under this theory is whether the same public disapproval would extend to the union between a stepparent and stepchild. The response to the question may well be, "it depends." If the stepparent had assumed a parenting role during the stepchild's minority, then the subsequent marriage or sexual relationship between the two would arguably offend community norms about incestuous behavior. On the other hand, if no real family ties had ever existed between them, then a subsequent sexual relationship between an individual and the adult child of his or her former spouse would be more likely to escape criticism.

Another important model for understanding the regulation of marriage and sexual relationships between close relatives emphasizes the stability of the family.[11] According to this theory, the incest ban strengthens and stabilizes family relationships by removing the potential for sexual relationships and jealousy within the family household. A related social benefit accrues

---

8. *See* ALA. CODE § 13A–13–3 commentary at 558 (1982) (noting that the "notion of 'tainting of blood' . . . does not apply to . . . stepchildren and adopted children," who are nevertheless included in the criminal incest statute); Carolyn S. Bratt, *Incest Statutes and the Fundamental Right of Marriage: Is Oedipus Free to Marry?*, 18 FAM. L.Q. 257, 267–81 (1984) (criticizing the genetic justification for incest regulation); WOLFRAM, *supra* note 3, at 138–47 (discussing the relationship between the genetic theory and the decline of regulation in the stepfamily).

9. *See* MODEL PENAL CODE PART II § 230.2, comment at 402 (Official Draft & Revised Comments 1980).

10. *See id.* at 406–07; Bratt, *supra* note 8, at 285–89 (discussing "[t]he conundrum posed by the use of legal sanctions for violations of moral principles" in this setting).

11. *See* JOSEPH SHEPHER, INCEST (A BIOSOCIAL VIEW) 135–50 (1983) (discussing the theories of Sigmund Freud and the family socialization school as they relate to incest regulation).

when family members reach out to others; the resulting formation of sexual ties and new family units outside the family of origin strengthens the larger social structure.[12] As with the application of community norms, these concerns would be raised by sexual relationships in the stepfamily when step-relatives actually function as members of a family unit. In other cases, the concerns about rivalries, insecurity, or insularity within the family would be less relevant.

Matthew Bacon, a noted eighteenth-century legal scholar, summarized the policies embodied in the English incest law in his treatise entitled *A New Abridgement of the Law*. His summary essentially reiterates each of the justifications for the regulation of family relationships examined here.

> [I]ncest, between the ascending and descending line, is contrary to the law of nature . . . because it destroys the natural duties between parents and children; for the parent could never preserve or maintain that authority that is necessary for the education and government of his child; nor the child that reverence that is due to the parent in order to be educated and governed, if such indecent familiarities were admitted. There likewise seems to be a natural reason . . . that it is necessary to cross the strain, in order to continue the species.
>
> . . . [I]f a concourse between brothers and sisters might be allowed, or their marriages be tolerated, . . . the frequent opportunities they have with each other, would fill every family with lewdness, and create heart-burnings and unextinguishable jealousies between brothers and sisters, . . . and it would confine every family to itself, and hinder the propagating [of] common love and charity among mankind . . . .[13]

A final justification involves the protection of weak family members from sexual overreaching by more powerful relatives, especially during childhood.[14] According to this rationale, legal regulation should extend to those stepfamilies where, by virtue of the roles assumed by the parties, the potential for overreaching exists. Indeed, numerous studies of abusive families have established the relevance of this protective concern in the stepfamily context.[15]

---

12. *See* Herbert Maisch, Incest 47–49 (1972) (discussing the theory that incest regulations strengthen the larger social structure).

13. IV Matthew Bacon & Henry Gwillim, A New Abridgment of the Law 526–27 (1st Am. ed. from the 6th London ed. 1811).

14. *See* Model Penal Code Part II § 230.2, comment at 407 (Official Draft & Revised Comments 1980).

15. *See, e.g.*, W.D. Erickson et al., *The Life Histories and Psychological Profiles of 59 Incestuous Stepfathers*, 15 Bull. Am. Acad. Psychiatry Law 349 (1987);

Thus, the various theories that explain and justify the legal prohibition of incestuous relationships emphasize the welfare of individual family members, the stability of the family unit, and the religious and moral interests of the larger society. They do not, however, provide a consistent guide for the proper treatment of stepfamily members. The religious rationale supports the complete prohibition of marriages and sexual relationships between stepparents and children and other steprelatives; the genetic rationale supports no regulation whatsoever; and the community norm, social, and protective theories support the regulation of stepfamilies some of the time.

An additional complication arises in the analysis of this topic because the laws regulating several distinct types of behavior have generally been classified together as incest regulations. Thus, the laws in this field determine the legitimacy of the marriage contracted between a surviving spouse (stepparent) and the adult child (stepchild) of his or her deceased partner. At the same time, this system of rules must address the criminal responsibility of a stepparent who engages in sexual activity with the minor stepchild with whom he or she resides. Both the marriage regulation and the criminal law, which direct the outcomes in these two situations, are classified generally as incest regulations. In the biologic family, both the attempted marriage and the sexual relationship between a parent and his or her child would easily be characterized as incestuous and unlawful under the relevant regulations in every state. A single line of analysis may not, however, produce a satisfactory outcome in the two hypothetical situations involving stepfamily members.

The problem is illustrated in the Model Penal Code. There, a single provision criminalizes marriage, cohabitation, or sexual intercourse between designated family members.[16] The drafters intentionally excluded all steprelatives from this provision with the following explanation: "Because there are situations where persons related by affinity should be permitted to marry, it therefore follows that they should not be included within the incest prohibition."[17] A more refined approach has been taken by a number of state legislatures, which treat the regulation of marriage, the regulation of sexual activity outside of marriage, and the regulation of sexual activity with a minor as discrete matters. As described in the remainder of this chapter, this approach better enables lawmakers to weigh the competing policy

---

Hilda Parker & Seymour Parker, *Father-Daughter Sexual Abuse: An Emerging Perspective*, 56 AM. J. OF ORTHOPSYCHIATRY 531 (1986); Patricia Phelan, *The Process of Incest: Biologic Father and Stepfather Families*, 10 CHILD ABUSE AND NEGLECT: THE INT'L J. 531 (1986); *Child Sexual Abuse Victims in the Courts: Hearings before the Subcomm. on Juvenile Justice of the Senate Comm. on the Judiciary*, 98th Cong., 2d Sess. on Oversight Hearings to Consider the Testimony of Children in Sexual Abuse Cases (1984).

16. *See* MODEL PENAL CODE PART II § 230.2, at 397 (Official Draft and Revised Comments 1980).

17. *Id.*, comment at 415.

considerations in each distinct situation where sexual relationships may be formed in the stepfamily.

IV. The Right to Marry

State laws impose numerous limitations upon the individual right to freely select a marriage partner, including restrictions on underage marriages, bigamous marriages, same-sex marriages, and incestuous marriages.[18] Within the last category, the laws in every state prohibit marriage between parent and child, between grandparent and grandchild, and between siblings. There is, however, no universal rule regarding marriage between more distant blood relatives, such as first cousins, or between persons related by marriage.

Civil law sanctions invalidate any attempt by relatives to create a prohibited marriage. The legal status of marriage involves many benefits, rights, and duties between the spouses and in relation to third parties. The declaration that a marriage is void entails a refusal by the state to recognize this status. Invalidity is a harsh sanction when a significant legal consequence, such as inheritance rights or the status of children, depends upon marital status. Beyond this civil law sanction of invalidity, any attempt to create a proscribed marriage may be treated as a criminal offense.

The table in the appendix to this chapter reveals that only nineteen states currently extend their civil and/or criminal marriage prohibitions to steprelatives. Lawmakers in these jurisdictions have determined that the policies discussed in the preceding section, relating to genetics, community mores, family harmony, and the protection of weak family members, justify a ban on the marriage of steprelatives as well as blood relatives.

The decision of the Tennessee Supreme Court in *Rhodes v. McAfee*[19] provides a focal point for analyzing this issue. In *Rhodes*, the court invalidated the fourteen-year union between B.E. Plunk and Gladys Griggs under a state law banning stepparent-child marriages. The stepfather, B.E. Plunk, first married Gladys's mother, Tula Griggs; thereafter, Gladys resided for a number of years in the household created by her mother and stepfather. Five children were born during the marriage of B.E. Plunk and Tula Griggs, which ended in divorce in 1943. Regrettably, the *Rhodes* opinion does not indicate the parties' ages nor the duration of this first marriage. In 1944, B.E. Plunk married his stepdaughter Gladys Griggs, and the couple subsequently had three children. The *Rhodes* case involved Gladys Griggs's

---

18. For general discussion of state marriage restrictions and the constitutional questions they raise, see Bratt, *supra* note 8, at 259–67; Leonard P. Strickman, *Marriage, Divorce and the Constitution*, 15 Fam. L.Q. 259, 279–97 (1982); Note, *The Constitution and the Family*, 93 Harv. L. Rev. 1159, 1248–70 (1980).

19. Rhodes v. McAfee, 457 S.W.2d 522 (Tenn. 1970).

claim to the economic rights of a surviving wife, particularly homestead and dower rights in B.E. Plunk's property, following his death in 1958.

The Tennessee marriage statute applied in *Rhodes* expressly prohibited stepparent-child marriages. The opinion of the Tennessee Supreme Court emphasized the public policies embodied in the incest provision, including the moral standards of the community and the harmony and stability of the family. According to the court, the statute was properly applied to deny the marital relationship between Gladys Griggs and B.E. Plunk.

> The statutes here at issue . . . are expressive of settled public policy in this State regarding public morals and good order in society. . . . This case is a good example of why such marriages are prohibited. The stepdaughter lived in the home with the mother and stepfather . . . [and her] status in this family would be closely akin to the natural children of a mother and stepfather . . . . If there were no statutes prohibiting such marriages, there not only could but very likely would [be] discord and disharmony in the family.[20]

From the court's viewpoint, the family first created by the marriage of B.E. Plunk and Gladys Griggs's mother was analogous to the biologic family for these purposes.

The *Rhodes* opinion neglected to consider a countervailing concern, namely, the serious hardship incurred by Gladys Griggs, who was denied the legal status of a surviving spouse following fourteen years of de facto marriage. The holding may also have impacted harshly on her three children, depending upon the treatment of children born outside of marriage under the laws of Tennessee at that time. Of course, hardships to individuals are the inevitable burden imposed by any rule of law that invalidates de facto unions. The marriage law of Tennessee still reflects the view that this type of burden is justified by the public policy concerns identified in the *Rhodes* opinion.[21]

In contrast, most other states have eliminated all civil and criminal restrictions on marriages between stepparents and children. Here, greater weight has been assigned to the interests of individuals in the position of Gladys Griggs than to the traditional policies that justified the ban on marriages between close steprelatives.[22]

---

20. *Id.* at 524.

21. *See* TENN. CODE ANN. § 36–3–101 (1991).

22. The English Parliament has limited the ban on steprelative marriages to situations where family-related policy goals are most likely to be accomplished. The Marriage Act of 1986 provides that the marriage between stepparent and stepchild, or between stepgrandparent and stepgrandchild, "shall not be void by reason only of that relationship if both the parties have attained the age of twenty-one at the time

Even in states, such as Tennessee, that retain a statutory ban on step-relative marriages, the courts have sometimes circumvented these restrictions. The first theory relied upon by the courts is the voidable marriage doctrine, which provides that a defective marriage cannot be challenged after the spouses have died, if the marriage is classified as "voidable" rather than "void."[23] In *Tyson v. Weatherly*,[24] for example, the Supreme Court of South Carolina invoked this doctrine to preserve marital property rights between the deceased stepmother/wife and her deceased stepson/husband, in the face of a statute that prohibited their marriage. However, the majority of states that draw a distinction between void and voidable marriages classify incestuous marriages as void, thereby foreclosing this theory of relief.

A second judicial theory, which has been applied to avoid the rigid application of marriage restrictions, is a doctrine known as the derivative theory of affinity. The theory assumes that a relationship created by affinity, such as the stepparent-child relationship, automatically terminates when the marriage creating it ends by death or divorce. Accordingly, application of this theory results in an automatic lifting of the ban on marriage between stepparent and stepchild when the prior marriage between the stepparent and the stepchild's natural parent terminates, either by their divorce or the natural parent's death.[25]

For example, the Iowa Supreme Court applied the derivative theory of affinity in *Back v. Back*,[26] a case factually similar to *Rhodes v. McAfee*, to validate the marriage between a stepdaughter and her stepfather. By holding that the stepfather-stepdaughter relationship had automatically terminated when the stepfather divorced his stepdaughter's mother, the court was able to recognize the subsequent marriage of these "former" steprelatives. In *Back*, the Iowa Supreme Court acknowledged that its holding

---

of the marriage and *the younger party has not at any time before attaining the age of eighteen been a child of the family in relation to the other party."* Marriage (Prohibited Degrees of Relationship) Act 1986, § 1, *reprinted in* 27 HALSBURY'S STATUTES OF ENGLAND 590 (4th ed., reissue 1992) (emphasis added). *See* P.M. BROMLEY & N.V. LOWE, BROMLEY'S FAMILY LAW 32–43 (7th ed. 1987) (discussing the English Marriage Act).

23. *See* D. Tolstoy, *Void and Voidable Marriages*, 27 MOD. L. REV. 385, 386 (1964).

24. Tyson v. Weatherly, 52 S.E.2d 410 (S.C. 1949).

25. The Court of Appeals of Alabama added an unusual twist to this derivative theory of affinity by limiting the doctrine to situations where no issue were born during the marriage between the stepparent and the stepchild's natural parent. Thus, a stepson who married his stepmother following his father's death was not guilty of criminal incest, because "there [were] no issue of [the] marriage [between his father and stepmother] to continue the relationship." Henderson v. State, 157 So. 884, 884 (Ala. Ct. App. 1934).

26. Back v. Back, 125 N.W. 1009 (Iowa 1910). *But see* Rhodes v. McAfee, 457 S.W.2d 522 (Tenn. 1970) (rejecting the derivative theory of affinity).

essentially nullified the state statute prohibiting stepparent-child marriages by limiting its application to the period of the original marriage between the stepparent and the stepchild's natural parent; during this time, the concept of monogamy and the law of bigamy already prevented the stepparent from taking a second spouse.[27]

The interplay between courts and legislatures in this area is highlighted by a provision in the Massachusetts marriage statute, which expressly rejects the derivative theory of affinity. The Massachusetts law clearly states that "[t]he prohibition of the . . . sections [banning marriages between relatives by affinity] shall continue notwithstanding the dissolution, by death or divorce, of the marriage by which the affinity was created."[28] This provision clearly removes all discretion from the courts in Massachusetts to invoke the theory of the *Back* case.

In summary, the laws in most states no longer prohibit marriages between close steprelatives. A number of important considerations enter into the analysis of any restriction on the freedom to select a marriage partner. First, individual autonomy in this area deserves protection in the absence of compelling reasons to limit individual choice. Furthermore, the enforcement of marriage restrictions typically imposes serious burdens on the parties to de facto unions, as illustrated by the outcome in *Rhodes v. McAfee*. Of course, compelling policies relating to family stability, the welfare of individual family members, and the morals of the community continue to justify the universal prohibition of marriage between close biologic relatives. Currently, however, the lawmakers in most states do not find these concerns to be sufficiently compelling to justify a similar prohibition in the stepfamily.

V. Sexual Activity Outside of Marriage

The regulation of sexual activity between steprelatives under criminal statutes is more widespread than the regulation of marriage, described in the preceding section.[29] The appendix to this chapter identifies the statutes in each state that utilize family relationship as a factor in defining criminal

---

27. The Iowa legislature subsequently deleted steprelatives from the civil marriage statute.

28. Mass. Gen. Laws Ann. ch. 207, § 3 (West 1987); *see also* 22 Op. Att'y Gen. 492 (Conn. 1942), *cited in* Conn. Gen. Stat. Ann. § 46b–21 Notes of Decisions (West 1986).

29. There are exceptions to the general rule that the states tend to regulate stepfamily sexual activity outside of marriage more than they regulate marriage between steprelatives. Rhode Island, Maryland, Massachusetts, Oklahoma, and the District of Columbia include steprelatives in their marriage statutes but not in the criminal statutes prohibiting sexual activity between close family members. *See* the appendix to this chapter.

sexual activity. The statutes fall into two basic categories. First, forty-four states retain general criminal incest laws that punish sexual activity between designated relatives, without regard to age; ninteen include steprelatives in these provisions. A second category of statutes, enacted in approximately one-third of the states, combines the age of the victim with the parties' family relationship as elements of the criminal offense. Almost all of the statutes in this second category are broad enough to include stepfamily relationships. Indeed, concerns about protecting minor stepfamily members find expression in the formulation and enforcement of many of the laws in this field. Still, a final tally of the various state regulations reveals that stepfamilies are completely excluded from the criminal incest laws in approximately one-third of the states.

The following Alabama statute exemplifies the traditional incest provisions, which punish marriage and/or sexual activity without regard to the age of the parties.

> [A] person commits incest if he marries or engages in sexual intercourse with a person he knows to be, either legitimately or illegitimately . . . [h]is ancestor or descendant by blood or adoption; or . . . [h]is brother or sister of the whole or half-blood or by adoption; or . . . *[h]is stepchild or stepparent, while the marriage creating the relationship exists*; or . . . [h]is aunt, uncle, nephew or niece of the whole or half-blood.[30]

In the nineteen states, including Alabama, that include steprelatives in this type of statute, two important variables must be addressed: the particular steprelationships to be regulated and the duration of the limitation.

Although the Alabama legislature has defined criminal incest to include marriage or sexual intercourse between broad categories of biologic relatives, among steprelatives only the stepparent and stepchild are included. Not surprisingly, all of the states that regulate stepfamilies include the stepparent-child relationship in the relevant criminal statutes. As disclosed in the appendix to this chapter, other jurisdictions have added stepgrandparent-grandchild relationships and/or stepsibling relationships. The courts have generally declined to expand on these statutory categories. For example, in *State v. Handyside*,[31] the Washington Court of Appeals rejected the prosecutor's argument that "stepchildren" in the criminal incest law should be broadly construed to include the eight-year-old and ten-year-old stepgranddaughters of the defendant. According to the court, the intent of the legislature to restrict the regulation to stepparents and their stepchildren was clear on the face of the statute.[32]

---

30. ALA. CODE § 13A–13–3 (1982) (emphasis added).

31. State v. Handyside, 711 P.2d 379 (Wash. Ct. App. 1985).

32. *Id.* at 380; *accord* State v. Moore, 262 A.2d 166 (Conn. 1969) (holding that the statutory term "stepchild" did not include "niece-in-law").

The second variable factor in the general incest laws that regulate stepfamily behavior without regard to the victim's age relates to the duration of the statutory restrictions. Specifically, lawmakers in each state must determine whether prohibitions on sexual activity continue after the marriage that created the steprelationship comes to an end through death or divorce. This is the same issue, involving the so-called derivative theory of affinity, that arises in the context of laws regulating marriage, discussed in the preceding section. Under the Alabama criminal statute, quoted previously, the stepparent-child prohibition endures only "while the marriage creating the relationship exists."[33] Under this provision, a stepparent and stepchild would be free to engage in a sexual relationship following termination of the stepparent's marriage to the stepchild's natural parent, either by divorce or the parent's death.

Other state statutes are silent on this issue. In *State v. Gish,*[34] the Court of Appeals of Georgia refused to restrict the state incest law by adopting the derivative theory of affinity. The stepdaughter in *Gish* was six years old when the defendant married her mother. Following his wife's death, four years later, the defendant successfully resisted the efforts of another party to assume legal custody of his stepdaughter. Finally, ten years later, he was convicted of incest under the Georgia statute, which defined the offense to include sexual intercourse between a "father and daughter or stepdaughter." The court rejected the defense that the girl had ceased to be the defendant's stepdaughter upon her mother's prior death.

> As a general rule, affinity ceases upon the death of the blood relative through whom the relationship of affinity was created. . . .
> . . . [W]e hold that because of the creation and continuation of the familial relationship between Gish and the victim who resided in his home pursuant to a court order personally sought by Gish, that an actual affinity was perpetuated as a continuation of, and persisted independently of, the affinity which originally arose from the marriage by the [stepfather] with his stepdaughter's natural mother.[35]

Thus, a broader definition of the stepparent-child relationship was required in order to accomplish the purposes of the state incest statute.

The traditional incest statutes are frequently applied in cases, such as *State v. Gish,* where the victim is a child. However, there is no age requirement in these laws, and prosecutions may be based on the sexual relationship between consenting adults. Recently, an appellate court in Oregon

---

33. ALA. CODE § 13A–13–3 (1982); *see also* MO. ANN. STAT. § 568.020(1) (Vernon 1979) (incorporating derivative theory of affinity into criminal statute regulating marriage and sexual activity); TEX. PENAL CODE ANN. § 25.02(a)(2) (West 1989) (sexual activity); UTAH CODE ANN. § 76–7–102(1) (1990) (sexual activity).

34. State v. Gish, 352 S.E.2d 800 (Ga. Ct. App. 1987).

35. *Id.* at 801.

upheld the conviction of a stepfather for incest based on his sexual relationship with an adult stepdaughter. In *State v. Buck*,[36]the court rejected the defendant's request to read an age limitation into the criminal incest statute.

Numerous policy interests may justify the regulation of sexual activity between adult stepfamily members. First, the vulnerability of children in the family may continue beyond their age of majority. Second, the interest in stability and harmony in the stepfamily may justify restrictions between adult members. Finally, the broad application of criminal prohibitions without regard to age may vindicate the views of the community about moral behavior in the stepfamily. Of course, there is no nationwide consensus about this issue; indeed, in a majority of states, there is no criminal regulation of sexual activity between adult stepfamily members. In contrast, the forty-four states with traditional criminal incest laws all extend their prohibition on sexual activity to adult relationships in the biologic family.

The age factor plays a key role in the second category of incest statutes, which have been enacted in approximately one-third of the states. Here, the legislative focus is on situations where a power imbalance exists in the family, similar to the authority exercised by parents over their children. For example, the North Carolina legislature has incorporated the in loco parentis doctrine into the "sexual offenses with certain victims" felony statute. Specifically, the statute proscribes sexual activity on the part of "a defendant who has assumed the position of a parent in the home of a minor victim."[37] Similarly, West Virginia defines "custodian" in the "[s]exual abuse by a parent, guardian or custodian" statute to include "the spouse of a parent . . . where such spouse . . . shares actual physical possession or care and custody of a [minor] child with the parent."[38] Both statutes would apply to stepfamilies where the stepparent plays an active parenting role with respect to minor stepchildren.[39]

In *People v. Garrison*,[40] a stepfather was convicted of the offense of "criminal sexual conduct" under the following Michigan statute.

---

36. State v. Buck, 757 P.2d 861 (Or. Ct. App. 1988).

37. N.C. GEN. STAT. § 14–27.7 (1986).

38. W. VA. CODE §§ 61–8D–1, –5 (1992).

39. A number of the criminal statutes that include de facto parent-child relationships also expressly include stepparent-child relationships. *See* ALASKA STAT. § 11.41.434 (Supp. 1992) (including stepchild victim under eighteen years or member of household under sixteen years); MICH. COMP. LAWS ANN. § 750.520b, .520c (West 1991) (including minor victim who is related by affinity to the defendant or a household member); N.J. STAT. ANN. § 2C:14–2(a)(2) (West Supp. 1993) (same). In Ohio, the crime of sexual battery requires the relationship of parent, stepparent, custodian, or person in loco parentis, although the victim need not be underage. *See* OHIO REV. CODE ANN. § 2907.03 (Baldwin 1992).

40. People v. Garrison, 341 N.W.2d 170 (Mich. Ct. App. 1983).

> [A] person is guilty of criminal sexual conduct . . . if he or she engages in sexual penetration with another person [who] is at least 13 but less than 16 years of age and . . . the actor is a member of the same household as the victim[,] the actor is related to the victim by blood or affinity to the fourth degree[, or] the actor is in a position of authority over the victim and used this authority to coerce the victim to submit.[41]

In *Garrison*, the Michigan Court of Appeals identified the multiple concerns addressed by this single statute.

> Under prior law, incest, which was based on a familial relationship unrelated to age, carried a less severe penalty than did statutory rape. The first-degree criminal sexual conduct statute evidences a strong legislative intent to specify several situations in which the chance for sexual abuse of young persons is acute.[42]

The court found that these protective concerns were germane to the *Garrison* case, where the stepfather was convicted of criminal sexual conduct based on acts of sexual intercourse with his wife's thirteen-year-old daughter.

The stepfather's conviction in *Garrison* was based on his status under the statute as a "member of the same household" with his stepdaughter. The court ruled that this requirement was satisfied, even though the stepdaughter resided with her father during the school year and lived with her mother and the defendant only during the summer months. The evidence established that the stepdaughter had experienced the "close and ongoing subordinating relationship . . . with a member of . . . her family" contemplated by the statute.[43] The *Garrison* court affirmed the defendant's conviction for criminal sexual conduct and sentence of life imprisonment.

The reference in the *Garrison* opinion to the Michigan statutory rape law highlights the overlap in purpose between this type of criminal provision and the incest statutes that require a minor victim. As described by the court in *Garrison*, the statutes that combine age with family relationship acknowledge the special public and private interests involved when an adult abuses his or her custodial authority. Frequently, there is an enhanced trauma for the victim, greater disapproval by the community, and a distinct stigma attached to the actor, when sexual overreaching occurs in these special circumstances. Where the legislatures have enacted special laws to

---

41. *Id.* at 172. The criminal sexual conduct provision is currently codified in MICH. COMP. LAWS ANN. § 750.520b (West 1991).

42. *Garrison*, 341 N.W.2d at 173.

43. *Id.* It is unclear from the *Garrison* opinion why the stepfather was not prosecuted on the alternative basis of his relationship of affinity to the minor victim.

address these interests, as in Michigan, they have typically included stepfamilies.

In summary, the laws in every state regulate nonmarital sexual conduct between close relatives. The traditional criminal incest laws prohibit such behavior without regard to the factors of age and consent. Currently, most states have broken with the religious and historical heritage that included stepfamily members within these regulations. Furthermore, the traditional incest statutes have been replaced or supplemented in many jurisdictions by other criminal laws that are specifically targeted at protecting weak family members against sexual abuse. These laws are limited to situations where a power imbalance is likely to exist within the family and include such factors as the age of the victim or the special custodial relationship of the parties. Minor stepchildren typically fall within the scope of these protective provisions.

The appendix to this chapter documents the resulting pattern of regulation within the stepfamily. Notably, in approximately one-third of the states, stepfamily members are completely excluded from the statutes that prohibit sexual activity between close family members. The lack of a national consensus on this important issue reveals the complexity of the underlying policy analysis, which involves both the definition of the family and, in the case of adult relationships, the acceptable limitations on individual freedom in the area of intimate association.

APPENDIX Family Relationship as a Factor in Marriage Statutes and in Criminal Statutes

State	Marriage Statute (Civil)	Steps Included	Criminal Statute/Activity	Steps Included	Special Features
Alabama	—	—	Ala. Code § 13A–13–3 (1982)/marriage and sex	SP,SCH	—
Alaska	Alaska Stat. § 25.05.021 (1991)	No	Incest: Alaska Stat. § 11.41.450 (Supp. 1989)/sex Sexual Abuse of a Minor: Alaska Stat. §§ 11.41.434, 436 (Supp. 1992)/sex	No SCH	— Victim is member of household under 16 years old, or minor stepchild
Arizona	Ariz. Rev. Stat. Ann. § 25–101 (1991)	No	Ariz. Rev. Stat. Ann. § 13–3608 (1989)/marriage and sex	No	—
Arkansas	Ark. Code Ann. § 9–11–106 (Michie 1991)	No	Ark. Code Ann. § 5–26–202 (Michie 1987)/marriage and sex	SCH, SGCH	—
California	Cal. Civ. Code § 4400 (West 1983)	No	Cal. Penal Code § 285 (West Supp. 1993)/marriage and sex	No	—
Colorado	Colo. Rev. Stat. § 14–2–110 (1987)	No	Incest: Colo. Rev. Stat. § 18–6–301 (1986 & Supp. 1992)/marriage and sex	SCH	Marriage to stepchild is defense

(continued)

State	Marriage Statute (Civil)	Steps Included	Criminal Statute/Activity	Steps Included	Special Features
			Aggravated Incest: Colo. Rev. Stat. § 18–6–302 (1986 & Supp. 1992)/marriage and sex	SCH	Victim under 21 years old
Connecticut	Conn. Gen. Stat. Ann. § 46b–21 (West 1986)	SP, SCH	Conn. Gen. Stat. Ann. § 53a–191 (West Supp. 1993)/marriage	SP, SCH	—
Delaware	Del. Code Ann. tit. 13, § 101 (1981 & Supp. 1992)	No	Del. Code Ann. tit. 11, § 766 (1987 & Supp. 1992)/sex	SP, SCH, SGCH	—
District of Columbia	D.C. Code Ann. § 30–101 (1988)	SP, SCH, SGP, SGCH	D.C. Code Ann. § 22–1901 (1989)/marriage and sex	No	—
Florida	Fla. Stat. Ann. § 741.21 (West 1986)	No	Fla. Stat. Ann. § 826.04 (West 1976)/marriage and sex	No	—
Georgia	Ga. Code Ann. § 19–3–3 (1991)	SCH	Ga. Code Ann. § 16–6–22 (1992)/sex	SCH	—
Hawaii	Haw. Rev. Stat. § 572–1 (1985)	No	Haw. Rev. Stat. § 707–741 (Supp. 1988)/sex	No	—
Idaho	Idaho Code § 32–205 (1983)	No	Idaho Code § 18–6602 (1987)/marriage and sex	No	—

State	Citation		Criminal Statute		
Illinois	Ill. Ann. Stat. ch. 40, para. 212 (Smith–Hurd Supp. 1992)	No	Sexual Relations Within Families: Ill. Ann. Stat. ch. 38, para. 11–11 (Smith–Hurd Supp. 1992)/sex	SP	Victim over 18 years old
			Sexual Assault: Ill. Ann. Stat. ch. 38, para. 12–13 (Smith–Hurd Supp. 1992)/sex	SP, SCH, SGP	Victim under 18 years old
Indiana	Ind. Code Ann. § 31–7–1–3 (Burns 1987)	No	Ind. Code Ann. § 35–46–1–3 (Burns Supp. 1992)/sex	Steps deleted in 1987	—
Iowa	Iowa Code Ann. § 595.19 (West 1981 & Supp. 1993)	Steps deleted in 1985	Sexual Abuse: Iowa Code Ann. § 709.4 (West Supp. 1993)/sex	Affinity within 4th degree	Victim 14 or 15 years old plus affinity or household member
			Incest: Iowa Code Ann. § 726.2 (West Supp. 1993)/sex	No	—
Kansas	Kan. Stat. Ann. § 23–102 (1988)	No	Incest: Kan. Stat. Ann. § 21–3602 (1988)/marriage and sex	No	—
			Aggravated Incest: Kan. Stat. Ann. § 21–3603 (1988)/marriage and sex	SCH, SGCH, SSIB	Minor victim
Kentucky	Ky. Rev. Stat. Ann. § 402.010 (Baldwin 1990)	No	Ky. Rev. Stat. Ann. § 530–020 (Baldwin 1984)/sex	SP, SCH	—

(continued)

State	Marriage Statute (Civil)	Steps Included	Criminal Statute/Activity	Steps Included	Special Features
Louisiana	La. Civ. Code Ann. art. 90 (West 1993)	No	La. Rev. Stat. Ann. § 14:78 (West 1986)/marriage and sex	No	—
Maine	Me. Rev. Stat. Ann. tit. 19, § 31 (West Supp. 1992)	Steps deleted in 1981	Me. Rev. Stat. Ann. tit. 17–A, § 556 (West Supp. 1992)/sex	No	—
Maryland	Md. Code Ann., Fam. Law § 2–202 (1991)	SP, SCH, SGP, SGCH	Md. Ann. Code art. 27, § 335 (1992)/sex	No	—
Massachusetts	Mass. Gen. Laws Ann. ch. 207, §§ 1, 2 (West 1987)	SP, SCH, SGP, SGCH	Mass. Gen. Laws Ann. ch. 272, § 17 (West 1990)/marriage and sex	No	—
Michigan	Mich. Comp. Laws Ann. §§ 551.3, .4 (West 1988)	SP, SCH, SGP, SGCH	Mich. Comp. Laws Ann. §§ 750.520b, .520c (West 1991)/sex	Affinity to 4th degree	Age 13–15 plus affinity or household member
Minnesota	Minn. Stat. Ann. § 517.03 (West 1990)	No	Minn. Stat. Ann. § 609.365 (West 1987)/sex	No	—
Mississippi	Miss. Code Ann. § 93–1–1 (1973)	SP, SCH	Miss. Code Ann. §§ 97–29–5, –27 (1973)/marriage and sex	SP, SCH, SGCH	—
Missouri	Mo. Ann. Stat. § 451.020 (Vernon 1986)	No	Mo. Ann. Stat. § 568.020 (Vernon 1979)/marriage and sex	SCH	—
Montana	Mont. Code Ann. § 40–1–401 (1991)	No	Mont. Code Ann. § 45–5–507 (1991)/marriage and sex	SCH	Consent of adult SCH is defense

State					
Nebraska	Neb. Rev. Stat. § 42–103 (Supp. 1992)	No	Incestuous Marriage: Neb. Rev. Stat. § 28–702 (1989)/marriage	No	—
			Incest: Neb. Rev. Stat. § 28–703 (1989)/sex	SCH	Minor victim
Nevada	Nev. Rev. Stat. Ann. § 125.290 (Michie 1993)	No	Nev. Rev. Stat. Ann. § 201.180 (Michie 1992)/marriage and sex	No	—
New Hampshire	N.H. Rev. Stat. Ann. § 457:1,:2 (1992)	Steps deleted in 1987	Incest: N.H. Rev. Stat. Ann. § 639:2 (Supp. 1992)/ marriage and sex	SCH	—
			Aggravated Sexual Assault: N.H. Rev. Stat. Ann. § 632–A:2 (1986 & Supp. 1992)/sex	Affinity	Victim age 13–15 plus affinity or living in same household
New Jersey	N.J. Stat. Ann. § 37:1–1 (West 1968)	No	N.J. Stat. Ann. § 2C:14–2 (a),(c) (West Supp. 1993)/sex	Affinity to 3rd degree	Minor victim plus affinity or in loco parentis
New Mexico	N.M. Stat. Ann. § 40–1–7 (Michie 1989)	No	N.M. Stat. Ann. § 30–10–3 (Michie 1989)/sex	No	Minor victim plus position of authority
New York	N.Y. Dom. Rel. Law § 5 (McKinney 1988)	No	N.Y. Penal Law § 255.25 (McKinney 1989)/marriage and sex	No	
North Carolina	N.C. Gen. Stat. § 51–3 (1984)	No	Incest: N.C. Gen. Stat. § 14–178 (1986)/sex	SCH	—
			Sexual Offenses: N.C. Gen. Stat. § 14–27.7 (1986)/sex	No	Minor victim plus in loco parentis

(continued)

State	Marriage Statute (Civil)	Steps Included	Criminal Statute/Activity	Steps Included	Special Features
North Dakota	N.D. Cent. Code § 14–03–03 (1991)	No	Incest: N.D. Cent. Code § 12.1–20–11 (Supp. 1991)/marriage and sex	No	—
			Sexual Assault: N.D. Cent. Code § 12.1–20–07 (1985)/sex	No	Supervisory authority plus age limit
Ohio	Ohio Rev. Code Ann. § 3101.01 (Baldwin 1992)	No	Ohio Rev. Code Ann. § 2907.03 (Baldwin 1992)/sex	SP	Also person in loco parentis
Oklahoma	Okla. Stat. Ann. tit. 43, § 2 (West 1990)	SP, SCH	Okla. Stat. Ann. tit. 21, § 885 (West 1983)/marriage and sex	No	—
Oregon	Or. Rev. Stat. § 106.020 (1990)	No	Or. Rev. Stat. §§ 163.505 (1), .525 (1990)/marriage and sex	SCH	—
Pennsylvania	23 Pa. Cons. Stat. Ann. § 1304(e) (1991)	No	18 Pa. Cons. Stat. Ann. § 4302 (Supp. 1993)/marriage and sex	No	—
Rhode Island	R.I. Gen. Laws § 15–1–1 to –3 (1988)	SP, SCH, SGP, SGCH	R.I. Gen. Laws § 11–6–4 (repealed 1989)	—	—
South Carolina	S.C. Code Ann. § 20–1–10 (Law. Co-op. 1985)	SP, SCH, SGP, SGCH	S.C. Code Ann. § 16–15–20 (Law. Co-op. 1985)/sex	SP, SCH, SGP, SGCH	—
South Dakota	S.D. Codified Laws Ann. § 25–1–7 (1992)	SP, SCH	Incest: S.D. Codified Laws Ann. § 22–22–19.1 (Supp. 1993)/sex	SP, SCH	Victim under 21 years old

			Rape: S.D. Codified Laws Ann. § 22–22–1(6) (Supp. 1993)/sex	No	—
Tennessee	Tenn. Code Ann. § 36–3–101 (1991)	SP, SCH	Tenn. Code Ann. § 39–15–302 (1991)/sex	SP, SCH	—
Texas	Tex. Fam. Code Ann. § 2.21 (West 1993)	No	Tex. Penal Code Ann. § 25.02 (West 1989)/sex	SP, SCH	—
Utah	Utah Code Ann. § 30–1–1 (1989)	No	Utah Code Ann. § 76–7–102 (1990)/sex	SP, SCH	—
Vermont	Vt. Stat. Ann. tit. 15, §§ 1, 2 (1989)	Steps deleted in 1975	Vt. Stat. Ann. tit. 13, § 3252(a)(4), (b)(1) (Supp. 1992)/sex	SP, SCH	Minor victim
Virginia	Va. Code Ann. § 20–38.1 (Michie 1990)	No	Va. Code Ann. § 18.2–366 (Michie Supp. 1993)/sex	No	—
Washington	Wash. Rev. Code Ann. § 26.04.020 (West 1986)	No	Wash. Rev. Code Ann. § 9A.64.020 (West 1988)/sex	SCH	Minor SCH
West Virginia	W. Va. Code § 48–1–2, –3 (1992)	No	Incest: W. Va. Code § 61–8–12 (1992)/sex; Sexual Abuse by Custodian: W. Va. Code § 61–8D–5 (1992)/sex	SP, SCH; SP who shares custody	—; Victim under 16 years old
Wisconsin	Wis. Stat. Ann. § 765.03 (West 1993)	No	Wis. Stat. Ann. § 944.06 (West 1982)/marriage and sex	No	—
Wyoming	Wyo. Stat. § 20–2–101 (1987)	No	Wyo. Stat. § 6–4–402 (1988)/sex	SP, SCH	—

Note: SP = stepparent, SCH = stepchild, SGP = stepgarandparent, SGCH = stepgrandchild, SSIB = stepsibling, Steps = steprelations.

CHAPTER 12 **Conclusion**

The family law system defines numerous rights and duties for adults and children, based on the parent-child relationship. Many important doctrines, such as the laws of child support and parental custody, create enforceable rights among the family members themselves. Other legal rules impose special rights or responsibilities upon third parties who interact with the family. For example, state statutes defining the vicarious liability of parents for the torts of their children create a cause of action for the victims of children; conversely, wrongful death statutes impose liability on wrongdoers, based on the existence of the victim's family relationships. Taken together, all of the family-related rules of law, in areas as diverse as torts, crimes, taxation, support, inheritance, and custody, define a complete legal status for parents and children in biologic and adoptive families.

Stepparents and stepchildren, and the individuals who interact with them, have sought protection under many of these same legal doctrines. The ultimate question raised by such stepfamily claims is whether the stepparent-child relationship is regarded as a family status in the eyes of the law. As revealed in the pages of this book, the answer remains terribly unclear.

First, the relevant issues are controlled, for the most part, at the state level. And so, the rights of stepfamily members frequently depend on where they live. For example, in Missouri, all stepchildren are entitled by statute to support from their residential stepparents;[1] in Hawaii, only poor children enjoy this right;[2] and in Pennsylvania (and the large majority of states), stepchildren have no support claims against their residential stepparents.[3] The same variety exists among the fifty states as to many other matters.

Furthermore, within each jurisdiction, the various issues affecting stepfamilies have been resolved in the legislature and courts, as they arise on an ad hoc basis. As a result, the existence of a rule recognizing the stepparent-child relationship for one purpose rarely affects the future decision making of lawmakers regarding other stepfamily issues. Thus, in a case that denied wrongful death benefits to dependent stepchildren in

---

1. See Mo. Stat. Ann. § 453.400 (Vernon 1986).

2. See Haw. Rev. Stat. § 577–4 (1985).

3. See Commonwealth ex rel. McNutt v. McNutt, 496 A.2d 816 (Pa. Super. Ct. 1985).

Washington state, the dissenting justices of the supreme court observed that the state child support statute "require[d] stepparents to support their stepchildren," and that "[t]he trend in the law is toward according stepchildren rights equal to those of natural children."[4] The majority, however, did not consider this trend to be relevant in resolving the wrongful death issue.[5]

In spite of all the inconsistencies, an important generalization can be made about the current treatment of stepfamilies in the law. For the most part, the stepparent-child relationship is not regarded as a legal status. Most often, the continuing adherence of lawmakers to a traditional family model forecloses the additional recognition of ties between stepparents and their stepchildren. Time and again, lawmakers have expressed protective concern about the nuclear family and reluctance about complicating the family law system by recognizing the stepfamily. For example, a judge in California gave the following reasons for denying a stepfather's request for visitation with his stepdaughter following the end of his marriage to the girl's custodial mother.

> [The stepfather] absolutely has no relationship to the child bloodwise or otherwise. . . . I can't accept I should burden all of the parties in this matter, including [the stepfather], with conflicts, struggles and disruptions for years to come because of [the stepfather's] present emotional state in connection with the child.[6]

The rules of law that do confer particular benefits or responsibilities based on the stepparent-child relationship are regarded as exceptions to this general principle of nonrecognition. The process by which limited rights and duties are defined in the stepfamily involves both the legislatures and courts and is best understood by reference to the development of particular doctrines.

For example, the stepparent-child relationship has gained the most widespread acceptance in the law of workers' compensation, which generally permits surviving stepchildren to collect benefits when a stepparent is killed in an industrial accident. In every jurisdiction, the basic provisions of the workers' compensation program, including the list of eligible beneficiaries, are established by the legislature. Many of the state statutes include dependent stepchildren, or a category of de facto family members that is broad enough to include many stepfamily relationships. Even in states

---

4. Klossner v. San Juan County, 605 P.2d 330, 333–34 (Wash. 1980) (dissenting opinion).

5. *See id.* at 332–33.

6. Halpern v. Halpern, 184 Cal. Rptr. 740, 743, 747 (Ct. App. 1982) (quoting the trial court opinion).

where the statutory categories are limited to traditional family relationships, the courts have frequently construed the laws broadly to include step-children. In reaching this result, judges have relied upon the common law in loco parentis doctrine, which is the most broad-based judicial theory for extending family benefits to nontraditional families; the doctrine provides that the adult who assumes parental responsibility will be treated as a parent for selected legal purposes. Thus, the courts and legislatures have created an almost uniform rule nationwide regarding the recognition of stepfamilies in the field of workers' compensation. The major exception appears in the law of Colorado, where the state supreme court denied the claim of a deceased worker's dependent stepchildren under a state statute that was limited on its face to traditional families.[7]

By way of contrast, in another important field of statutory law that provides economic protection for families, the state legislatures have totally ignored stepfamilies, and the courts have done little to fill the gap. The inheritance statutes in every state govern the distribution of property when a person dies without a will. Children are everywhere included as primary heirs in this process. The California statute alone recognizes stepchildren as primary heirs, but only in extremely narrow circumstances; stepchildren may inherit as the children of a deceased stepparent only if "it is established by clear and convincing evidence that the . . . stepparent would have adopted the person but for a legal barrier."[8] Stepparents and stepchildren are absent from the lists of primary heirs in all other state statutes. Further-more, the courts have consistently refused to apply the in loco parentis doctrine to identify "parents" and "children" outside of biologic and adoptive families in intestacy cases. Instead, the only judicial relief has come under the doctrine of equitable adoption, which requires clear proof that the de-ceased adult during his or her lifetime promised to adopt the claimant. Very few stepchildren have been able to pass this test as the basis for inheriting as children of their deceased stepparents.

Issues of stepparent support, custody, and visitation arise in many stepfamilies, especially after the marriage between the custodial parent and stepparent ends. As to support, the consistent statutory rule nationwide denies recognition to stepfamily ties after the marriage has ended.[9] Limited recognition may be available in the courts under two theories, the law of implied contracts and the doctrine of equitable estoppel. In fact, the proof required to establish an implied contract to provide child support, or the

---

7. *See* Tri-State Commodities, Inc. v. Stewart, 689 P.2d 712 (Colo. Ct. App. 1984).

8. CAL. PROB. CODE § 6408(e) (West 1991).

9. *But see* N.D. CENT. CODE § 14–09–09 (1991) (extending support duty "dur-ing the marriage and so long thereafter as [the stepchildren] remain in [the step-parent's] family").

elements of an equitable estoppel claim, is rarely present in the stepfamily. Thus, enforceable child support obligations are unlikely to exist in this setting.

There is much more variation from state to state in both the procedural and substantive laws governing stepchild custody and visitation, than in the area of child support. Thus, when the stepparent finds a forum to raise custody issues, the outcome may very well depend upon where the family resides. The substantive standards governing custody disputes between stepparents and biologic parents appear both in statutes and case law. At one extreme, the stepparent may be required to prove the parent's unfitness before his or her request for custody will be entertained. At the opposite end of the spectrum, other states employ a pure best interests of the child standard, which weighs the benefits of parental custody against the benefits of placing a child with the stepparent. The legal standard applied is outcome determinative in many cases.

To select just a few more examples, the laws governing inheritance taxation and wrongful death recoveries further illustrate the lack of consistency in the treatment of stepfamilies from state to state and within each jurisdiction. Among the states with special inheritance tax statutes that impose lower tax bills on bequests to certain relatives, most include stepchildren in the category of preferred beneficiaries. In contrast, stepfamilies are omitted from the large majority of wrongful death statutes, which create a cause of action for eligible surviving relatives against the person who negligently or intentionally kills a family member. In both the inheritance taxation and wrongful death fields, in the absence of legislative recognition, the courts have been totally unreceptive to requests from stepchildren for beneficial treatment under judicial doctrines, such as in loco parentis, equitable adoption, or equitable estoppel. This posture is inconsistent with the approach taken by the judiciary in the fields of workers' compensation and even the laws of inheritance and child support, where the doctrines of in loco parentis, equitable adoption, and equitable estoppel, respectively, have been applied.

It is impossible to reconcile all of the differences in the legal treatment of stepfamilies. Certainly, justifications can be presented as to any given judgment by a state legislature or court. For example, both the legislatures and courts have likely been generous to stepfamilies in the field of workers' compensation, because the system in most states is a remedial, administrative system involving limited recovery amounts. Thus, the problems of mushrooming family benefits and judicial inconvenience, which frequently justify the refusal to recognize nontraditional families, are less relevant here. Conversely, the impact of opening the doors to nontraditional claimants in the law of inheritance would arguably displace significant economic expectations on the part of current heirs and impose a new burden on the probate courts. As a result, both the legislatures and courts consistently refuse to consider the claims of nontraditional family members in this field.

It becomes more difficult to rationalize many other variations in the law, such as why the legislatures in some, but not all, states recognize stepchildren as wrongful death beneficiaries, or why judges in certain jurisdictions have been willing to employ the equitable adoption doctrine in the field of inheritance but not to resolve wrongful death claims. These inconsistent approaches to stepfamily issues are explained in part by the manner in which the laws have developed, namely, issue by issue and state by state in both the legislatures and the courts. But another consideration is equally important. Lawmakers, as they go about the task of addressing the various legal issues that affect stepfamilies, have no shared understanding about the nature of the stepparent-child relationship. The range of views expressed in judicial opinions about the relationships established in individual stepfamily cases is most revealing in this regard.

Furthermore, lawmakers who acknowledge the family-related aspects of the stepparent-child relationship must simultaneously be willing to expand the traditional definition of the family. This process raises the most basic questions about the role and the goals of the family law system. Not surprisingly, there is no current consensus among lawmakers, lawyers, or the members of society about these basic issues.

There is, however, a trend toward more comprehensive understanding and analysis in this field. First, a great deal of work has been completed, and agendas for the future established, by social scientists who provide empirical information about stepfamilies.[10] This work will surely be helpful to those who study the legal aspects of relationships in the stepfamily. Second, legal scholars are attempting to assess the overall impact of existing legal doctrines on stepfamilies and to consider proposals for change in the future;[11] this book is intended to be a contribution to the effort. Finally, in 1987, the Family Law Section of the American Bar Association began work on a project that is intended to culminate in a model act defining rights and duties between stepparents and stepchildren.[12] The effort to evaluate stepfamily issues on a more comprehensive basis is a laudable one.

The families of the twenty-first century will include a large number of stepfamilies. Their interests in certainty and protection under the law will demand continuing attention. Ongoing development in the law of stepfamilies will be necessary if the family law system is to meet the needs of the families of the future.

---

10. *See, e.g.*, REMARRIAGE AND STEPPARENTING: CURRENT RESEARCH AND THEORY (Kay Pasley & Marilyn Ihinger-Tallman eds., 1987).

11. *See, e.g.*, David L. Chambers, *Stepparents, Biologic Parents, and the Law's Perception of "Family" After Divorce, in* DIVORCE REFORM AT THE CROSSROADS (Stephen D. Sugarman & Herma Hill Kay eds., 1990).

12. *See* Joel D. Tenenbaum, *Legislation for Stepfamilies—The Family Law Section Standing Committee Report*, 25 FAM. L.Q. 137 (1991).

Index